GOAT CASTLE

GOAT CASTLE

A TRUE STORY
OF MURDER, RACE, AND
THE GOTHIC SOUTH

Karen L. Cox

THE UNIVERSITY OF NORTH CAROLINA PRESS

CHAPEL HILL

Designed by April Leidig

Set in Ehrhardt by Copperline Book Services, Inc.

Manufactured in the United States of America

The University of North Carolina Press has been a
member of the Green Press Initiative since 2003.

Jacket illustrations: photos of Glenwood ("Goat Castle") and Octavia Dockery
and Dick Dana courtesy of the Earl Norman Photograph Collection,
Historic Natchez Foundation, Natchez, Miss.; photo of Emily Burns
courtesy of Birdia Green and Phyliss Morris, Natchez, Miss.

Library of Congress Cataloging-in-Publication Data

Names: Cox, Karen L., 1962– author.

Title: Goat Castle : a true story of murder, race, and the gothic South /
Karen L. Cox.

Description: Chapel Hill : University of North Carolina Press, [2017] |
Includes bibliographical references and index.

Identifiers: LCCN 2017013168 | ISBN 9781469635033 (cloth : alk. paper) |
ISBN 9781469635040 (ebook)

Subjects: LCSH: Murder—Mississippi—Natchez—History—20th century. |
Judicial error—Mississippi—Natchez—History—20th century. | African
Americans—Segregation—Mississippi—Natchez—History—20th century. |
African Americans—Civil rights—Mississippi—Natchez—History—
20th century. | Merrill, Jennie, 1864–1932. | Dana, Dick, 1871–1948. |
Dockery, Octavia, 1865–1949.

Classification: LCC HV6534.N28 C69 2017 | DDC 364.152/30976226—dc23
LC record available at https://lccn.loc.gov/2017013168

For Phoebe

CONTENTS

Prologue

I

ONE

Reclusive Aristocrats

17

TWO

The Residents of Glenwood

35

THREE

Pink and Sister

53

FOUR

Murder at Glenburnie

63

FIVE

The Investigation

73

SIX

Jim Crow's Investigation

87

SEVEN

National Scandal

103

EIGHT

Sideshows

117

NINE

Cold Justice

131

TEN

Hollow Victory

147

ELEVEN

Longing for Home

161

Epilogue

169

Acknowledgments

177

Notes

183

Bibliography

205

Index

213

FIGURES

Map of Natchez as tourist destination 2

Jennie Merrill in her youth 18

Ayres Merrill Jr. 19

Duncan Minor in his youth 26

Reverend Charles Backus Dana 36

Octavia Dockery as a young woman 44

Glenwood, or "Goat Castle" 49

Emily Burns with her family, ca. 1913 55

George Pearls, aka "Pink" 59

Glenburnie 64

Duncan Minor with Sheriff Clarence "Book" Roberts 74

Murder map 76

Chief Deputy Joseph Stone 79

Maurice O'Neill 83

Emily Burns with her mother, Nellie Smith 91

Octavia Dockery and Dick Dana in Adams County jail 110

Goat Castle library 121

Octavia Dockery's bedroom 123

Dick Dana's bedroom 123

Dick Dana alongside piano 126

Dick Dana and Octavia Dockery with goats 148

Goat Castle flyer 149

Octavia Dockery, 1933 152

Female prisoners in sewing room at Parchman 163

GOAT CASTLE

PROLOGUE

Like most late summer evenings in Natchez, it was hot and steamy that Thursday when sixty-eight-year-old Jane Surget Merrill settled in her home, Glenburnie, to wait for her cousin Duncan Minor to arrive. Known by locals as "Miss Jennie," she had become increasingly reclusive, rarely leaving her estate except to run errands in town. One of the few guests she welcomed was Duncan, also sixty-eight, who would saddle his horse every night at his nearby estate, Oakland, and ride the short distance to see Jennie, returning home just before dawn broke. Their ritual was decades old, but on that night in August 1932, it would come to an abrupt end.

On his ride to Glenburnie, two local black citizens, Willie Boyd and M. C. Hacher, waved Minor down. Boyd reported that while he was on his way to church, he heard what sounded like gunshots and screaming coming from Glenburnie. Alarmed, Duncan urged his horse to gallop the rest of the way, arriving at a house cloaked in darkness. He called out for Jennie, but no one replied. He fumbled for a lantern, only for the light to reveal that her home had been ransacked. Furniture lay askew. There was evidence of a struggle and the walls were smeared with blood, but there was no sign of his cousin. One of her hired hands rushed to a nearby store to phone the sheriff of Adams County, and in a matter of hours Duncan's worst fears were confirmed: Jennie had been murdered. Within days, the crime would make headlines nationwide.

Natchez had once been a fine jewel in the crown of the region's Cotton Kingdom, and the writers covering the story of Jennie Merrill's murder couldn't help but remark on her connection to the town's planter aristocracy. They wrote about her life of privilege as a belle of the Old South, but also about her

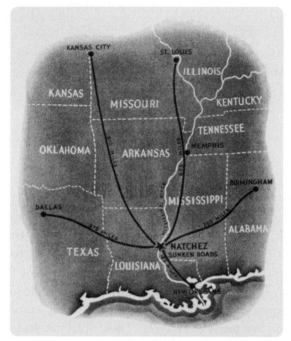

During the 1930s, tourists regarded Natchez as the epicenter
of what had been the Old South. ("The Old South Still Lives,"
Better Homes and Gardens, February 1938.)

retreat into seclusion in recent years. Poignant as the story of a murdered scion
of the southern aristocracy may have been, however, the media's focus quickly
shifted to her eccentric neighbors Richard "Dick" Dana and Octavia Dockery,
who were arrested for her murder. They, too, were descendants of southern
elites but lived in squalor at Glenwood, a two-story Greek Revival mansion
that was falling down around them. The press called it "Goat Castle," a reference to its once grand status as a southern mansion as well as to the four-legged
residents who shared the home with the odd pair. Years later the crime became
known as the "Goat Castle murder" with Merrill's death an afterthought.

The press's obsession with the southern gothic spectacle of Glenwood and
its residents and of the southern aristocracy in decline meant ignoring another
side of the story. The only person to stand trial for Jennie Merrill's murder was
an African American domestic named Emily Burns. She was no guiltier of the
crime than Dana or Dockery, but in the Jim Crow South, the arrest and convic-

tion of a "Negro" was expected. Like so many other southern blacks who were caught in an unjust legal system, Emily Burns was virtually erased from community memory, becoming a footnote in a saga that had gripped the nation.

The murder of Jennie Merrill and the vivid spectacle of Goat Castle captured America's attention throughout the fall of 1932. It made such an impression that newspapers and popular magazines made reference to it for several years after. And yet, the actual facts of the case have long given way to vague community memories, speculation about who killed Jennie Merrill, and even ghostly legend. In the Natchez City Cemetery, however, headstones serve as reminders of what was very real. Jane Surget Merrill is buried in the Merrill family plot. The long granite ledger marking her grave is etched with a large Celtic cross, her name, and the day of her death—August 4, 1932. Less than a hundred yards away, Dick Dana, born Richard Henry Clay Dana, is buried in the small gated plot of his family. A modest marker bears only his name and birth and death dates. Less than ten yards from his final resting place is a simple headstone that marks the grave of Octavia Dockery, who lived with Dick Dana and served as his guardian. A local group of citizens placed it there in the months following her death. "Mistress of Goat Castle" is carved below her name. It was a title she both reviled and reveled in.

The grave of Emily Burns, tried and convicted as an accessory to first-degree murder in Merrill's death, will not be found there. She is buried in an unmarked grave in Skinner's Cemetery on a shady hillside off of Liberty Road, where the members of her church, Antioch Baptist, are laid to rest. And while stories about the Goat Castle murder have circulated for decades in Natchez, memories of Emily Burns are practically nonexistent. Sentenced to spend the rest of her life at the Mississippi State Penitentiary in late November 1932, she was swiftly forgotten, as were the facts that led to her conviction.

The course of this case may seem perfectly ordinary. In the Jim Crow South, justice for the murder of a white woman often meant the conviction of a black person. In Mississippi, blacks convicted of petty crimes could end up at Parchman, the state penitentiary. There, they labored in the cotton fields like their slave ancestors had before them, working under the supervision of a gun-toting white man on horseback. While a murder conviction often meant death by execution, Emily Burns instead received a life sentence because the jury could not agree on her punishment. And yet, almost eight years to the day when she arrived at the prison, Governor Paul B. Johnson suspended her sentence. She quietly returned to Natchez, where she lived until her death in September 1969.

So why *did* the national media pick up this story and follow it daily until the trial ended? Why did newspapers and magazines continue to publish articles about the crime for decades? Why was the case a cause célèbre? Part of the answer lay in the popularity of true crime stories in the 1930s. During the Depression, true crime sold newspapers and magazines and served as a cheap form of entertainment for Americans during desperate economic times. Such stories frequently involved the demise of prominent individuals and were fixated on the salacious details of family dysfunction. The murder of Jennie Merrill in Natchez, Mississippi, had all of this and then some.

Generally, such stories were only of local interest. But Jennie Merrill's murder made national news. One *New York Times* headline about the case hints at why it attracted such attention:

Neighbor Pair Held in Natchez Murder, R. H. Dana and
His Housekeeper Charged with Slaying Miss Merrill over Goats.
Three Members of Aristocratic Families, All 60 or More,
Lived Lives as Recluses.[1]

Murder, aristocracy, recluses, and goats—these were subjects more likely to be found in a southern gothic novel, and in fact journalists immediately drew parallels to the fiction of Edgar Allan Poe, and later, William Faulkner's novels about the social decay of old southern families. But this was no fictional tale. The eccentric personalities and the economic, and even mental, decline among these descendants of once respected families was all true, and it drew reporters and voyeuristic tourists alike to Natchez that fall and for years to come.

The basic facts of the crime are straightforward. Near dusk on the evening of August 4, 1932, someone shot and killed Jennie Merrill—by all accounts a very petite woman—during an attempted robbery in her home, Glenburnie. The perpetrators then carried her body about one hundred yards from the house, where they dumped it in a thicket. Merrill's neighbors Dick Dana, sixty-one, and Octavia Dockery, sixty-seven, were among the first to be taken in for questioning and, within a few days, charged with murder. Their constant feuding with Merrill made them likely suspects. Yet despite the fact that their fingerprints were retrieved from inside of Merrill's home, a judge released them on their own recognizance to return to Glenwood after a ten-day stint in the Adams County jail.

Meanwhile, two African Americans were targeted as murder suspects. One was fifty-seven-year-old Lawrence Williams, an Adams County native who had migrated to Chicago years before. He had come to Natchez in July in hopes of finding work, which was difficult to come by during the Depression, especially for a black man. While there, he met Emily Burns, a widowed thirty-seven-year-old domestic who, along with her mother, took in boarders to supplement her income. Williams, known in Chicago as George Pearls, appears to have struck up a romance with Burns, and after knowing her for less than a week, he moved to the home she shared with her mother on St. Catherine Street.[2]

Within hours of Jennie Merrill's murder, he vacated town so swiftly that he left behind his trunk of personal belongings. While making his way home to Chicago, a police deputy in Pine Bluff, Arkansas, stopped Williams for reasons unrelated to the crime in Natchez. The deputy shot and killed him, he said, for resisting arrest and allegedly refusing to answer questions. The gun found among Williams's possessions, it turned out, used bullets that were subsequently matched with the type recovered from the crime scene in Natchez. A few days later, the Adams County sheriff, tipped off by a local who had met Williams, recovered Williams's trunk and arrested Emily Burns and her mother, Nellie Black. Burns later gave a coerced confession after a week of intense questioning. Several weeks later, on the Friday after Thanksgiving, a jury of twelve white men from Adams County convicted George Pearls, alias Lawrence Williams, posthumously, after which Emily Burns stood trial as his accomplice. Her conviction was swift. At most, she was at the scene of the crime, but she did not kill Jennie Merrill.

These were the facts, yet almost from the outset, journalists were obsessed with Dick Dana and Octavia Dockery and their home, Glenwood. The dilapidated mansion had been Dana's childhood home and was his inheritance. For years he had boarded in different homes throughout Natchez, but around 1916 Dick and Octavia moved into Glenwood, where they lived out the rest of their lives. Technically, because of his inability to pay property taxes, Dick Dana no longer owned the property. But neither of them had anyplace else to go. And so, he and Octavia lived there for more than three decades without ever paying taxes or rent while repeated attempts to evict them failed. The two were, for all intents and purposes, squatters among the ruins of what had once been a respectable abode. The contrasts between what had been and what was now was not lost on reporters.

While the first headlines focused on Jennie Merrill's death—"Rich Woman Recluse Slain In Mississippi" and "Elderly Recluse Slain in South"—they soon gave way to "Weird Mississippi Murder Traced to Row over Goats" and "Southern Goat Castle Scene of a Tragedy" and others like it.[3] A jailhouse photo of Dick and Octavia accompanied the articles. Stern and unsmiling, she looked like a weathered farm wife. She wore a straw hat, and a smock covered her morning dress. Dick's hair looked unkempt. He had not shaved for several days, and he wore filthy coveralls. He sat to her left with his hands in his lap and had a wild-eyed expression that suggested he might be mentally off-kilter, which indeed he was. His interviews with the press could be rambling and nonsensical. Octavia seemed to enjoy the attention and actually welcomed interviews with reporters as a ploy to shape a narrative of her life as a one-time southern belle who had fallen on hard times.

And then there were the goats. They not only roamed the grounds of Glenwood but also feasted on the wallpaper and books inside its walls. The home had long ago descended into shocking condition. It was ankle-deep in filth and overrun with animals—ducks, geese, chickens, cats, dogs, and especially goats. By the time of the murder, Glenwood had literally become "Goat Castle." Indeed, the goats lived better than the humans with whom they shared the house. In the days following their arrest, photographs and descriptions of the home's condition also circulated, along with references to Dana as a "Wild Man" and Dockery as the "Goat Woman." *This* intrigued the public and sold newspapers, which is why generations later, locals still refer to it as the "Goat Castle murder." In many ways, the lives of Jennie Merrill, Duncan Minor, Lawrence Williams/George Pearls, and Emily Burns—all central figures in this crime—have been overshadowed.

———

America's fascination with stories about the Old South helped drive the reports coming out of Natchez, especially because of Merrill's connection to great planter wealth. Goat Castle aside, the town was home to numerous antebellum mansions, the kind that Hollywood tried to recreate in movies of the era, so many of which were set in the pre–Civil War South. They were also homes that attracted visitors even before there was a definable tourism industry for the South's plantation heritage.

Since the dawn of automobile tourism, and particularly after Henry Ford began producing the affordable Model T, tourists from the Northeast and Midwest traveled to Natchez to see its architectural treasures. They trespassed on the grounds of the grand estates just to catch a glimpse of the magnificent homes with stately names like Melrose, Dunleith, and Stanton Hall. During the spring of 1932, only a few months before the Merrill murder, several of the homes were opened to the public for the very first time in their history. Many of the direct descendants of the families who built the houses still lived in them, and some greeted their guests dressed in their ancestors' clothing. Their efforts proved wildly successful, and magazine writers lauded pilgrimage festivities as an authentic representation of life in the antebellum South. Throughout the 1930s, popular magazines, as well as national and regional newspapers, encouraged their readers to travel to Natchez. The garden club promoted the opportunity to experience what life was like before the Civil War, made possible not only by the homeowners but also by local blacks in the role of house slaves and carriage drivers.[4]

Jennie Merrill's murder and the notoriety of Goat Castle, however, stood in stark contrast to the pilgrimage motto "Come to Natchez, Where the Old South Still Lives."

It was no small feat to reach Natchez in the early 1930s. There were no airports, and what counted as a highway was not much more than a dirt road. For travelers from a western state like Texas, the Mississippi River presented an additional challenge once they arrived in the town of Vidalia, Louisiana, directly across the river from Natchez. Ferries provided the only way across until a bridge was built in 1940. And yet, during the depths of the Great Depression, thousands of American tourists sought out Natchez. They boarded ferries and crossed the Mississippi River, drove their cars over treacherous terrain, and traveled by trains from the Northeast and the Midwest to venture to this remote location to experience what impressed them as a living, breathing, and genuine example of the Old South.

Why Americans ventured to Natchez has a lot to do with its history, a history that made the town a temptress of sorts. As journalist David Cohn wrote in an issue of the *Atlantic Monthly* in 1940, "Natchez was a lady." She was the oldest settlement on the lower half of the Mississippi River and earned her name from her original inhabitants, the Natchez Indians. Her suitors included the French (who established Fort Rosalie in 1716), the English (following the Seven Years' War with England, the fort was ceded to the British in 1763), the Spanish (from 1779 to 1798, during which time Natchez began to take shape as a city laid out in the common grid pattern under territorial governor Manuel Gayoso de Lemos), and finally the Americans in 1798, when Lady Natchez came under the control of the U.S. government.

The town has had its fair share of famous visitors throughout its history, even before the Civil War. When it was the capital of the Mississippi Territory, former vice president Aaron Burr was first arrested near Natchez for conspiring to create a separate nation, though he was released and later acquitted on charges of treason. Two decades later, the American naturalist John James Audubon spent a few months there painting birds; he also enrolled his sons at nearby Jefferson Academy, a military school for young boys. P. T. Barnum brought the Swedish singing sensation Jenny Lind to Natchez in 1851, where she performed to a sell-out crowd, as she had done in cities across the United States.

Northerners from Pennsylvania, New York, New Jersey, Maine, Connecticut, Maryland, and Massachusetts came, too. Between the 1830s and the 1850s, they purchased large tracts of land in Louisiana and Mississippi, staking their claim to the profits of the region's cotton boom. While stately homes were built for families of wealth in Natchez proper, the life of a country gentleman was to be found in the gently rolling hills on the outskirts of town. There, planters created large estates, which, in addition to very grand homes, included outbuildings and slave quarters. Melrose typified this model.

Melrose was built for the McMurran family during the 1840s. The home sat back from the main road, and in the nineteenth century travelers made the long approach to Melrose in a horse-drawn carriage. Bouncing along the dirt path, guests of Melrose passed through a romantic landscape. At the entryway was an ornamental pond and, later, a bog surrounded by cypress trees dressed in Spanish moss, after which visitors drove through a canopy of tall trees. As the home came into view, it seemed to grow larger in size. House slaves greeted guests and took their trunks and baggage, leading them into the house through the imposing portico. The McMurrans filled their home with "all that fine taste and a full purse" could afford—silk draperies, painted canvas floor coverings, and ornate rococo-style furniture. A hand-carved mahogany punkah, operated by slaves, shooed flies away from the food served on the long dining room table, as well as provided dinner guests with a gentle breeze. Service itself had been modernized, relative to the antebellum era, through a system of bells linked between the main house and the brick dependencies where house slaves were quartered.[5]

Such estates were often filled with the best porcelain and silver money could buy and objets d'art from Europe. In fact, traveling through Europe was seen as a rite of passage for the sons of the planter elite before they assumed their role in the family business. Frederick Quitman, for example, took a six-month tour of Europe that included the British Isles, Switzerland, Venice, and Milan following his graduation from Princeton in 1853. Only then did he return to manage his father's sugar plantation. Not everyone lived as well as the planters, however, and Natchez was not always ladylike.[6]

Down below the bluffs, the area known as "Natchez Under-the-Hill" had a different historical reputation altogether. It was one of the most notorious river landings on the Mississippi River, peopled with gamblers, thieves, swindlers, and prostitutes. Boatmen, who traveled up and down the river loading cotton and unloading slaves, frequented its saloons, and knife fights were a regular feature on the levee below Natchez proper. Still, it was the wealth and the mansions above the bluffs that defined Natchez.

The town was an important link in the global market for cotton, much of which was shipped directly to New York and Liverpool, England. The booming British textile industry created the demand for the cotton coming from the lower Mississippi valley. A labor-intensive crop, cotton required substantial numbers of slaves, and as demand for it increased, America's domestic slave trade rapidly expanded, too. Between 750,000 and one million enslaved people were forcibly relocated to the Deep South, roughly two-thirds of whom were sold through the mechanisms of the slave trade. For most, their first stop was the port of New Orleans. By 1850, it was the third-largest city in the country and the epicenter of America's domestic slave trade. Most of them were purchased by slave traders in the Upper South states of Maryland and Virginia, where tobacco farming had depleted the soil and was being replaced by other less labor-intensive crops. As a result, slave trading became a business of supply and demand. Planters in the Upper South had the supply, and the demand for slaves resided in the Deep South. Between October and January, New Orleans annually received ships filled with slaves from Maryland and Virginia. Once they arrived in the Crescent City, they were thrown into one of the high-walled pens, or holding areas, in the city's slave market. To entice potential buyers, slave traders dressed men in suits, while female slaves wore gingham dresses. They were among the thousands of men, women, and children sold on a daily basis whose final destinations were the plantations of Louisiana and Mississippi. Many were taken and sold in slave markets upriver, including Natchez, the second-largest slave market in the Deep South outside of New Orleans.[7]

The town was integral to this slave network. It had active slave markets as early as 1801, but its most famous, and the largest, was the slave market known as the Forks of the Road, where Washington Road and Liberty Road intersected. The Forks, established after an 1830 ordinance was passed to keep traders out of the city limits, served as the basis of operations for numerous slave traders, including the firm of Franklin and Armfield. Isaac Franklin of Tennessee purchased property at the Forks for the express purpose of slave sales, while his nephew John Armfield operated the firm's slave pen in Alexandria, Virginia. Together, they became two of the most active slave traders in the United States, buying slaves for low prices in Virginia and then selling them for considerable profit in Natchez. Like other slave traders at the Forks, they built rudimentary pens to hold the human chattel they brought to the area from other slave markets. Rectangular in shape and built from wood, they offered nothing in the way of human comforts because they were considered temporary shelter. Joseph Ingraham, in his book *The South-West by a Yankee* published in 1835, described the shelter for slaves as "old unoccupied buildings, and often tents or booths, pitched upon the common." He also detailed the march of slaves from the river landing, below the Natchez bluffs. "Passing through the city in procession, sometimes dressed in a new uniform, purchased for them in New Orleans, but often in the brown rags in which they left Virginia preceded by a large wagon carrying the surplus baggages; they are marched beyond the city limits" to the Forks of the Road.[8]

Since Congress abolished the African slave trade in 1808, Natchez planters relied on the domestic slave trade to meet their needs. In addition to the slaves shipped to New Orleans from Baltimore, Maryland, and Alexandria, Virginia, and eventually brought upriver to Natchez, slave traders marched thousands more overland. These coffles of slaves—large groups bound together by chains— were force-marched from Virginia to Tennessee. Then, just outside of Nashville, they traveled down the old Indian trading path known as the Natchez Trace. By the time they reached Natchez, a journey of several weeks, they had walked more than a thousand miles.

Once there, they were prepared for their sale to the owners of area estates who held thousands of acres in Adams County and neighboring Jefferson County and across the river in Concordia Parish, Louisiana. "The slaves are made to shave and wash in greasy pot liquor, to make them look sleek and nice," wrote William Anderson, who was sold in Natchez in the early nineteenth century. "Their heads must be combed, their best clothes put on, and when called out to be examined, they must stay in a row—the women and men apart—then they are picked out and taken to a room and examined." Men and women, husbands and wives, were often sold separately. Anderson also described children being torn from their mothers' arms and sent away, never to be seen again. The "weeping and crying" he heard disturbed him, but the reaction of the slave owners was to quell the noise by beating the slaves with a lash. These scenes were repeated for decades and took place within sight of Monmouth, Linden, and D'Evereux—the mansions owned by some of the wealthiest of the town's slave owners.[9]

When the Civil War erupted, the world that Natchez planters enjoyed came to a swift end. Union troops arrived there in August 1863 after having seized Vicksburg, another town that sat atop bluffs farther upriver from Natchez. Planters in Natchez had divided loyalties, both Union and Confederate, but regardless of their sympathies, the Yankees moved quickly to seize control of their estates. While officers fashioned headquarters inside the mansions, soldiers pitched tents on the grounds around them. Those who remained loyal to the Union, some of whom entertained federal troops while they occupied Natchez, were the most fortunate.

Down below the bluffs, the federal army established a slave contraband camp and, most alarming to Natchez residents, placed black soldiers on street patrol. The Union occupiers also placed black troops at the Forks of the Road slave market, where they were quickly joined by slaves who had abandoned local plantations. The very existence of black soldiers struck fear into the hearts of white Natchezeans, but having them stationed at the Forks sent the message that the days of chattel slavery were numbered.

A *New York Times* correspondent traveling with the army commented on what the locals likely took for granted—the city's riches. "It contains more wealth in proportion to its inhabitants than perhaps any town in the whole country, either North or South. It is a common saying here that if a man is not worth a million, he is not considered well off," he wrote. The wealthiest planters and largest slaveholders were, according to the *Times* reporter, "the most stubborn Union men," which included Jennie Merrill's father, who owned plantations in Louisiana and Mississippi, several hundred slaves, and Elms Court—one of the most beautiful homes in the area.[10]

Confederate defeat and the end of slavery marked the beginning of the town's long decline, but for the thousands of slaves who toiled in the cotton fields that made Natchez planters wealthy and helped build the mansions that tourists still see today, it was the dawn of a new day. Of the four million humans in bondage at the war's end, a large majority worked on plantations in the lower Mississippi valley. According to the U.S. Census in 1860, slaves constituted the majority of the population in this area. In Adams County, slaves made up 72 percent of the total population, in neighboring Jefferson County the figure was 81 percent, and in Concordia Parish just across the river from Natchez, 91 percent of the population was enslaved.[11] Their emancipation ended the economic domination of planters in the Cotton Kingdom, some of whom left and went back north, while others stayed and tried to return their lands to profitability in the absence of free labor. Sharecropping replaced slavery, and while cotton still dominated the regional economy for decades, Natchez was no longer the center of opulence.

In the latter decades of the nineteenth century, a Jewish mercantile class played a key role in the town's economic recovery. A few of these merchants became cotton planters, but their financial success came as agents in the plantation supply and cotton-buying business, accomplished by working with both white planters and black sharecroppers. Natchez had a vibrant Jewish community going back to 1843, and during the later years of the nineteenth century Jews made important civic improvements and also participated in politics. In the early 1930s, the mayor of Natchez was a Jewish merchant, Saul Laub, whose wife was a member of the Natchez Garden Club. The glory days of the southern aristocracy, however, had long since passed.[12]

During the early twentieth century, very little new industry had emerged. The town was accessible by train, but there were no good roads in Mississippi to make it worth investing in a town as remote as Natchez. Sure, there was the river, but steamboats and ferries were outmoded forms of transportation. There wasn't even a bridge across the river. So, like a debutante waiting for someone to sign her dance card, Natchez sat on the sidelines of modernity for decades.

Still, the magnificent homes and estates built from that wealth remained. Aside from being weatherworn or needing repairs, by 1932 not much had changed these antebellum structures for almost a century. Some of the descendants of the original families still lived in them. And the descendants of slaves? Many joined the Great Migration of African Americans to northern cities searching for what author Richard Wright called "the warmth of other suns." Wright would know.

He was born in Adams County, and, like other black Natchezeans, his family, too, went north. Still others became part of the black middle class who located their businesses—barbershops, restaurants, funeral homes, and juke joints—along St. Catherine Street. They worked side by side with Italian immigrant families, like Eduardo and Maria Stallone, who operated a grocery store there. This was also the street where they attended their churches, the largest of which was Holy Family—the first Catholic congregation for African Americans in Mississippi.

Yet for so many more it was almost as if time had not passed. Except for earning meager wages, their lives often resembled those of their grandparents. They continued to work for white families in Natchez—cooking for them, cleaning their homes, washing and ironing their clothes, and maintaining the grounds of the estates. Some were able to purchase farmland, but they were sharecroppers, too. And while they were free, the constant state of indebtedness to the landowners made it feel like freedom in name only. Those who lived in town rented ramshackle houses because they couldn't afford to own one. Entire black neighborhoods emerged within spitting distance of the Forks of the Road, where so many of their ancestors had been bought and sold. This is important to understanding why outsiders felt as if Natchez was nothing short of a time capsule of the Old South—six decades after the Civil War.

Americans in the 1930s were fascinated by this image of the region, and it was a fascination with a long history, extending back in time to the early nineteenth century, when plantation novels were all the rage. In the twentieth century, the new medium of film also captured this nostalgia for the plantation South. Movies sought to bring southern romance to life, but it was always Hollywood's version in which the main attraction was often the setting itself —the large, white-columned mansions peopled by ladies in hoop skirts and black house slaves all too happy to serve their white masters. It was a well-established image long before the publication of Margaret Mitchell's *Gone with the Wind*. In fact, two years earlier, Stark Young's book *So Red the Rose* had been the best-selling novel on the Old South. Its setting? Natchez.[13]

As it turned out, Natchez had all of this southern romance in spades, and it was no movie set. It was real. Charleston and Savannah also drew visitors seeking southern pastoral romance, but in the Deep South, no city other than New Orleans could boast such a large collection of antebellum houses as Natchez, which included Jennie Merrill's ancestral home, Elms Court.

Still, beneath the patina of a glamorous southern civilization presented by the garden club, many visitors were also curious about that other house. The one with the goats. The one where the "Wild Man" and the "Goat Woman" lived. The one where Poe's and Faulkner's fiction came to life.

This book returns to the Deep South of the 1930s—to Natchez, Mississippi —when Jennie Merrill was killed and descriptions of Goat Castle riveted the nation. It revisits the facts of the case and the personalities involved, placing them in the context of their time. As the story unfolds, the history of both black and white Natchezeans before, during, and after the crime help to explain what actually became of the descendants of both slave owners and the enslaved at a time when writers waxed nostalgic about the South's pastoral traditions or, in some cases, held up a mirror to its decline. This account of events also engages the contemporary issues at play—particularly race relations— that are critical in understanding how the region moved from slavery to Jim Crow in the decades following the Civil War. Finally, Natchez itself helps us to better understand the nation's idealized image of the South during this decade, since, for so many, Natchez *was* the Old South.

Many have tried to make sense of this crime. Several journalists and local citizens felt compelled to write about it. In 1933, Homer G. Wells, a Memphis-based crime writer, authored a five-part series of the crime for the pulp magazine *Master Detective*, published under the title "The Crimson Crime at Glenburney Manor." During this same year, Natchez resident Zaida Marion Wells published her seventeen-page booklet, *The Merrill Murder Mystery*, exploring the crime. Howard University professor Sterling Brown visited Natchez in the early 1940s. He briefly noted the crime, calling Glenwood a "perverse attraction for tourists," which it was. Harnett Kane, a best-selling author from New Orleans, included a chapter about the murder in his book *Natchez on the Mississippi* (1947), referring to Goat Castle as a "peep show for the nation." Fifteen years passed before anyone sought to write the full story. Charles East, former editor for the Louisiana State University Press, researched the case for years and submitted his book proposal, which he called "Natchez Gothic," to American Heritage Publishing in 1962. The editors turned him down, so he continued his research; he died in 2009 having never written the book. In 1985, two local Natchezeans, businessman Sim Callon and journalist Carolyn Vance Smith, published their book, *The Goat Castle Murder: A True Natchez Story That Shocked the World*. While it presents the basic outline of the story, it includes next to nothing on the black principals in the case, leaving many questions unanswered. And yet, it has had the most influence over how locals and tourists have learned about the events of that year. Its impact is also evident in the most recent book to examine the crime, *The Goat Castle Murder*, a fictionalized account by novelist Michael Llewelyn. As a work of historical fiction it fabricates dialogue, and sometimes the "facts" are simply the myths that have been repeated in Natchez for decades. Llewelyn, like so many others, treats the experience of Emily Burns with only passing interest. By doing so, the story remains incomplete. That is, until now.[14]

———————

What follows is a historical pilgrimage to Depression-era Natchez and what was arguably its "crime of the century," a story that captured the nation's attention. Based on extensive local research, it makes stops at sites pivotal to the case and introduces the key personalities involved. Along the way, it offers historical lessons on how the South's culture changed, including the conditions that contributed to Jennie Merrill's death and led to Emily Burns's incarceration. At the center of the story is Natchez—a character in its own right. Its history and its setting, overlooking the bluffs of the Mississippi River, only add to the crime's mystique.

The journey begins.

CHAPTER ONE

RECLUSIVE ARISTOCRATS

Jennie Merrill's life should have played out differently. Women born into the southern planter class, particularly the privileged group to which she belonged, were being prepared for marriage from the time they were young girls. They received an elite education while their mothers taught them the social skills required of genteel women. Once married, young women from well-heeled Natchez families were expected to entertain the members of their elite social circle or risk being the subject of community gossip—or worse, shunned. And it was assumed that they would bear children to preserve bloodlines, as well as the family fortune. The changes wrought by the Civil War, however, complicated those expectations.[1]

Jennie's full name—Jane Surget Merrill—signaled her elite status and connections to the world. The Surget and Merrill families were among the wealthiest in the antebellum South. At his death in 1856, Jennie's grandfather Francis Surget was not only one of the wealthiest planters in the South but also one of the richest men in America. He had amassed a cotton empire that extended across Louisiana, Mississippi, and Arkansas, and he owned more than a thousand slaves. When his daughter Jane (Jennie's mother) married Ayres P. Merrill Jr. in 1852, he gave them a home—Elms Court—as a wedding gift. Merrill expanded the 1837 Greek Revival mansion to include decorative ironwork and a double-tiered gallery on the front facade, making it one of the most beautiful of the suburban villas in Natchez. This was the home where Jennie was born, yet the timing of her birth—August 1863—forever changed her life's expected trajectory.[2]

The Civil War, a war so many of Mississippi's planters hoped to avoid, cast its long shadow over the state in the summer of 1863. Just upriver from Natchez, in Vicksburg, Major General Ulysses S. Grant battled Confederate com-

Photographs of Jennie Merrill near the time of her death do not exist.
This one, taken when she was around twenty, illustrates her petite frame.
(Courtesy of the Dicks Family Collection, Historic Natchez
Foundation, Natchez, Miss.)

mander General John C. Pemberton for control of the town and, consequently, the Mississippi River. After suffering severe casualties, Grant laid siege to the town, choking off troops and civilians alike from food and supplies. The siege lasted forty-seven days before Pemberton surrendered, on July 4, effectively ceding the river to Union control.

One month later—the very month Jennie Merrill was born—federal troops arrived in Natchez. Strategically, the town was not as important as Vicksburg; nevertheless, it supplied the army with food and a place to rest. Many Natchez planters, in fact, held Union sympathies. Jennie's father, Ayres Merrill, Jr., certainly did. His ties to the North were both personal and professional. He

Jennie's father, Ayres Merrill Jr., n.d. (Courtesy of the Thomas H. and
Joan W. Gandy Photograph Collection, Louisiana and Lower Mississippi
Valley Collections, Special Collections, Hill Memorial Library,
Louisiana State University Libraries, Baton Rouge.)

was descended from Merrills in Pittsfield, Massachusetts, and he conducted
business with cotton factors in New York. Merrill had a lot to lose. A successful planter, the 1860 census showed that he owned nearly one hundred slaves
in Adams County and another three hundred across the river in Concordia
Parish. He and others opposed the war because they knew it would bring a
dramatic end to slavery, the Cotton Kingdom it supported, and the lifestyle to
which area planter families had grown accustomed.[3]

In many ways Jennie's family was fortunate. Several days before Union
troops arrived in his hometown, the thirty-eight-year-old Merrill joined a
group of men from Natchez who traveled to meet with General Grant in Vicksburg. They sought to demonstrate their loyalty in an effort to protect their
land from being confiscated. The men also hoped to still be able to hire former
slaves to harvest that year's cotton crop. Going to see Grant was not without

its risks, as they might be taken into custody by Union troops or be killed by Confederate guerrillas.[4]

Merrill also reached out to Brigadier General Thomas Ransom, commander of the post at Natchez, and found him receptive. Ransom defended Merrill to Grant, describing him as "one of the few sound Union men of the region." As he explained, "During all of his difficulties he has [bravely] maintained his position and, pistol in hand, defied the mob [of Confederate guerrillas] that threatened to burn his residence and hang him." Ransom also endorsed Merrill's request to allow him to hire slave contraband — those slaves taken by federal forces — in order to harvest his cotton before it ruined in the fields. As the Natchez commander noted, "Being a young man he has passed through great trials and dangers & suffered great pecuniary loss."[5]

While Grant approved Merrill's request, hiring former slaves who were now considered "contraband of war" was both risky and futile — risky for newly free slaves and futile for planters like Ayres Merrill. According to a Union soldier with the Twelfth Wisconsin, there were "about four thousand contrabands in Natchez" in early 1864, yet "very few have gone to work on the abandoned plantations." The reason? Confederate guerrillas. They were "so numerous that but few plantations will be worked during the coming season," the soldier reported. He also warned of the mortal danger of going back to work for men like Merrill. "Already the negroes on two or three plantations have been captured and murdered," he wrote, adding, "The rebels are determined that if they can't have the benefit of these plantations, no one else shall."[6]

Aside from Merrill's request to harvest his cotton, Grant also approved his appeal to take his young family north, to New York City, where they waited out the war in a home on Washington Square. While there, Ayres formed a partnership with Walter Goodman, a cousin by marriage, as cotton factors and general commission agents who purchased, sold, and leased southern land as well as plantation-related machinery until the death of both men in 1883.[7]

Despite his losses in Mississippi in both slave labor and cotton, Merrill's investments were diverse, and he remained a wealthy man. Even sequestered in New York, he contracted to build a magnificent home in Newport, Rhode Island. The mansion, named Harbor View, was under construction when Merrill's wife, Jane, died during childbirth at the age of thirty-six. The house had promised a new beginning for the young family, but Ayres, now a widowed father of six young children, would spend little time in Newport after his wife's death. He sold Harbor View less than five years after its construction.[8]

In the years immediately following the war, several of the Merrill children were of school age and, as before the conflict, attended the best schools money could buy. Jennie was about eight years old when her father enrolled her at St. Mary's Hall, a private academy for young girls in Burlington, New Jersey. The school, founded in 1837 by the Episcopal bishop George Doane, offered girls an education as intellectually engaging as that received by their male peers. By providing her with an elite education, Jennie's father continued the antebellum tradition of preparing daughters for marriage with members of their class. Ayres proved to be an engaged and doting father throughout her boarding school experience, writing her frequently, encouraging her in her studies, and keeping her up to date on her siblings at Elms Court.[9]

Jennie was not yet a teenager when, in 1876, her father's Union loyalties paid dividends. During his second term of office, President Grant submitted Ayres Merrill's name as his choice for U.S. ambassador to Belgium. Besides having proven his loyalty, Merrill was also Harvard educated, well traveled, and a French speaker. Congress swiftly approved Merrill's appointment in January of that year, and by the spring, the family was headed for new adventures in Europe.[10]

Jennie Merrill enjoyed a brief but very privileged time in Brussels. Because of her father's status as ambassador, she and her siblings frequently circulated among European elites. Although she was not quite the age of a debutante, Jennie certainly enjoyed the life of one while there, as did her older sisters, Catherine and Minnie. When Grant and his wife, Julia, toured Europe after his second term as president, Catherine and Minnie were involved in their visit to Belgium. The sisters accompanied the Grants on their tour of the Bois de la Cambre, the beautiful park in Brussels adjacent to the Sonian Forest. Known in the press as the "Misses Merrill," they were guests at a dinner attended by numerous European dignitaries, hosted by the king and queen of Belgium to honor the former president.[11]

Both Minnie and Catherine grew quite popular in social circles, and wherever they traveled they garnered public attention. In an article titled "The Beauties of America," a journalist wrote that the sisters "have been poetically called 'Night and Morning.' Miss Minnie Merrill, the former, is a perfect brunette of the Spanish type and is spoken of as one of the handsomest brunettes in America." Catherine, with "hair the shade that Titian loved to paint," was also considered a great conversationalist. Whether "in the casino or ballroom of Spa, she held undisputed sway."[12]

The rest of the family was on its way to Paris when Minnie and Catherine were entertaining in Spa, Belgium. The Merrills' final destination, however, was the French city of Nice, where they were scheduled to spend the winter months. The family's true purpose in going there was in hopes of improving the health of Ayres Merrill. Several months before, at the age of fifty-two, the Belgian ambassador had a paralytic stroke that caused him to be bedridden. Its severity not only prevented him from performing his duties as ambassador but also required his children to play an even more significant ceremonial role in his absence. This is why Jennie's sisters entertained the Grants on their tour of Belgium and why her older brother, Dunbar, was the person to greet the former U.S. president and his wife upon their arrival. Now, as the Merrill family traveled south, her older sisters' exploits served to distract the public from their father's condition.[13]

The ambassador's health did not improve. U.S. newspapers documented his stroke in April 1877, and by October some predicted he would have to resign. Yet Merrill stayed on, perhaps for his children's sake, for two years following his stroke. Then, in May 1879, the family—including Jennie, her sister Catherine, and brothers Ayres III, Dunbar, and Frank—boarded the SS *Zeeland* in Antwerp and set sail for the United States.[14] They disembarked in Philadelphia, a common port of entry for ships on the Red Star Line, before returning to New York. Minnie stayed behind in Belgium, where she married and began a family in Antwerp. The following year, Ayres and his young family moved to Pittsfield, Massachusetts, where his father had been born. Then, in September 1883, Jennie's father died in Ocean County on the New Jersey coast, where he had gone in a final effort to improve his health. He was only fifty-seven years old. He had been gone from Natchez for years, and only in death did he return.[15]

Jennie Surget Merrill, a young woman of twenty, now found herself in a world without the protection or sage counsel of her father. She was smart and well traveled and had moved in elite circles among royalty in Europe. Her inheritance included plantations in Concordia Parish, Louisiana, and she had the means to live and travel wherever she pleased. And while she could always return to Natchez, which she did from time to time, it would be several years before she returned for good.

For nearly two decades after her father's death, Jennie spent time in various cities, including New Orleans, Louisville, Memphis, and Baltimore, but she clearly preferred to be in New York. She spent her early childhood there, and friends and family from Natchez either had homes in the city or visited there on vacation. The Merrill name still had cachet, and she used it to her advantage. Though Jennie left no letters detailing her activity, fragmentary evidence from newspapers reveal that, by her late twenties, she found her calling as a member of the King's Daughters—a philanthropic and religious order founded in New York City in 1886 by women with ties to the Methodist, Presbyterian, and Episcopal churches.[16] This was a period of enormous growth for women's clubs in the United States, and in fact the King's Daughters grew to 125,000 members in just four years. This "sisterhood of service" was a perfect outlet for young, elite women like Jennie, eager to apply their talents for organization, public speaking, and reform in an era when women were not supposed to have careers. The service-oriented work of the order and the opportunity to maintain a high public profile clearly appealed to her.[17]

Jennie Merrill was personally moved to assist and improve the living conditions of immigrant mothers living in the slums of New York. She became an acolyte of Jacob Riis, the Danish-born journalist who photographed the conditions of tenement housing in New York and documented the plight of immigrants in his book *How the Other Half Lives*, published in 1890. He lectured widely and drew people to his cause by sharing his photographs of tenement families in dramatic fashion via a projector known as a stereopticon. Jennie was one of them. After hearing one of Riis's lectures in Chautauqua, New York, she became a champion of tenement reform.[18]

As a member of the King's Daughters, Jennie Merrill ginned up interest in Riis's work by going on her own speaking tour in several cities. She made speeches in advance of those being given by Riis and personally visited tenement slums in New York. Her concern for immigrant children, in particular, drew her to support the construction of a settlement house that contained a mothers' training school, a day nursery, and a kindergarten supplied with trained nurses. The Henry Street settlement, as it became known, was a direct response to Riis's argument that children who were reared in tenements would become an "army [of] tramps" and a burden on society if left to their own devices.[19]

Jennie was twenty-eight years old when she went on the speaking circuit. She always traveled at her own expense and as a prominent representative of the King's Daughters. Following her appearance in Baltimore, local papers described her as "a highly cultivated and interesting young lady" and reported that she gave presentations on the subject "with an intelligent and graceful ease that fixed the attention of her audience, which was [also] moved by her personal magnetism." She called the proposed settlement house a place where "the poor may learn to help themselves" and regarded it as but a small step "towards the complete reform of the tenement-house system in New York." Her dedication eventually led her to call for an audience with Cardinal James Gibbons—the archbishop of Baltimore—to encourage him to support the King's Daughters as they reached out to the "degraded, the outcast, and the miserable in the slums of New York, who were living not only in great physical want, but also beyond the reach of spiritual influences." Merrill told the cardinal that the King's Daughters sought not to interfere with the work of churches; rather, their "mission is to seek out those who belong to no church, who acknowledge none, and to bring them within reach of saving influences." Persuaded by Merrill's visit, the cardinal endorsed the project.[20]

Jennie Merrill's career as a reformer, her speaking tours, and her ability to attract attention for her reform work gave her life a purpose. And, while she had her suitors, she chose to live independently, to travel, and to pursue a life of public service during the very years of life when most women considered marriage. However, as the nineteenth century came to a close, Jennie, now in her mid-thirties, returned to Natchez for good where she lived a quiet life—quite the opposite of all she had known before.

Had it not been for the Civil War, Jennie Merrill would have grown up with the expectation of marrying a man who could secure the family's wealth and land. This custom usually meant marrying a son—who might have been a cousin—from among elite families in Natchez. The tradition of marrying cousins did not die out with the war, and in Jennie's case, two such men vied for her attention, though neither succeeded in securing her hand in wedlock.[21]

A few months after burying her father in Natchez, Jennie and her brother Dunbar traveled to Memphis, where they visited with their cousins the Goodmans, who were the children of Walter Goodman, with whom Ayres Merrill had set up his cotton factor firm in New York right after the war. It was during this time that the youngest Walter Goodman, who worked as a clerk in his father's merchant business, fell for Jennie. During an extended stay with his family, Jennie and Walter became better acquainted, and they later exchanged letters throughout 1884. Though only Walter's letters survive, they reveal a young man completely smitten with Jennie, who by now was truly a woman of the world. "My Dearest Love," he wrote her in the fall of 1884, "I miss you more than I can express. . . . Could I follow the dictates of my heart I could write volumes, the substance of which might be told in three words—*I love you.*" Jennie's feelings are unknown, but Walter's last known letter to her provides a clue, as he closed with "yours in devotion, but *without* hope of your love."[22]

The truth of the matter is that Duncan Gustine Minor, another of Jennie's cousins, was pursuing her at the same time. She had known Duncan since childhood. Their mothers were first cousins. On his father's side, Duncan's ancestry could be traced directly to Stephen Minor, who served as the last Spanish governor of the Natchez District. And, like Jennie, he was related to the Surgets, whose wealth was unsurpassed by other families in the area. When Duncan's parents married, his mother, Kate, brought considerably more assets to the union. She had inherited several valuable plantations around Natchez, which mostly she, and not her husband, managed with much success.[23]

Duncan and Jennie were both born in 1863, the same year that Union troops took possession of Natchez.[24] Yet unlike the Merrills, who fled north to wait out the Civil War, the Minors remained, at least until late 1864. Much to the chagrin of their Confederate-sympathizing neighbors, John and Kate Minor remained unabashedly loyal to the Union. According to Kate, her husband considered the war "a lost cause from the beginning, and that it was foolish of them [Confederates] to undertake it." As she recalled, "We had been North in 1860, and we both went home impressed with the folly of such an undertaking." During the Union occupation of Natchez, from August 1863 through the end of war, the Minors' home, Oakland, became a gathering place for federal officers. Thomas H. Spain, the Minors' former overseer, noted that "in a week after [U.S. troops] came to Natchez, John Minor's house was a perfect hotel for [Union] Officers, Generals & all; and remained so" until war's end. This not only irked neighbors but also raised the ire of local Confederate guerrillas and required John Minor to request "a guard to keep his house, to keep the Confederates away," especially since he had been entertaining "Yankee officers."[25]

Local women were civil but cool toward Kate Minor. According to Julia

Duncan Minor at twenty.
(Courtesy of the Dicks Family Collection,
Historic Natchez Foundation, Natchez, Miss.)

Nutt, also a loyalist, the ladies of Natchez "were compelled to be polite to her" because of her wealth and status in the community, but "there was little visiting between her and the ladies." In late 1864, the Minors received a pass to head north like other loyalists from Natchez. They waited out the war in New York, most likely at the home of Kate's uncle Jacob Surget.[26]

There were consequences for maintaining such loyalty to the Union. Kate Minor remarked that her husband felt "that his treatment from his old friends and associates had been such that he didn't care whether he lived or died." And following the war, his health worsened. During the summer of 1869, he traveled to New York seeking a reprieve from the Deep South's heat, and perhaps its hatred. There, after a terrible fall at his hotel, he sustained a head injury and died. Kate Minor carried on the family's business as she always had, managing her large plantations in Mississippi and Louisiana. Business-savvy and intelligent, she petitioned the Southern Claims Commission in 1871 to compensate her for Civil War losses. The commission, set up by the federal government, determined the validity of claims made by loyal southern Unionists regarding property loss. Kate's original claim was for more than $64,000, of which she received little more than $13,000 after nearly a decade of litigation.[27]

Still, Minor's finances exceeded those of many of her former friends in Adams County. In addition to the lands she owned at her husband's death, Kate inherited several more plantations from her uncle Jacob Surget and eventually formed a partnership with her brother James to administer their properties. Throughout her life, U.S. Census takers listed her as either a "Planter" or "Plantation Manager."[28]

Once he became old enough, Kate's son Duncan assumed responsibility for managing his mother's plantations in Mississippi and Louisiana. His mother first sent him north for an education, continuing a decades-old tradition among elite planter families. Duncan attended St. Paul's School, a college preparatory school in Concord, New Hampshire. He later enrolled at college at Princeton. It was a brief foray away from Natchez, after which he returned to the family home, Oakland, where he assisted his mother with the management of her extensive landholdings, much of which he eventually inherited. And there he remained—enamored of Jennie Merrill.

From the time he was a young man, Duncan Minor loved Jennie Merrill. While no letters attest to her feelings in return, his intense devotion to her lasted a lifetime. In one of his earliest surviving letters to her, dated April 1883, he had just returned to Natchez from New Orleans, where he spent time with her. Both were nearly twenty years old, and though he was smitten, his letter indicates that she did not feel the same. "It was such a trial to leave you for I was having such a nice time, notwithstanding the fact how little I saw of you, and I think if I had remained there longer I should have become bold there as [in Natchez]," he wrote, suggesting that she kept him at bay when they were away from their hometown. Yet Jennie had clearly reprimanded him prior to his leaving New Orleans, which caused him to offer her reassurances. "I see the senses of what you told me and will do all in my power to please you in all things," he wrote. "As for smothering, I feel sure that I will never do it again, for it is foolish for a man to smother by [love] as I have been doing lately."[29]

When Jennie visited Natchez in the spring of 1885, she stayed at her family's home, Elms Court, where Duncan sent her notes daily. In one, he hinted at the ritual that became theirs when Jennie eventually returned to Natchez.

My Precious One

I trust that you are able to be up this morning as I had so hoped that you would be yesterday. I have been thinking about you and wondering how you are ever since I got up this morning.

So please let me know how you are and I will be on my way this evening.

With my whole love—

Always yrs.
Duncan G. Minor

Restless as ever, Jennie went to New Orleans two weeks later and left Duncan behind to pine for her in Natchez. "I can't tell you how blue this separation makes me," he pouted. Even when she remained in town at Elms Court, she could be distant. Failing to see or hear from her, Duncan was beside himself. "Please write me how you are my Love, and stop this thru word business [allowing others to tell him how she is doing], as my heart is so full that it is nearly breaking, and it is only you that can give me comfort."[30]

By the time Duncan's surviving letters to Jennie picked up again in 1889, she was back in New York and moving from place to place. She was quite independent, and it becomes clear that his letters and impatient love for her have proven irritating. In letters that used to begin with "My Precious," there are no longer salutations. Not able to determine her whereabouts, he wrote to her in November 1889:

Is there any need of saying the letter contained in your card was a great surprise to me and cause of deep regret, but it is well deserved and you cannot be blamed for it. I hardly know if you desire these lines to ever reach you, as you send no address but will send to the same one as before hoping that they will [be forwarded]. Judging from the first mark I take it that you are in Baltimore; although I do so trust not ill, as the handwriting would seem to indicate.

For fear of erring to [an even] greater degree (if it is possible) I will send no more, but if there is any mercy for such as I, write me upon receipt of this.

Duncan Minor[31]

As the years passed, it became more obvious that his feelings were unrecip-
rocated. Again, during another of her visits to Natchez, she was distant. "Why
do you write me such miserable little," he complained in one note; "you must
know that it would make me anxious to know your reason why you do not
wish me to come over before Sunday." Finally, in the last letter from Duncan
known to exist, dated August 24, 1900, he writes, "Why is it there is nothing
from you, the days pass by, each one increasing my anxiety and still no mis-
sive of any kind to allay my fears?" The last line of his note, though, suggests
that Jennie may have toyed with Duncan. On the one hand, she ignored his
attempts to communicate with her, which caused him great consternation. On
the other hand, she made him feel guilty if he failed to write. As he told her,
"Of course, you will say that my not writing sooner is proof [I don't care] but
you are mistaken if intentional on your part."[32]

Jennie Merrill returned to Natchez for good, sometime in the late 1890s. But
why? In the earlier part of that decade, she was an avid tenement reformer in
New York who supported the work of Jacob Riis and led a life with purpose. She
also had such an independent streak that neither Walter Goodman nor Duncan
Minor was able to convince her to marry. But when Riis died in 1896, perhaps
her career as a speaker and reformer died with him. Wealthy as she was, she
could have continued to travel, but she had inherited plantations in Louisiana
and perhaps needed to return to manage them. She had never really lived full-
time in Natchez, and after leading such an exciting life as a young woman in
both Belgium and New York City, returning to Natchez, a small town seem-
ingly bypassed by modernity, must have been a disappointment. Yet return she
did. By now Elms Court had new owners, so she rented Gloucester, a nearby
house. A few years later, in 1904, she purchased Glenburnie, a house built in
1833 that sat on several acres of land just across the Kingston Road from where
she was born. This probably pleased Duncan, who still lived with his mother,
Kate, and it is about this time that he began his evening ritual of saddling his
horse at Oakland and riding to Glenburnie around dusk, where, after more than
twenty years of waiting, he could finally spend time alone with Jennie.[33]

By all accounts, Jennie became increasingly reclusive. Until the day she died,
she continued to wear the fashions of the 1890s, as she had when she lived in
New York — dresses with mutton sleeves and Princess Eugenie hats. Her pri-

mary human interactions were with Duncan and local black men and women she hired to cook for her and maintain her property. As needed, she went into town to do her banking, and eventually she purchased a 1919 Model T Roadster for basic errands around Natchez, running through stoplights and stop signs as she went. "Every policeman in Natchez knew [she] never waited for a red light, but nobody gave her a ticket," her mechanic would later say. She lived a discreet life until early 1916, when she acquired new neighbors on the adjacent property, Glenwood. Little did she know that their arrival next door would mark the beginning of a relentless, years-long feud that would disrupt the quiet solitude she had sought.[34]

Dick Dana and Octavia Dockery may never have moved to Glenwood had Duncan Minor had his way. When Dana failed to pay property taxes on the estate for 1911, the county tax collector sold it at public auction. Duncan Minor was the highest bidder and acquired Glenwood and its forty-five acres for the sum of forty-six dollars in 1912. Yet only a few years later, probably at the suggestion of Octavia Dockery, local attorney Laurens Kennedy sent Minor a letter asking him to reconvey the property to Dana because he had no place else to live. "It is believed that your and Mr. Dana's friendship in the past will cause you to do this, as you will not lose anything thereby, and it is his home," he wrote.[35]

Minor was unmoved by this appeal. Three years had passed since the sale, long past the two-year statute of limitations for reconveying property to the original owner. Besides, owning the estate offered both him and Jennie privacy, as Glenwood sat adjacent not only to Glenburnie but also to land he owned as well. As far as he was concerned, the case was closed.

What Duncan did not anticipate was Octavia Dockery. Though not married to Dick Dana, she came to his defense by filing a bill of complaint in January 1916 to force Minor to reconvey the property to Dick Dana. The case, entered into court as *R. H. C. Dana by his next friend, Miss Octavia Dockery, Complainant vs. Duncan G. Minor, Defendant* was significant. As "next friend," Dockery was acting on Dana's behalf because he was unfit to look after his own interests. The case against Minor, in fact, rested on Dockery's argument that Dana had been "in ill health of body and mind to such an extent he was and is incapacitated to attend to his personal affairs, business or otherwise." As a consequence, she asserted that the tax deed that Minor purchased was null and void and that the land and house should be returned to its rightful owner—Dick Dana. The property was Dana's inheritance, and though he had only lived there intermittently since his youth, personal circumstances required that he be able to return.[36]

Octavia proved she was a worthy opponent in court. Minor's attorneys alleged that when he purchased the property for the taxes on Glenwood, Dana was in "truth and fact . . . sane and of sound mind" and still was. But in his "lunacy" hearing on February 6, 1917, a jury declared that "R. H. C. Dana" was non compos mentis and appointed chancery clerk Pat Mulvihill Jr. his guardian. Glenwood and its grounds, sold for taxes in 1912, could now be redeemed despite the fact that Dockery filed a suit on Dana's behalf well after the two years provided by law. Why? Because a clause in the state's property statute provided a redemption for persons of unsound mind. For the time being, Dockery had saved Glenwood for her friend Dick Dana and for herself. If she had failed, not only would they both be homeless, but Dana may have spent the remainder of his days in one of the state's so-called lunatic asylums.[37]

Now the pair had rights to Glenwood. Octavia put out a small garden and raised chickens to sell their eggs. She also acquired some hogs and goats that proved to be as wily as Dick Dana. They ambled throughout the woods on the estate and could be difficult to round up. They also made themselves comfortable on the neighboring property. Sometimes the owner shot at them, but most of the time she held them for damages and reported the trespassing to the sheriff. Octavia had never met Jennie Merrill, but she resented her just the same.

Jennie's Glenburnie estate was about half the size of her neighbors'. It included the house, two ponds, and some outbuildings, including former slave cabins. The only livestock she owned was one milk cow. Her plantations in Concordia Parish may have been for farming, but not her town estate. The land around her home was largely planted with bushes and flowers. She seemed particularly fond of lespedeza, a Japanese clover, which flowered and grew well in Natchez's temperate climate.[38]

Much to her chagrin, her new neighbors' hogs also enjoyed the lespedeza and regularly ambled over to Glenburnie to forage. From the time Dick and Octavia moved next door, Jennie Merrill had a hog problem. And she would soon come to find out that she had a foe in Octavia Dockery. During the years they were neighbors, Jennie filed several lawsuits against Octavia for the damage caused by hogs—to her corn patch, her ponds, and finally her lespedeza. For every infraction, Merrill phoned the sheriff's office. She made so many complaints that Sheriff Mike Ryan told her attorney, Abraham Geisenberger, that he had "made so many trips out there [to Glenwood]" he could not recall them all.[39]

When hogs trespassed onto her estate, Merrill would write a curt note to Dockery and send one of the men she hired to do her yard work to deliver it. On one occasion, for example, she made Henry Rollins take a note to Octavia demanding that she pay a fee for keeping the hogs fed and watered. Another time the hogs trespassed, Jennie simply sold them. Octavia generally paid the fees but also filed complaints of her own.[40]

As far as Jennie Merrill was concerned, Octavia Dockery was not her social equal. Under oath, she stated, "I have never spoken to Miss Dockery in my life." This was intentional. When Jennie communicated with her neighbor, she either sent a note by a servant or called the sheriff to take care of disputes, clearly signaling that the woman next door was beneath her. As someone descended from Surgets and Merrills, Jennie simply never dealt personally with the likes of Octavia, despite Dockery's own claims to an Old South lineage.[41]

After a year of troubles with her neighbors' hogs, Jennie Merrill filed another suit against Octavia Dockery in April 1917. Angered by the damage the swine caused to her property, Merrill again contacted the sheriff's office. As he had done many times before, Sheriff Ryan drove out to Glenwood, but this time he issued a writ of seizure for the hogs, described as "four black and white sows, one black and white barrow, and 14 more or less shoats."[42] It might have been a simple case of resolving a dispute between two neighbors, but neither of these women was simple.

The case—of damages caused by trespassing hogs to Jennie's lespedeza and one of her ponds—eventually made its way to Mississippi's state supreme court and in the process would reveal the ongoing battles between the two women to be as much a conflict about class as it was over hogs.

The attorneys in the case had their hands full with Jennie and Octavia. During questioning, Jennie's responses were brusque and impatient, perhaps because she had filed so many complaints to no avail. Her response to Laurens Kennedy, Dockery's attorney, was typical. In trying to determine the alleged damages to her property, he asked, "Did you show me and him [the justice of the peace] that pond?" Her reply was combative. "That is the pond in the corn suit where the hogs came over and destroyed every bit of my corn. This is another suit entirely," she snapped. "I wish you would get these suits straight in your head. You don't seem to know what you are trying." And when asked if she had any hogs, she shot back, "No, sir. I have never had one and I wouldn't have one in 25 miles of me if I could help it," adding, "I can't do anything over there for her hogs. I am tormented to death with them."[43]

Octavia, on the other hand, proved to be a cunning witness in her own defense. She knew exactly how to elicit sympathy among the jurors and, as it suited her purpose, selectively failed to recollect conversations and events. When asked where Merrill lived, she replied, "I understand she lives next to me — on the North of me." And in a follow-up question, she took the opportunity to suggest something about Jennie's social mores. "I understand that Miss Merrill and Mr. Minor lives over there — that's the best of my understanding." Dockery essentially testified that they lived together — unmarried.[44]

Octavia also displayed a dry sense of humor, especially when it came to the suggestion that her hogs had been "trained" to do their foraging at Glenburnie. "I never could train a hog, except train them to eat," she answered, adding, "If I owned all [the hogs] reported to [be mine] out there, I would be rich." The implication about riches was not lost among the jurors.

In fact, when her attorney questioned her about how she made her living, she made sure to distinguish herself from her wealthy neighbor. "I am about [like] the old hen said. 'I have to keep scratching to make a living.' I sell country produce, milk, eggs, in fact everything that can be made on a farm, I make it and sell it." Her response was one that the jurors, who were not descendants of planter elite, could appreciate.[45]

Much of Jennie's case rested on the writ of seizure issued by Sheriff Ryan. Here, Dockery was very cagey. She recalled that the sheriff served her "a paper" and, she testified, that "he read it by the lamp light to me." Yet when she was told that the writ described the several hogs she owned, her memory seemed to fail her. "I don't remember nothing about it," she answered. According to the sheriff's testimony, he intended to seize the hogs, but Dockery claimed they were not hers. When Jennie's attorney asked about it, she answered his question with a question. "You can serve anything by lamp light, but can you seize anything by lamp light?" Then when asked if she accompanied Sheriff Ryan to look for the hogs, she demurred, "I am not accustomed to walking around over the country with a man after dark."[46]

When her testimony centered on the messages Henry Rollins delivered to her at Glenwood, Dockery took the opportunity to slight Merrill again. "Did you ever tell that old colored witness [Rollins] these were your hogs trespassing over there?" Geisenberger asked. To which she replied, "He come over and told me there [were] some hogs over there, and that he despised her." While Geisenberger ignored her comment and continued his questioning, it turns out that there may have been some truth in what Dockery said about Rollins's feelings toward Jennie Merrill, because it was rumored in the African American community that "Miss Merrill would work her help holding a .22 rifle over them."[47]

Testimony from the justice of the peace weakened Jennie's case further. He had accompanied the sheriff to Merrill's property numerous times to view the alleged damages, but not only did he not see any damage, he also was unable to recall individual visits to Glenburnie because "there [have] been so many suits between Miss Merrill and Miss Dockery . . . [that] I can't keep track of them," he said.[48]

Merrill's suit for damages was unsuccessful, resulting in a judgment for the defendant. And in the years to come, Jennie's neighbors' hogs continued to trespass while their home fell further into wrack and ruin.

Duncan continued his nightly horseback rides to see Jennie at Glenburnie. By 1930, Jennie, now sixty-six, took in a live-in maid named Effie Stanton. She didn't socialize as she had in her youth and preferred Duncan's company or that of her relatives at Elms Court. She went into town on rare occasion to shop or conduct business with the bank, but on the whole she spent most of her time at home.

Just two years later, journalists would represent Jennie to the public as an "aristocratic recluse" whose father had been the Belgian ambassador. They would also write about her in relation to the woman who had become her late-in-life nemesis. The woman with the hogs—and, apparently, more than a few goats.

CHAPTER TWO

THE RESIDENTS OF GLENWOOD

The first time Odell Ferguson visited Glenwood, Dick Dana was swinging through the trees on a grapevine. Ferguson and his father were cutting timber when they spotted the tall and lanky Dana perched on a limb high above them. As soon as Dick saw them, Odell recalled, "He let go of the grapevine, fell to the ground, got up and ran into the house." Odell was fourteen years old, an age when boys still liked to climb trees and swing on grapevines. Dana was a grown man of fifty-three.[1]

If bloodlines were guarantees of success, then the boy who was born Richard Henry Clay Dana had plenty to draw from. The Danas became household names during the nineteenth century. They included Richard Henry Dana, an attorney and the popular author of *Two Years before the Mast* (1841), a classic account of life at sea, and Charles Dana Gibson, the artist famous for his drawings of women popularized in the image of the "Gibson Girl." There was also Charles Anderson Dana, assistant secretary of war in Abraham Lincoln's administration who later became editor and part owner of the influential *New York Sun* in 1868. During the paper's heyday, Dick's older brother, also named Charles, became a writer for the *Sun* in November 1889. As he explained in a letter to Dick, "Through the influence of Mr. Charles A. Dana I was appointed on the editorial staff of the *New York Sun*. I started with a little better salary than is generally paid to new men, since then I have been promoted and now I am doing very well."[2]

Many of Dick Dana's direct ancestors were involved in the ministry. After graduating from Dartmouth University in 1828, his father, Charles Backus

Dick Dana's father, the Reverend Charles Backus Dana,
in his vestments, n.d. (Courtesy of the Earl Norman Photograph
Collection, Historic Natchez Foundation, Natchez, Miss.)

Dana, received his divinity degree from Andover Theological Seminary in 1833. Following a brief tenure as an instructor at the Presbyterian-affiliated Mount Hope College in Baltimore, he became rector of one of the most famous Episcopal churches in the country — Christ Church of Alexandria, Virginia. Famously known as "Washington's church" because George Washington and his family worshipped there, it was also the seat of worship for another important Virginia family — the Lees. Beginning in 1834 Dana served Christ Church for twenty-six years, ministering to the faithful, which included Robert E. Lee and his family, with whom the rector became friends.[3]

Charles Backus Dana cut a stern figure in his portraits and photographs. Dressed in his vestments, he had a receding hairline of dark brown hair and sported mutton chops. Whether it was his humorless appearance or his dedication to the ministry, Charles did not marry until he was fifty-four years old. When he did, it was to a woman half his age. Elvira Close, a parishioner originally from New York, was only twenty-seven when she wed the rector in Alexandria in July 1860. At the time of their marriage, two other women were living in the rector's home, including a sixty-five-year-old white housekeeper and a young mulatto slave woman. Less than six months after their union, the newlyweds left for a new parish far away from Alexandria in the Deep South state of Mississippi. There, Charles became the rector of St. James Church in Port Gibson, a small town about halfway between Natchez and Vicksburg. Why he left after serving Christ Church for nearly three decades is a mystery, though his marriage to a parishioner half his age perhaps did not sit well with his congregation. A new church in a faraway parish offered the rector and his wife a fresh beginning.[4]

The difference between states was stark. As rector of Christ Church, Dana had served a large congregation of well over 150 parishioners, but at St. James his flock numbered fewer than 75. As a consequence, Dana ministered twice per month to a second, and much smaller, church in nearby Grand Gulf, spending much of the rest of his time trying to expand the number of communicants at St. James. Yet more pressing challenges lay ahead. Dana and his wife, Elvira, arrived in Port Gibson in mid-January 1861, just as sectional tensions between North and South were heating up. A few months later, the Civil War erupted, and it had a demonstrable impact on the couple as well as on the churches Dana served. Although Dana's 1862 report to the Diocese of Mississippi revealed that "a considerable addition [had] been made to the number of communicants," he also conveyed that because of "the disturbed condition of the country, and the stringency of its monetary affairs," he was forced to postpone building a new church. The couple also experienced personal changes that year as Elvira Dana became pregnant and gave birth to the couple's first son, Charles, in August.[5]

Less than a year after Charles Jr. was born, the Danas bore witness to the Civil War firsthand. As part of General Ulysses S. Grant's plan to take control of the Mississippi River, his troops made their way toward the Danas' new hometown. During the Battle of Port Gibson in early May 1863, Union forces engaged and defeated Confederate troops who were less than half their number, demonstrating both the strength of the Union army in Mississippi and the inability of Confederates to defend against it. Ultimately, the Union victory paved the way for the fall of Vicksburg.[6]

According to legend, Grant considered Port Gibson "too beautiful to burn," sparing it the destruction other southern towns experienced during the war, but this was no consolation to Reverend Dana. Following the war, in 1866, the family moved to Natchez, where Charles Dana began his tenure as rector of Trinity Episcopal Church. It, too, had experienced hardship, and when he arrived there in January, the reality of what the war had wrought could be seen in the congregation itself.

In his 1867 report to the Mississippi Diocese, Dana described the dire state of Trinity Episcopal in Natchez after the war. "The condition of the parish," he wrote, "was greatly depressed. Many families that had previously belonged to it had removed to other parts of the country, or were residing in Europe, while of those who remained in the city, comparatively few could do much to sustain the Church." Membership had dropped significantly from 253 communicants in 1861 to just 120 in 1866. Many of them had left during the occupation of Natchez, few had come back, and still others never returned. Despite this, Dana remained hopeful. The number of church members was growing, and the coffers showed signs of recovery.[7]

Dana's own finances improved when he moved to a larger church with a better rector's salary. He purchased a large home, called Glenwood, on the outskirts of town. Built in 1841, the wood frame house stood two stories and had four chimneys, a large front veranda, and a balcony that spanned the entire front of the home. In 1871, while living at Glenwood, the Danas welcomed another son, Richard, whom they called Dick. By now the rector was sixty-five years old. He barely had time to enjoy his new house in Natchez and scarcely had time to get to know his infant son when, in 1873, he died.

Elvira was now a widow with two young sons—Charles, eleven, and Dick, two. She and her boys stayed on at Glenwood for several more years, at least until her death in February 1886 at the still youthful age of fifty-three. Dick, now fifteen, was orphaned. He had never really known his father, and by the time of their mother's death, his brother, Charles, had already left Natchez for New York. After four years in the army, Charles took up a career as a journalist, following in the footsteps of other Danas by going to work for the *New York Sun*.[8]

Charles enjoyed several years with the newspaper during its heyday. Then, when the United States declared war on Spain for sinking the battleship *Maine* in Havana Harbor—a war that the *Sun*'s editor vocally supported—he determined to join the army, just ten days after the official declaration of war.

He enlisted at Fort Slocum, New York, on May 5, 1898, and signed on for a potential three years of service, but his service ended swiftly after just three months. Charles died in Puerto Rico, not from battle wounds but from disease. Just thirty-six years old when he died, he had never married, nor did he have any offspring. Glenwood, the family home in Natchez, now belonged solely to his younger brother, Dick.[9]

It is unclear who cared for Dick Dana following his mother's death. He did attend the Chamberlain-Hunt boarding school in Port Gibson to complete his secondary education. When he came of age, he enrolled at Vanderbilt University in Nashville, Tennessee, attending for just two years, between 1888 and 1890. Dick was an accomplished musician, and according to local legend he followed his brother to New York, where he pursued a career as a concert pianist. While there is no evidence proving that he went north, one fact is clear: if he went, he did not stay long. Another legend suggests that he returned to Natchez following an injury to his fingers—said to be have been caused by a fallen window sash—which ended his musical aspirations.[10] Whether he had any real career to pursue is questionable, but it is true that an injury left the fingers of his right hand deformed. By 1900, Dick Dana, now twenty-eight, lived in Natchez, but not at his family's home of Glenwood. Instead, he boarded in the home of local musician Duncan Baker, along with his family, on Pearl Street.[11]

By 1906, Dick had moved on from the Bakers' home to board in the home of Richard Forman and his wife, Nydia, on Main Street.[12] Among the residents were Forman's daughter, Sadie, born to his first wife, and another boarder, Archibald Dickson, a bookkeeper with a local lumber company. Nydia's unmarried sister lived there, too. Her name was Octavia Dockery.

Octavia was not a native Natchezean. This alone may have given Jennie Merrill sufficient reason to dismiss her socially. She was from the very rural town of Lamartine, Arkansas, where she was born in 1866. Her grandfather John Dockery and his family, which included Octavia's father, Thomas, moved to Arkansas in the early 1850s. Like so many families, the Dockerys had migrated west from states in the Upper South to take advantage of the antebellum cotton boom. Originally from Montgomery County, North Carolina, in the 1840s, they first moved to Hardeman County, Tennessee, just east of Memphis. They farmed there several years before eventually making the move to Columbia

County, Arkansas, where John Dockery became one of the area's largest land and slave owners. He named the area where they settled Lamartine. When he died in 1860, his wife, Ann, and their son, Thomas, now twenty-seven, assumed management of Dockery's plantations and slaves.[13]

By 1860, John Dockery's investment in land and slaves left his family in exceptional financial shape. Ann's real estate was valued at $15,000, and her personal property, which included forty-five slaves, was worth $75,000, which meant they were among the wealthiest families in the state.[14] Thomas's personal property, including the eight slaves he inherited, was worth $10,000. This was nowhere near the wealth of planters in Natchez, several of whom owned hundreds of slaves; nonetheless, the Dockery family was still quite successful. But families like theirs, who had not invested beyond slaves and land, had the most to lose—and did—in a war to end slavery.[15]

As of 1860, Thomas Pleasant Dockery, who married Mississippian Laura West the year before, was a new father with a sizable inheritance. Like other southern men his age, he looked forward to expanding his investments in the cotton and slave economy of the Arkansas delta. The Civil War changed all of that.[16]

Thomas Dockery's commitment to protect his state and property led him to put his life on the line as an officer in the Confederate army. As a colonel, Dockery commanded two different Arkansas regiments—the Fifth Infantry and, later, the Nineteenth Infantry. Colonel Dockery's troops participated in the Battle of Port Gibson and were later captured during the siege of Vicksburg. Having ascended to commander of his brigade after the death of his superior, Dockery was captured by Union forces on July 4, 1863, where, after taking an oath of loyalty to the U.S. government, he was paroled. His loyalty was not worth the paper on which it was signed, however. Promoted from colonel to brigadier general just a few weeks later, Dockery returned to Arkansas on August 10, 1863, where he led his men in several engagements against federal forces until the spring of 1865, when Confederate troops in the state finally surrendered.[17]

Like many former Confederate officers, Thomas Dockery would always be associated with his military exploits and addressed publicly by his military title. Yet General T. P. Dockery, as his name often appeared in print, felt Confederate defeat on a bitter, personal level. He had lost his property, including slaves, and the war ruined him financially. When he returned to Lamartine at war's end, he and his wife, Laura, would soon welcome another daughter, Octavia. Dockery turned to civil engineering to try to rebuild his fortune, and for a few years he worked to establish a railroad between Little Rock and Shreveport. But the project was unsuccessful. In 1874 he made a failed bid to be the Arkansas secretary of state, and a few years later he left the state for Texas, where he found work with the city of Houston.[18]

When the former Confederate general left home, he did not take his young family with him; he instead situated them with a relative while he sought to resuscitate his finances. Laura and their daughters, Nydia and Octavia, moved to Laura's native Coahoma County, Mississippi, where they lived with Pleasant Thomas Mask—a young maternal uncle of Thomas Dockery. Mask, a physician, was just forty-seven years old and already a widow. He took in Thomas's wife and their two young daughters, supporting them for a few years until Laura died in September 1880.[19]

Thomas Dockery, now a fifty-year-old widower, moved to New York, taking Nydia and Octavia with him. There he worked as a stockbroker investing funds for the city of Houston, Texas. Nydia was in her early twenties by this time, and her younger sister was a teenager. Octavia always claimed that she attended the Comstock School for Girls—a private boarding school located on West Fortieth Street in Manhattan—and there is no reason to believe she did not. It must have been an exciting time for the young ladies from rural Arkansas, though any happiness they may have enjoyed soon turned to sorrow as they witnessed their father's personal decline.[20]

The former Confederate general did not fare well in New York. Only a few months after Laura's passing, he quickly married a young woman from Copenhagen, Denmark, named Frederika Toelle, described as "fair, slim, and ladylike" yet "timid" with a "sad face." Wed in Connecticut, the couple moved to the city, where she found work in a private home as a seamstress. A short two months later the marriage fell apart—as did Dockery's life. For three days in a row in March 1884, the *New York Times* reported on his public outbursts. The headline for March 22 announced "Gen. Dockery on the War-Path: After Thrashing Two Men He Thirsts for More Blood." The following day it read "Accused by His Wife: Gen. Thomas P. Dockery Arrested for Abandonment." Then finally, on March 24, the paper noted "Mrs. Dockery in Hysterics: The General Declines Mr. Jackson's Offer to Fight," indicating that the former general's life was swiftly unraveling.[21]

The trouble began when Dockery went to the office of J. C. Chew, a Houston attorney, where the two men argued about issues of compensation before Chew insinuated that Dockery was a liar. According to the *New York Times*, Dockery "dealt Mr. Chew a lusty blow to the face," followed him into the hallway when he tried to get away, and then "knocked him down, kicked him, and pulled his long beard energetically." When another man interfered, Dockery hit him, too.[22]

The following day, Thomas was arrested for abandoning his young wife. Frederika had filed a complaint against her husband for deserting her, and, in fear for her life, she went to live with the couple for whom she worked. According to Frederika's testimony, her husband abandoned her because he said he was "broke." In his defense, the general stated that he never cohabitated with his wife. Nonetheless, the judge in the case decided in Frederika's favor, and Thomas was made to pay her ten dollars per week. After leaving his wife, Dockery briefly stayed with Nydia and Octavia in the city's Buckingham Hotel. His dire financial situation—as evidenced by his fight over compensation and Frederika's abandonment suit—was so severe that the hotel held his daughters' trunks of personal belongings for a two-hundred-dollar debt *he* owed.[23]

His reputation as a Confederate hero was about all Thomas Dockery had left, and occasionally it paid off. When President Grant died in August 1885, a group of ex-Confederates living in New York selected Dockery and others to represent southern soldiers in the military parade that was organized in Grant's honor.[24] The *New York World* also printed his story about Grant's kindness to him after his capture in Vicksburg. While Dockery was a prisoner of war, his first wife, Laura, traveled there in hopes of seeing him. When she met General Grant, he assured her that Thomas was alive and well and that she would soon be reunited with her husband. "For the gentle and feeling manner in which General Grant treated her," the paper reported, "Mrs. Dockery never ceased to bless the brave man who today will be laid in his last resting place."[25]

Confederate nostalgia, however, did not pay bills, and Thomas Dockery was unable to care for his daughters. The sisters remained in New York for a few more years and then left following Nydia's marriage to Richard Forman in Manhattan. Forman, a resident of Jefferson County, Mississippi, was already widowed and had adult children. At fifty-five, he was the same age as Nydia's father. Forman had been pursuing Nydia since 1885, when he first asked the general for his daughter's hand in marriage, writing, "I would be happy to have her father visit us at any and all times, and it would be my earnest desire that her sister Octavia would make our house her home until married." Unbeknownst to Forman, one of Thomas Dockery's friends wrote him a letter about the man who had just proposed to Nydia. He described Forman's appearance as "quite old," noting that he was "homely and ill shaped, displaying the tremulous activity of an old man." Dockery may not have desired such a marriage for Nydia, but he was unable to care for either daughter, and so in January 1888 she wed the much older Mr. Forman.[26]

As promised, Octavia was welcomed into the home of her newlywed sister. The Formans first returned to Richard's hometown of Fayette, Mississippi, in Jefferson County, before moving to Natchez around 1896. The sisters' father stayed in New York, where in February 1898, at the age of sixty-five, he died penniless in a rooming house. Nydia arranged for Thomas Dockery to be buried in the Natchez City Cemetery, a city where he never lived but where his daughters could pay their respects.

In many ways, Thomas Pleasant Dockery's life was a symbol of what became of the Civil War generation—the generation who hoped to maintain the slave economy of the Old South in order to sustain and increase their own wealth. Like so many of the men he led into battle, he lost everything in defense of that dream. Still, for generations of southern whites who knew of his exploits as a Confederate, he was a hero. Dockery may not have been able to leave his daughters an inheritance, but his reputation as a war hero was intact, and Octavia wove this into her own life's narrative. It would prove valuable indeed during some of her darkest days.

By the time Octavia returned to Mississippi, she was a young woman in her mid-twenties. When she was born in Lamartine, Arkansas, the daughter of a successful planter, it was 1866. Confederate defeat had changed the world around her. Not only did she not grow up to be a plantation mistress, but she had also spent her life moving from state to state as her mother died and her father fell apart emotionally and financially. Bound to her sister's household, she returned to Mississippi with no means to support herself.

Even so, Natchez seemed to suit Octavia Dockery, a slim-figured redhead with angular facial features. She was a "New Woman," a term used in the late nineteenth century to describe women who were educated, were more carefree

Octavia Dockery as a young woman, ca. 1890s.
(Courtesy of the Thomas H. and Joan W. Gandy Photograph
Collection, Louisiana and Lower Mississippi Valley Collections,
Special Collections, Hill Memorial Library, Louisiana
State University Libraries, Baton Rouge.)

than their mothers, and dreamed of a career before marriage. Octavia fancied
herself a writer. This is not to say that she didn't have her suitors; she did. It
is just that the attention she craved wasn't from men but from publishers. A
Natchez attorney named Richard Reed found this out the hard way when she
cut short his attempt to court her after declaring his "supreme love." Octavia's
response, he told her, left him feeling that "a companionship socially was de-
cidedly obnoxious." The harshness of her reply, Reed told her, "caused a pain
that almost deadened my sensibilities to suffer (and I wish sometimes that it
would)."[27]

Octavia's "ambition to gain a standing as a writer," as Reed noted, nonetheless impressed him even as his efforts to gain her affection were met with
resistance. The two remained friends, and he even offered her advice on how
she could achieve her goals. In a letter to her dated 1892, when she still lived
in Fayette County, Reed wrote, "I think, Octavia, that it would be difficult for
you to get a paper accepted by the Leading Monthlies," noting, "There is such

a crowd of writers seeking to gain recognition in the well-established publications." So he suggested a different plan of starting their own publication. "You cannot expect success all at once," he admonished. "A gradual improvement & progress is the surest and most stable," he wrote, adding that she should become an editor.[28]

Reed's letter also impressed upon her his true motivation for writing. "Having all these matters in mind and realizing my love for you, and believing you love me, I again bring up the subject of our getting married, and make the proposition that we do so, and without further delay." He insisted that the matter be decided swiftly, and he would make plans to take her to New Orleans "where they could be married." His persistence was never rewarded.[29]

A few years later, another attorney named Thomas Bulger began to pursue Octavia. "I have fallen in love with you and am getting most anxious to know if you are willing to be my darling," he wrote her in the summer of 1896. His letter suggests the slightest hint of her motivation for considering marriage when he says, "If you mean what you say about marrying a lawyer I will promise to love you more than you can ever know." The two seem to have had a courtship that lasted until the fall of that year when, in the only other known correspondence from Bulger, he writes how happy he was to receive her letter. "This is the sweetest letter of [all]. . . . I know you are the sweetest little woman in the world and I love you so devotedly as can be," he wrote, adding, "I will bring your ring when I come. I must put it on your finger in person and you must give me a sweet kiss. Then I know you are mine." Yet in spite of his best efforts, Thomas Bulger was no more successful than Richard Reed. He, too, failed to secure a marriage with Octavia.[30]

Why Octavia never married is unclear, yet her determination to be a published writer never waned. And she did have modest success. While the regional literary magazine the *Sunny South*, published in Atlanta, turned her down, her work was printed in the Philadelphia-based magazine *The Blue and the Gray*. In 1893, the magazine carried a few of her writings, including a short story titled "Held by the Enemy." Significantly, Octavia named the protagonist "Laura," after her mother. It is a story of romance set during the Civil War in which Laura is rescued from the Yankees by a Confederate captain, whom she falls in love with and marries the following year. Like many stories of the era, it invokes the trope of the loyal slave speaking in dialect. While it is amateurish, it shows how Octavia, a woman just one generation removed from the war, romanticized the era in which her mother lived (and continues to live in her story) rather than seeing it as the devastating time that it truly was for women like Laura Dockery.[31]

Octavia published other short pieces, including one about sugar production on Louisiana plantations, but little else. As the *Saturday Evening Post* recounted several years later, "Her verse was bad, but she esteemed it more than her beauty." Her writing never really brought her the public attention she hoped for. She couldn't have known it, but a few decades later, she would find it after all.[32]

———

As the nineteenth century became the twentieth, Octavia's chances of marriage swiftly dissipated. Now thirty-three, she claimed she was twenty-seven. She continued to stretch the truth about her age when, a decade later, in 1910, the census recorded her age as thirty. One can only imagine the incredulous look of the census taker when Octavia, nearly forty-four, insisted on such a youthful number. At the time, she listed her occupation as "magazine writer." Despite the fact that Octavia had become an "old maid" while living in Richard Forman's household, he kept his promise to her father that she would have a home until she married. He probably did not anticipate that his sister-in-law would still be there twenty-two years later.[33]

Sometime during the first decade of the new century, the Formans moved from their first home in Natchez at 145 Wall Street to 1016 Main Street. Richard Forman rented the homes he shared with his wife, his daughter, and sister-in-law, and at both locations they also took in boarders. At the house on Main Street, a forty-year-old bookkeeper at the local lumber company, Archibald Dickson, boarded with the Formans. Their other boarder was thirty-seven-year-old Dick Dana, who did not work but had his "own income," likely the remaining funds he inherited from his mother. It was during this time at the Forman residence on Main Street where Octavia Dockery and Dick Dana probably first met, marking the beginning of their peculiar relationship — a relationship that lasted for the rest of their natural lives.[34]

The fact that the Formans took boarders in their rented homes suggests that they struggled financially. This is supported by the fact that between May 1910 and February 1911 the Formans moved again, but this time to the home that was Dick's inheritance. Weathered clapboards, cracking plaster, and other signs of decay had taken their toll on the house, but they could all live there at no cost if only Richard Forman paid the property taxes on the place. And so, Richard, Nydia, his daughter Sadie, Octavia, and Dick Dana moved to the antebellum house on the outskirts of Natchez called Glenwood.

Sadly for Octavia, her sister, Nydia, with whom she had lived her entire life, died at Glenwood after a long illness, very likely cancer, in February 1911.[35] She was just fifty-one years old. A year later, Nydia's husband, Richard, also died. By now, his daughter Sadie rented a home on Rankin Street. Octavia and Dick — two people with no significant means of income and no one to support them — were left to fend for themselves.[36]

It had been clear to Octavia for several years that Dick Dana was unable to take care of himself, personally or financially. A diary he kept not long after he moved in with the Formans revealed a man whose brain was cluttered with incongruent thoughts. His scribbling was a stream of consciousness. "Mr. Forman insulting dog. Passed through streets of Natchez don't look at anyone. A piano toy at kitchen door." He was obsessed with dogs and snakes. And, in a surprisingly lucid passage, he wrote, "Doc says I am an old fool and got no sense. I am not a fool and got sense. He may think they can change me." Only he knew who "they" were, but Dick clearly suffered from some mental deficiency.[37]

Whatever income he now had likely came from Glenwood, because he never appeared to have had any gainful employment. The small estate Dana inherited from his mother, which could be rented to raise livestock or harvest timber, was barely sufficient to live on. And Octavia, now forty-seven, was past a marriageable age, and she had never earned much from publishing small articles in insignificant magazines.

It was time for her to face reality.

For a few years following her brother-in-law's death in 1912, Octavia boarded briefly at a home on Pine Street and even spent some time in Mobile, Alabama, with an extended family member. Dick's whereabouts for that time are unknown. He may have worked out a deal with Duncan Minor to stay at Glenwood now that Minor owned the property after paying the taxes. But Octavia returned to Natchez and pursued legal means to force Duncan to reconvey the property back to Dick Dana. Despite Dick's later recollections of a promise he made to Nydia on her deathbed that he would take care of her sister, the truth of the matter was Octavia looked after him—in part because she likely felt genuine concern for the man who had lost his grip on reality, but also because her own situation was precarious following the deaths of Nydia and Richard.

Glenwood passed through several owners during the years that Dick and Octavia lived on the property, often under threat of eviction. Yet Octavia was savvy. She countered every court order by locating loopholes in the law and, later, by using the local press to garner sympathy from the Natchez community. She had no choice, really, because eviction presented a scenario even more tragic than the derelict state of Glenwood.[38]

———

Living at Glenwood brought challenges of its own. First, there was the condition of the house, described in court papers as early as 1917 as "dilapidated." The house had no electricity or running water. The furniture that Dana's parents owned was still there, as was his father's library, which included hymn books and religious titles like *Twenty-Five Village Sermons* by Charles Kingsley, a well-known Anglican priest. The rector's collection also included books given him by Robert E. Lee, when the elder Dana first left for Port Gibson.

Yet the roof was rotten, and year by year Glenwood's condition worsened. Outside, chimneys crumbled, the second-story balcony became increasingly unstable, several windows were broken, and the front porch was rotting away. Inside, the wallpaper was falling off while dust and cobwebs gathered on everything. Octavia slept in an upstairs bedroom on a mildewed mattress she perched between chairs, even though it laid next to an impressive four-poster mahogany bed. Over the years, various animals—cats, chickens, geese—took up residence inside the home, including the couple's herd of goats, which chewed the wallpaper as far up as they could stretch their necks and ate pages from rare books they had pulled off of the same bookshelves where chickens had built their nests.[39]

Octavia never thought of herself as a housekeeper and, for reasons only she knew, appeared resigned to the filth that gathered year in and year out. She also had to figure out a way to support herself and Dick, whose behavior became increasingly erratic. Although he was finally declared non compos mentis in 1917, she did not become his legal guardian until 1923. Prior to that time, Dana was the ward of two consecutive chancery clerks in Adams County, including Pat Mulvihill Jr., who later became an Adams County sheriff's deputy.

Glenwood, or "Goat Castle," 1932.
(Courtesy of the Earl Norman Photograph Collection,
Historic Natchez Foundation, Natchez, Miss.)

In early 1919, Octavia went to Mulvihill to seek a five-year lease on Glenwood and proposed "that she would take care of [Dana] for the use of the property." Very likely, she knew that the estate could be sold out from underneath them, so she sought to strike a bargain with Mulvihill. He agreed and petitioned the chancery court, which then leased the home to her. As he noted, "[She] has lived on said property for several years and has supported and taken care of . . . [Dana] without any compensation," adding that if she "should decide to leave the premises, there would be no one to take care of [him]" and it would "be necessary that he be confined in the asylum."[40]

At the same time Mulvihill secured a lease for Octavia, she borrowed money in order to pay off encumbrances against the property, including the amount owed to Duncan Minor, who paid not only taxes on the property for a few years but also court costs to defend himself against Dockery when she filed a bill of complaint to have the property returned to Dick Dana. All told, taxes and other liens against Glenwood amounted to more than six hundred dollars, which Octavia promised to pay in full at the end of her five-year lease. Those five years came and went, and Glenwood was sold for debts owed. In fact, the property went through several owners while Dick and Octavia remained. At various times, she worked out an arrangement that allowed them to stay. Rents went unpaid, eviction notices were issued, and through it all, Octavia managed to hold on to the property by issuing her own bills of complaint and reminding the court that Glenwood was Dick Dana's inheritance.[41]

Dick was never much help to Octavia and had the potential to physically hurt her. In early 1931, people who lived nearby found her "knocked out in their small field." When deputies were called, she claimed it was a "negro," but they were convinced that Dana had beaten her.[42] Neither was he able to earn a living, and he spent the bulk of his days in the wild vegetation that grew around Glenwood—a gothic landscape of gnarled trees draped in Spanish moss and of palm fronds, weeds, and vines. The trees were his favorite. He climbed them and hid in their branches, where he stayed even when Octavia called for him to come inside after dark. His hair and beard grew long and scraggly. He rarely bathed and was rumored to wear little more than a burlap sack with a hole cut out for the head as he romped through the woods. Dick Dana was the human equivalent of what Glenwood had become.[43]

Octavia supported them both by milking cows and selling eggs and other produce that could be raised on the open land around the house. There was also a small shack on the property that sat adjacent to the Kingston Road, which she occasionally rented out. The old building had been a roadhouse in the nineteenth century nicknamed "Bucket of Blood" because of the frequent fights that broke out there. In the early 1920s, the building took on a new nickname: the "Skunk's Nest." Sheriff Clarence Roberts eventually shut it down, remarking, "It was as unsavory in reputation as it was smelly in name." Still, the building produced a smidgen of income for Octavia and Dick. For three weeks in July 1932, a ruddy-faced unemployed logger named John Geiger rented the place before Octavia forced him to leave for nonpayment of rent. He had originally moved into the old roadhouse with his family, but on the following morning his wife left him. Later, in his rush to vacate the premises, the twenty-eight-year-old Geiger left an old mattress, some broken furniture, and an old brown overcoat. No sooner had he left than Dick and Octavia showed up to scavenge the place for anything valuable. They dragged the filthy mattress back home and laid it across two chairs on the rotting front porch of Glenwood, where it became a perch for napping kittens. They also took the overcoat.[44]

At the time Octavia requested the five-year lease on Glenwood, the surrounding property badly needed a new fence both to keep in the livestock she owned—cows, hogs, and goats—and to prevent the destruction of crops she had planted. The lack of secure fencing meant that her livestock frequently traipsed elsewhere. They regularly made their way to the property next door, which led to even more headaches for her since the law required an Adams County sheriff's deputy to confiscate her errant hogs and goats.

But Octavia was no pushover. All she had been through had hardened her. The last thing she needed was a writ of seizure, so she returned the favor by contacting the sheriff for her own purposes and filed suits of replevin that forced Jennie Merrill to return livestock she kept as payment for the alleged damage. Glenwood was all she had, and she was prepared to defend it against a woman who looked down on her and who had known only wealth and privilege. So, Octavia scratched out a living at Glenwood, did her best to look after Dick, whose mental state continued to decline, and, as needed, met with local attorneys seeking loopholes to prevent their eviction.

Octavia's grievances with her neighbor, however, seemed to never end. Jennie's complaints to the sheriff's office were relentless, and every few years there would be another lawsuit for the damage caused by trespassing hogs or goats. That they were neighbors at all was a constant irritation for both women. By 1932, during the depths of economic depression, the costs of going to court with Jennie likely caused Octavia additional stress. "Miss Jennie" might be able to afford the constant stream of legal fees, but for the woman who eked out an existence on the neighboring property, enough was enough.

CHAPTER THREE

PINK AND SISTER

While the descendants of Mississippi's antebellum elite had experienced steep economic and social decline in the decades following the Civil War, the descendants of slaves barely moved the needle of progress in their favor during those same years. True, they were now free, but their former owners sought to curtail that freedom in every way possible through restrictive laws, discriminatory labor contracts, incarceration, and racial violence. These conditions made it extremely difficult, though not impossible, for black Mississippians to determine their own destiny.

Emily Burns and George Pearls represented the different paths southern blacks took in the twentieth century when they came of age. Born and raised in Natchez, Emily remained there, married, and worked as a laundress for white families in town. George was also born in Adams County, on one of its many plantations, under the name of Lawrence Williams. Yet around the time of the First World War, he left for Chicago seeking a better life. He joined the mass exodus of African Americans in the Great Migration, relocating to northern cities in search of jobs and the promise of personal freedom they were unable to experience in the world of the Jim Crow South.[1]

Emily was born around 1895, and like most black Natchezeans of her generation, her grandparents had been slaves. Her father, James Black, was born in Louisiana in 1865, just as the Civil War ended. Census records show that his father came from Mississippi and his mother from Maryland, though both ended up slaves in Louisiana. In the case of James's mother, her birth in Maryland meant that she was one of nearly one million men, women, and children who were transported to the Deep South as prime commodities in America's domestic slave trade in the decades before the Civil War.[2] It was a trade fed by the cotton boom that peaked in the 1830s and again in the 1850s, sending black lives to Louisiana and Mississippi to cultivate the crop that made millionaires out of families like the Merrills and the Minors of Natchez.

To put it another way, the life of Emily's paternal grandmother followed the pattern of other slave women who were born in Maryland. She was bought by a slave trader from a Maryland planter, separated from her family, and taken from the only home she had probably ever known. She was shackled alongside other slave women and men and put on a ship docked in Baltimore that was bound for the Port of New Orleans. Once in the Crescent City, she was placed in one of its slave pens. Then, as had happened to other slave women, her hair was combed, she was dressed for sale, and she was made to stand on the auction block. There a planter purchased her for the purpose of laboring in the fields of a Louisiana cotton plantation. She may even have made the journey by steamboat to Natchez, where she would have been enclosed in a slave pen at the Forks of the Road, the second-largest slave trading post in the Deep South outside of New Orleans, before finally being auctioned to a local planter.[3]

Emily's family history was woven into the fabric of American slavery on her mother's side, too. Her mother, Nellie Smith, was born in 1877, twelve years after the end of the Civil War and just as white leaders in the state reassumed control over state government and went to work dismantling what little progress had been made by Reconstruction. And while she was not born into slavery, her mother, Agnes Smith, born in 1852, and her grandmother Abigail Bell, born around 1835, had most certainly been slaves.[4] In fact, is it very likely that Emily's grandmother Agnes may have been fathered by a slave owner, since she was listed as "mulatto" in U.S. Census records. After growing up on a farm her mother owned out on Liberty Road, Nellie married James Black in 1894, when he was twenty-nine and she was a young woman of seventeen. A year after they married, they welcomed their daughter, and only child, Emily, into the world. So Emily grew up in an extended family of her parents, her grandmother, aunts and uncles, and numerous cousins.[5]

To understand the world into which Emily Black was born, one must understand Natchez as a place. Large as its black community was, it was a community relegated to the outskirts of town—in and around the Forks of the Road at the intersection of Washington and Liberty Roads. Washington (now D'Evereux Drive) fed into St. Catherine Street, which later became the center

Smith family photo, ca. 1913. Emily Burns, eighteen, sits on the far left of the center row, wearing a shirtwaist and tie. Her mother, Nellie Black, stands behind her. Emily's uncle George "Doc" Smith stands in the center, and her grandmother, Agnes Smith, sits on the far right. (Courtesy of Birdia Green and Phyliss Morris, Natchez, Miss.)

of black life—the very same street down which newly imported slaves were once driven from steamships on the Mississippi River to be sold.

The black population of Natchez grew in the aftermath of the Civil War as former slaves tested their newfound freedom through the simple act of moving from plantations to town. While most freedmen stayed on those lands as sharecroppers, many others chose to leave the places where they had been enslaved. They sought out more urban environments and new work arrangements, rejecting the grueling toil of cotton production. Among them were men and women who had labored on the plantations of Concordia Parish, Louisiana, just across the river from Natchez, or who had been slaves on plantations in Adams or nearby Jefferson Counties. They moved to the town of planter millionaires, where they saw for themselves the luxurious homes their former masters enjoyed, direct products of their slave labor.[6]

They built churches and schools, too, institutions that fed the spirit and the mind. On the outskirts of town along Liberty Road, they erected Antioch Baptist Church, the church Emily grew up in and where her extended family of aunts, uncles, and cousins worshipped. Organized on August 1, 1900, Antioch was initially a wooden structure that doubled as a school for local children. Emily herself may have learned to read and write there. And while the road on which Antioch was built was named for a town in Mississippi, there was a sweet irony in building a black institution on a thoroughfare named "Liberty," given that coffles of slaves were once marched in chains along this same route to be sold at the Forks.[7]

In the decades after the war, Natchez freedmen needed places to live. Few had the resources to build their own homes, so they relied on rental property —often no more than wooden shacks—erected by local whites. Most of them were located on the edges of town along St. Catherine Street and its alleyways and close to the old slave trading post where area planters had purchased their parents, or perhaps even them. By the early decades of the twentieth century, men like Charles Zerkowsky, a Polish Jew who ran a grocery store on St. Catherine, owned those properties and continued to rent them to African Americans, most of whom would never know the pride of home ownership in their lifetime. So they rented those little houses and duplexes that by the 1920s were already run-down shacks.[8]

Still, St. Catherine Street emerged as a vibrant corridor of activity and promise for the black community. It ran from the Forks to Zion Rest African Methodist Episcopal Church, founded and led by Hiram Revels. Revels, a free black man from North Carolina, had served as a chaplain to black troops during the Civil War and became the first African American U.S. senator in the history of the nation. Along St. Catherine, one could find O'Ferral's grocery, a gristmill, a filling station, churches, saloons, and mortuaries. African Americans made up the vast majority of inhabitants, yet there were also Italians, French, Irish, and Poles. Jews, Catholics, Baptists, and Methodists were all represented. Holy Family Catholic Church, the first African American Catholic church in the state, was among the houses of worship along St. Catherine. It was the most diverse area of the city.[9]

Whether with his parents or as a young man, Emily's father, James, was one of many African Americans who left behind the Louisiana plantation on which he was born for possibilities in Natchez. At least by 1912, and perhaps before, he worked as a laborer at the National Box Factory—a company that built wooden crates for shipping goods. The factory employed a large black male workforce yet paid them poorly, which is why thirty of them went on strike for better wages at the factory in 1920. Whether James participated is unknown; however, his income was such that he never owned a home and his small family always lived in rental property in and around St. Catherine Street near the Forks.[10]

Southern black women like his wife, Nellie, had far fewer employment choices. The vast majority of black women worked as domestics—cooking, cleaning, washing, and ironing for white families. They often labored long hours for little pay, as little as four dollars for six days a week and ten- to twelve-hour days, only to go home to do the same tasks for their own families. Being a laundress was unique among domestic work in that it gave black women the most autonomy, even if it was arduous, because the work could be done from home and away from white supervision. Nellie Black was a laundress, and as soon as Emily was old enough, she became one, too.[11]

Emily, who went by the familiar "Sister," grew up moving between those shacks along St. Catherine Street before her family eventually settled in one located between Cedar and Junkin Alleys, literally a stone's throw from the Forks. She was a short woman, around five feet tall, and carried a little extra weight, though not much. She had a fifth-grade education, so she could read and write. Like most black girls, her childhood was cut short in order to support her family. Probably between the ages of twelve and fourteen, she went to work helping her mother. She had no choice. Then, sometime in 1911, at the tender age of sixteen, she married a farm laborer named Edward Burns, who was ten years her senior. The couple never had children and lived with her parents on St. Catherine Street during their entire marriage until Ed's untimely death sometime in the late 1920s. Her father, James, also died around the same time, very likely in 1929.[12]

When the 1930s began, Emily Burns was thirty-five, widowed, and living with her mother, Nellie Black, now fifty-three and also a widow. They did what most black women with insufficient income in Natchez did: they took in boarders. In 1930, twenty-six-year-old Ed Newell became a lodger in the home Emily shared with her mother. He worked as an embalmer for the Bluff City Undertaking Company, one of several local black-owned businesses in town. His full name was Edgar Allan Poe Newell, a name appropriate to his occupation and one that foreshadowed what was to come from his association with Sister, even though he generally went by "Poe."[13]

So when summer came in 1932, Sister, now thirty-seven, was barely eking out an existence as a laundress. By then the country was in the depths of the Depression, and she and her mother were hanging on by a thread. In late July, her life took a turn for the better, at least so she thought, when a nice-looking man from Chicago came to town and showed her some attention. Not long after, he moved to the home she shared with her mother on St. Catherine Street. He introduced himself to her as Pinkney Williams. She called him "Pink."[14]

Pink was twenty years older than Sister when they met in the summer of 1932. A handsome man, he stood just five-feet-seven, and at 140 pounds he had a slim build.[15] He had dark brown skin, kept his hair cut short—typical of the time—and sported a mustache. While she knew him as Pink, she would later discover that he also went by Lawrence Williams and, in Chicago, was known as George Pearls. Nicknames and aliases were not unusual in the black community, since naming one another became a way of rejecting the history of having names given to them by slave masters. Sometimes they were needed to outwit the law, especially at a time when black men could be arrested and sent to jail—or worse, lynched—for the slightest affront to a member of white society. They may have also needed one for wooing women who weren't their wives. For Pink, it appears to have been a little of both.[16]

Pink was born in 1875 in Mississippi, and both of his parents were Louisiana natives, where they most assuredly had been slaves. Like Emily's parents, Pink grew up in Mississippi during a time of rapid social, economic, and political change. When the Civil War ended, the state's black population stood at 55 percent of the entire whole—in Adams County it was closer to 70 percent—and white Mississippians were hardly willing to accept the idea of former slaves circulating among them freely. For two years following the war, the period known as Presidential Reconstruction essentially left former Confederates in control of Mississippi. And only seven months after the war's conclusion, in November 1865, the state legislature enacted Black Codes with the intent of replicating the control whites had over blacks under slavery. These codes restricted freedmen's newly won rights of citizenship as they were unable to own guns, needed a license to preach the gospel, and had to prove they were employed by producing a written contract to authorities or else be arrested for vagrancy. The vagrancy laws were especially pernicious. If found guilty, a person could be fined as much as one hundred dollars, a sum most

George Pearls, also known as Lawrence Williams
and Pinkney Williams, or "Pink." This photo, printed
in the *Natchez Democrat* on August 23, 1932, likely
came from the trunk of his belongings taken
as evidence by sheriff's deputies.

freedmen simply didn't have. Those unable to pay were punished at the dis-
cretion of the local sheriff, who could "hire out said freedman, free Negro, or
mulatto to any person who [would] . . . pay said fine." This was simply another
form of slavery, since white men who paid the fines found ways of ensuring
that freedmen would never be able to work off the debt.[17]

Black men and women who remained on plantations after the war, and for
decades after, were afraid of their white employers, whom they still referred
to as "master." Planters continued to hire "riding bosses," men on horseback
whose job was to ensure productivity even if it meant flogging black tenants.
Their fear of "white folks" was very real. "We had to mind them as our children mind us," one woman recalled. "It was just like slavery time."[18]

Federal officer Colonel Samuel Thomas saw this firsthand. The U.S. government sent Thomas to Vicksburg, about seventy miles north of Natchez, to open an office of the Freedmen's Bureau to assist former slaves in their transition to freedom. When he testified before Congress in late 1865, he explained how whites in Mississippi not only defied attempts at Reconstruction but also willfully used violence to maintain control over freedmen. "The whites esteem the blacks their property by natural right," Thomas explained, "and however much they may admit that the individual relations of masters and slaves have been destroyed by the war and the President's emancipation proclamation, they still have an ingrained feeling that the blacks at large belong to the whites at large."[19]

Thomas's testimony, and that of other Freedmen's Bureau officials, convinced Congress it needed to take more definitive steps to institute real Reconstruction. Republicans ushered in the era of Radical Reconstruction, which lasted for eleven years, 1867–1876, in Mississippi, as it sought to fulfill the promise of citizenship for freedmen. More than two hundred black Mississippians held public office during those years, and the state sent the first two black senators to Congress—Hiram Revels, as mentioned above, and Blanche Bruce.[20]

White Mississippians, shocked by their reversal of fortune and control, were having none of it. They brought Reconstruction to an end through violence and intimidation. Ku Klux Klansmen hid beneath costumes, pretending to be the ghosts of Confederate soldiers. They beat or murdered Republicans and terrorized black men and women. And they did so with impunity as officials looked away, intimidated by the punishment inflicted on others.[21]

Pink, and Sister's parents, were born into this world of intimidation and violence and had to navigate it if they were to survive. And while James and Nellie stayed in Natchez, whites in the state gave black Mississippians justifiable reasons to join the migration of blacks from across the South to cities throughout the North in the early twentieth century. Pink chose Chicago.

There was a saying in the black community that "it's better to be a lamppost in Chicago than a big deal in Natchez."[22] Simply put, Natchez was small potatoes compared to the Windy City. Chicago was a vibrant metropolis, and there someone like Pink, who took on the name of George Pearls, could be part of a larger black community made up of thousands of like-minded folks from all over the South. The music that blared from local bars had a familiar ring, too—jazz and blues from New Orleans and Mississippi adapted to the rapid pace of city living.

He eventually settled in the village of Summit, a Chicago suburb located about twelve miles from the city. There he lived with his second wife, Meadie, a Texas native who was sixteen years his junior. His daughter from a previous marriage, Amelia Garner, lived nearby. By 1930, George and Meadie rented a house at 7727 Sixty-Second Street, just down the block from the Corn Products Refining Company, where he worked. At the time, the plant was the largest corn refinery in the world and manufactured products like cornstarch under the brand name Argo. In fact, the area where the couple lived was known as Argo before it was annexed by Summit.[23]

If there ever was a melting pot, Summit was it. One of the largest of Chicago's suburbs, the area had grown from fewer than six hundred residents in 1900 to more than sixty-five hundred in 1930. African Americans made up only 7.5 percent of residents in 1930, which stood in stark contrast to Natchez, where more than half of the population was black. The majority who lived there were natives with foreign parentage or who were themselves foreign-born: Poles, Croats, Slovaks, Russians, and even a few Mexicans. George and Meadie's neighbors reflected that diversity, as they included Polish, Lithuanian, and Mexican households in addition to families of black southern migrants from Alabama, Mississippi, Georgia, and South Carolina.[24]

George worked with many of those same people, black and white, at the refinery. But in 1932, the effects of the Great Depression meant that many of these men lost their jobs. This likely happened to George Pearls, which is why he left his Chicago suburb in the summer of 1932. Desperate, he returned to his native Mississippi, to familiar land and familiar work. He packed up a large steamer trunk of his belongings and set south, eventually landing not in Greenville, not in Jackson or McComb, but in Natchez. He made a conscious decision in choosing the Bluff City, not a random one, because it was his hometown and he knew the whites he had once worked for, including, for a brief time, Duncan Minor.[25]

As was common given the conditions of roads at the time, he traveled to Natchez by train, on the Illinois Central, which ran between Chicago and New Orleans. When he got to town he hitched a ride to 33 Beaumont Street, where Zula Curtis, a forty-six-year-old widow, ran a boardinghouse. He did not stay there long, maybe a week, when he moved his belongings to 230 St. Catherine Street in the duplex shared by Emily Burns, her mother, and their boarder Poe. Maybe room and board was cheaper, but it appears that George may have taken a personal interest in Sister and she in him. Nonetheless, he took the time to write his wife, Meadie, a letter:

> Dear Wife Just a few lines as to let you hear from me this leaves me well and I made my arivel [*sic*] to Natchez safe and dear I do hope this will fine [*sic*] you feeling better so I am in Natchez for awhile so I just wants to let you know where I am at so you be sweet and let me hear from you real soon. I will write you a long letter next time so this is all from your husband G. Pearls
>
> Address to 230 St. Catherine Street, Natchez, Miss.[26]

As the nation headed deeper into economic collapse, jobs nationally dried up, and if there was any work for black men in Adams County in 1932, it was most likely farm labor or piecemeal work doing odd jobs for local whites. That summer in Natchez, Pink struggled to find the most basic employment. Testimony collected after Jennie Merrill's death suggests that he had sought work from both her and Duncan Minor and was rebuffed. Minor later recalled that a Negro, who had given his name as Lawrence Williams, had been "insolent" when Minor turned him away. In truth, any black man who did not show deference to white authority was likely to be regarded as disrespectful. Perhaps Williams suggested to both Jennie Merrill and Duncan Minor that he knew they had the money to hire him, which is why they considered him "insolent." To whites like Jennie and Duncan, whose family wealth had been built on cotton and slaves, he was just another black face whom they did not know by name. Yet Pink remembered his treatment, and he was right to believe that they had money. Because they did. Even during the Great Depression, rich people were still rich.[27]

So, as July turned into August, Pink was desperate for income, though how he came to strike up a conversation with Dick Dana and Octavia Dockery remains a mystery. Perhaps, after being rejected for work by Jennie Merrill, he simply walked next door to Glenwood to see if he might be hired. The decaying old mansion and the poorly maintained land on which it sat should have instantly signaled to him that he would find no paid work there. And yet on Thursday afternoon, August 4, Pink found himself talking with Dick and Octavia.

CHAPTER FOUR

MURDER AT GLENBURNIE

Dick Dana and Octavia Dockery had struggled to make ends meet for years. It was bad enough that goats roamed their house; they were also reduced to killing and eating them, too. Octavia regularly waged court battles with the various owners of Glenwood who had purchased it for unpaid taxes, managing to keep the property in litigation and herself and her ward in a home. As the pair spoke with the black man who called himself Lawrence Williams, the three of them swiftly realized that they shared more in common than poverty. They all had a disdain for the "haves," especially for the owner of Glenburnie. In Octavia Dockery's case, her contempt for Jennie Merrill went back for more than a decade. Merrill had money but had gone after what little Octavia and Dick had because of some trespassing hogs and goats. Williams's anger stemmed from being dismissed by wealthy whites he believed should have hired him. He had worked in the corn refinery and lived in a Chicago suburb for so long, he had nearly forgotten what it was like to deal with white planters like Merrill and Duncan Minor. Both refreshed his memory.[1]

No one will ever know the actual content of their conversation, but together the three spoke about Jennie Merrill. Octavia assumed her old foe kept money in the house, since the Depression led people to safeguard their cash at home rather than risk keeping it in the bank. She also knew that Duncan Minor's nightly visits to Glenburnie were so regular, between 8:30 and 9:00 P.M., she could set her watch by him. So, she and Williams made the plan to rob Merrill that evening, just after sunset but before Minor arrived. All stood to benefit from any money found, but Octavia no doubt relished the idea of getting revenge on Jennie. And wild-eyed Dick found it all very exciting. Pink could return to his life in Chicago with money in his pocket and tell his wife that the trip to Natchez to find work had been a success. And Jennie Merrill would get her just deserts.

Glenburnie, 1932. (Courtesy of the Thomas H. and Joan W. Gandy Photograph
Collection, Louisiana and Lower Mississippi Valley Collections, Special Collections,
Hill Memorial Library, Louisiana State University Libraries, Baton Rouge.)

After his chat with Dick and Octavia, Pink walked through the small forest of
scraggly trees behind Glenwood and cut across Duncan Park, over the Mississippi Central Railroad, through George Kelly's estate, Melrose, and up Cedar
Alley before reaching the little shack on St. Catherine Street. He didn't speak
a word to Sister or her mother, Nellie, about the plan he had hatched with the
odd couple who lived alongside the Kingston Road, though he may have told
Poe where to meet him later that evening.[2]

After dinner, as the afternoon sun drifted downward, Pink asked Sister to
go on a walk with him. She willingly accepted, enamored by this man of the
world from Chicago. As they left St. Catherine Street they strolled back across
the Melrose estate, walking along the alley-like path adjacent to the railroad,
and then into Duncan Park. But their walk did not end there. Pink led them
farther into the nearby woods, navigating weeds, bayous, and unruly palm
fronds, until they came to an opening among towering moss-covered trees in

the middle of which stood a ramshackle, two-story antebellum house that local blacks called the "spooky mansion."[3]

As Sister waited in the opening, Pink walked toward the house to meet with the occupants of this decaying estate. She had never seen them before, and something about them appeared strange to her. Both appeared to be a good ten years older than Pink. The man was tall and his beard was long and graying. His hair was also long and stringy, as though it was never combed or washed. Even at a distance, he looked grubby. The woman was also on the tall side, wearing a straw hat and a threadbare morning dress. Her skin was tan and weathered.

Sister may have heard of the "Wild Man" and the "Goat Woman," because black folks had originally given them their nicknames, but it was something different to see both in the flesh.[4] She noticed that the pair talked with Pink as though they had already met him. During their walk, Pink had told Sister that he wanted to get money from Merrill but did not say what he had in mind. She swiftly realized, however, that he and these odd white people had plotted to rob Jennie Merrill. Terrified, Sister wanted to leave and head for home, but it was too late to escape. Pink threatened to kill her now that she knew of their plans.[5]

Only three hundred yards separated the Dana and Merrill estates, and as they prepared to head west to Glenburnie, Dick gave Pink an old brown overcoat, the one that he got from the Skunk's Nest when John Geiger vacated the place. Maybe he thought it would provide a good cover, as daylight turned to dusk.

Around seven o'clock the four of them—Pink and Sister, Dick and Octavia—headed toward Glenburnie. They fumbled their way through the woods and overgrowth, across the snaky portion of Glenwood, slipping through the wire fence as Octavia's goats had done a dozen times, except they weren't there for Jennie's roses. They wanted the old biddy's money.

Once they crossed onto Merrill's estate, they all noticed Jennie's German shepherd, who was her constant companion. Normally the dog had free rein, but after it killed one of Jennie's pet kittens, she had tethered it to a tree behind the rear of the house. One of the four, perhaps Pink or even Dick, untied the dog and put it inside a nearby barn. Now certain that the dog posed no threat, they decided to go under the house, where they sat quietly, listening. Pink wanted to determine Miss Merrill's location within the house. He heard the old woman humming, and then he motioned to Sister to stand watch outside. He placed the old overcoat in front of his face to protect his identity and gingerly climbed the steps of the front porch before going inside. Sister later confessed that her boarder Poe was there, too, convinced by Pink to join them when they ran into him in the dirt alley along the railroad.[6]

———————

Near dusk, Jennie Merrill went to her bedroom to light the silver oil lamp she used to read by. It provided her only light, since her home had no electricity. Her maid, Effie Stanton, was away, and the tenants who lived on her property were in their own homes or getting ready for evening church services. Her German shepherd was just out back and would let her know when company arrived. Of course, these days the only real company she entertained was her cousin Duncan Minor. Still in her bedroom slippers, she began humming a tune as she lay down in her bed to read, still wearing the combs that kept her hair off of her neck in the stifling August heat.

Jennie had received a substantial inheritance from her father, and though by 1932 she did not lead nearly the extravagant life she had in her youth, she was still a wealthy woman, even by Depression-era standards. She owned plantations in Concordia Parish, in addition to her home Glenburnie, and had several investments. Glenburnie, built in 1833, was modest compared to Elms Court, the house where she was born. It was a single-story home with a porch that extended across the front, upheld by Tuscan columns, and then wrapped around the right-hand side of the house. What people did not know, except for maybe her cousin Duncan and local bankers, is that she never kept more than a few dollars with her at any one time.

As she sat in bed reading by the light of the silver lamp, waiting for Duncan to arrive, she heard someone come through her front door. Moments later, she spotted a man walking toward her, hidden behind a brown overcoat. Why hadn't her dog barked when he came on the property? Who would enter her home unannounced? She may have recognized the middle-aged black man who recently asked her for money and something to eat. She had fed him but said no to giving him money.

What happened next, no one knows for sure. Louis Terrell, a local black citizen, said Pink showed some men a .32 Colt pistol earlier in the day down at Hedges Store and told them that he knew where to get "plenty of money" if he could find someone who "had the nerve" to go with him. He fired the gun several times into the air, Terrell said, "to show he was a bad man."[7]

Jennie had guns, too, and wasn't afraid to use them. She kept a similar pistol in her purse. Her car mechanic had seen it several times when she paid him to fix her car. She also owned a .22 rifle, which she allegedly leveled at local blacks she hired to work for her, as if she had forgotten that slavery had ended decades before. She had a reputation among her tenants for shooting at Octavia's trespassing livestock—the hogs and the goats—because they were always causing damage and ruin to her property. It is doubtful she feared her intruder.[8]

Pink's intention was to get money from Jennie Merrill, but she fought back. After hitting her in the face with the butt of his gun to try and knock her out, she managed to get up from her bed, running to get her purse in the dining room just outside of her bedroom door. A scuffle broke out between the two, and shots were fired. Was it Pink's gun? Or had he taken Jennie's own gun from her? Either way, a .32 pistol went off. A bullet missed her and landed in the door frame to her bedroom. She began to scream and Pink shot again, and then a third time. One bullet hit her in the upper left chest. Another bullet pierced her neck and tore through her jugular vein, fatally wounding her. Jennie seems to have tried to escape to her bedroom, which is where she fell to the floor, blood pooling around her.[9]

Sister, standing outside on the porch, heard the scuffle, the shots, and the screaming. Octavia and Dick went inside. The group needed to think fast. It was close to eight o'clock and becoming more difficult to see. Duncan Minor would be there soon. Poe handed the silver lamp from Jennie's bedroom to Sister and went back inside to help Pink. Jennie Merrill may have been a tiny woman— her car mechanic estimated she didn't even weigh ninety-eight pounds—but Pink did not have the strength to carry her alone. So he and Poe picked up Jennie's now lifeless body and took her through the dining room, where one of her bloody slippers and hair combs fell to the floor. They carried her through the door that led to the side porch, circling around to the front of the house, and then down the stairs while Sister held the lamp that lit their path.[10]

Once outside, the men carried the body toward the rocky driveway about one hundred feet from the house, where they slipped and dropped Jennie on the ground. They could not see it, but the second of her bedroom slippers fell off, along with another of her hair combs. She was still bleeding profusely, so that when they picked her up again, another pool of blood had gathered. As they rushed to dispose of the body, they headed toward the woods that separated Merrill's estate from Glenwood. They got about a hundred yards from Jennie's house before they tossed her body—face up—into a thicket near a deep ravine. Sister, who had accompanied them, threw the lamp in the weeds about twenty feet away. Pink yelled at her to pick it back up and light it, but she hesitated because she had no matches. So he grabbed the lamp and lit it himself.[11]

The three of them headed back toward the house, and as Sister stood watch outside, Pink and Poe went back in. Octavia and Dick were already there. They ransacked Merrill's home, pulling drawers from furniture, including an old washstand and a chifferobe. One of them went through Jennie's purse and another flipped the mattress on her bed looking for a stash of money, but there was none to be had. A woman was dead. And not just any woman—Jennie Merrill was planter aristocracy in a town that prided itself on that heritage.

The unlikely group scattered. Pink and Sister went back as they came—through the woods, crossing over railroad tracks, and then through the Melrose estate to a back road that led to her house on St. Catherine Street. Poe, who was likely at the scene of the crime, headed into town by Homochitto Street.

By the time they made it back to Sister's house, it was almost 9:30 P.M. As soon as they walked in the door, Pink hurriedly grabbed some matches and headed to the backyard, where he ripped off his bloody clothes, doused them in coal oil, and set them on fire. He made a small bundle of personal effects and put his pistol in a scabbard. Or was it Jennie Merrill's gun? His trunk was too large to carry, so he told Sister he would send for it later. Pink changed into a brown suit and put on a black hat and shoes. He made plans to have Poe drive him to Giles Point, where he would cross the river into Louisiana and head north. Sister joined him as he walked out into the darkness to meet Poe. They both got into Poe's car, and the three of them made the quiet drive beyond the city cemetery, where they stopped and Pink got out. There on the banks of the Mississippi River, in the pitch of night, Pink and Sister said their good-byes. It was the last time she ever saw him.[12]

Dick and Octavia scurried back to Glenwood in darkness, their only light Miss Jennie's oil lamp. But before they crossed the property line into Glenwood, Octavia likely commanded Dick to get rid of it in some weeds. For all of Octavia's scheming, the pair had returned with nothing but a neighbor's blood on their hands.

What had seemed simple to her hours earlier had become complicated in the extreme. Octavia may not have liked Jennie Merrill, but she had not fathomed that the plan to rob her would have ended so horribly. She had to know that she would be questioned about it. Just a few days before, she and Jennie had what was later described as an "unusually bitter clash" because Glenwood's goats had once again trespassed onto Jennie's estate and made a meal of her roses. She knew it would not be too long before the sheriff came to question them, and she needed to make sure that her ward didn't tell what he knew. Dick was still very excited by the drama that had unfolded that evening, and Octavia feared—rightly, as it turns out—that he was liable to slip up and say something that would draw suspicion.[13]

———

It was around 7:30 P.M. that Thursday evening when twenty-three-year-old Willie Boyd, a tenant on Merrill's estate, heard shots and screams and the hollering of a German shepherd coming from Glenburnie. His wife laughed at him. "It's probably Miss Jennie killing another one of Dana's goats," she said. Willie was curious but afraid to go see about it, so he walked over to a small black settlement where fifty-eight-year-old M. C. Hacher lived. He remarked to Willie that perhaps Miss Jennie's dog had killed another of her pet kittens and so she had shot it. Still, he was concerned, and he and Willie headed back up the Kingston Road toward the entrance of Merrill's estate where they planned to wait on Duncan Minor to arrive, which he did with regularity around 8:45 P.M. More important, they knew that as black men in Mississippi, it was unwise to go to the house of a white woman who lived alone, especially at this time of the evening, because whatever had happened, they could easily be arrested or even lynched.[14]

As they walked along the gravel road, they noticed a white man ahead walking away from the estate and called out to him to go with them to see what was happening at Merrill's home, but he refused. Was it Dick Dana? Perhaps. So they waited, and like clockwork, at 8:45 P.M., they saw Duncan Minor. He was riding one of the horses he kept at a local stable in town, traveling at a leisurely pace on his nightly visit to see Jennie. They waved him down, and Hacher had Willie tell Minor about the screams and the shots he heard earlier.[15]

Something was wrong, and it was now dark. Country dark. And no light could be seen coming from inside the house. Jennie usually waited up on him to arrive. Duncan grew more concerned as he approached the house with Hacher.

After he entered the front door, Duncan called several times for Jennie, but there was no answer. He fumbled for a small antique lamp that sat on the fireplace mantel and lit it. The faint glow of the little lamp revealed a gruesome scene. Blood was smeared on the walls and floor of the dining room and on the floor of Jennie's bedroom. But there was no sign of her. Her mattress lay askew on the bed. Drawers had been yanked from their places. Furniture had been tossed around. Jennie's empty purse was on the floor, along with one of her now-bloodied slippers and a hair comb. What had happened?

Duncan searched for Jennie outside. He told Hacher to help him, and they called out for Willie Boyd to join them. The small search party followed the trail of blood and went back and forth between the house and outbuildings and into the woods adjacent to the house but never saw her. Minor's instincts, however, were telling him she was out there. They searched for nearly an hour before Duncan realized that he'd better contact law enforcement. So, he directed Willie Boyd to go find the nearest telephone and call the sheriff.[16]

———

It was late that Thursday evening in August when some teenage boys, including Charlie Bahin, gathered on a street corner in their hometown of Natchez to chew the fat and enjoy what little bit of cool air might brush by them. It beat hanging out down on the bluff overlooking the Mississippi River battling swarms of gnats and mosquitoes. Besides, what else was there to do in their small town? No sooner had that thought crossed Charlie's mind than a loud siren blared from a car speeding down Pearl Street. Even more surprising to the boys was the fact that one of their pals, Barnett Serio, was driving.

Charlie and his friends started running to find out what was happening. They discovered a crowd gathered around the Gem Café near the corner of Main and Pearl Streets, where Barnett parked the car and ran inside to tell folks what he had just learned. There was a nervous tension in the air as men and women walked in and out of the Gem, where they heard the terrible news that Jennie Merrill had been murdered, or so they thought, since she had not been located.[17]

As Barnett told it, just after 10:00 P.M. his father, Joe, a deputy sheriff, had gotten a phone call from Sheriff Clarence Roberts to meet him at the Adams County jail on State Street. One of Jennie Merrill's young black tenants, Willie Boyd, had phoned the sheriff's office to let him know that Duncan Minor needed his help real quick. Miss Merrill was missing, and there was blood on the floors and walls of her house.[18]

Fifty-four-year-old Zaida Marion Wells was one of the townspeople who caught wind of something dramatic as she walked out of the Baker-Grand Theatre, where she had gone to see a movie with her friend Nettie Smith. As the women stood on the corner of Pearl and State Streets, they had a clear view of the county jail. They watched and could see sheriffs' deputies going toward the jail with guns. Then, what seemed like a short time later, another group of men arrived. Across State Street at city hall, several policemen hurried down the steps to a waiting car and sped away.

Zaida and Nettie walked back to the Gem Café, where they heard talk of murder. Now the activity at the jail made sense. The two women, especially Wells, wanted to drive out to Glenburnie, but it wasn't proper for women to drive alone after dark. So they asked Charlie Bahin and another teenage boy to get in Wells's car to accompany them out to the Kingston Road where Jennie Merrill lived. As they drove along the gravel road that fronted Miss Jennie's estate, Zaida slowed her car down to a creep as the entire group of them stared out of the windows looking for—what? They did not know. All they could see in the darkness were the search party lights that waxed and waned through the woods like fireflies.[19]

Nothing so exciting had happened in Natchez since nearly four thousand visitors had come to their little town only a few months earlier to tour the Bluff City's antebellum mansions—relics of another time when the town of Natchez had cachet in the larger world. But this was a different kind of excitement —the kind that caused old women to gasp and young hearts to race.

CHAPTER FIVE

THE INVESTIGATION

While word spread throughout Natchez that something sinister had taken place on the edge of town, Sheriff Clarence Powell Roberts and his deputy Joe Serio drove swiftly to Glenburnie to meet with Duncan Minor and begin the investigation. By now it was close to 11:00 P.M., and Duncan's efforts to locate Jennie had been futile. Roberts's first priority was to locate her, so he called on his deputies, former sheriff Walter Abbott, chief of police Mike Ryan, and several patrolmen to assist him. A posse of local citizens armed with lanterns and flashlights also joined in the search and spread across the estate, which by now was pitch-black. Yet even in the dark, the sheriff and his deputies knew this landscape. They had walked it many times with Jennie Merrill as she pointed out the damage done by the neighbors' hogs and, lately, their goats.

Clarence Roberts, now almost forty years old and unmarried, had not dreamed of becoming an officer of the law. Born in 1892 in the little village of Gloster, Mississippi, he was one of five children and the only son of Quitman and Calpernia Roberts. He first followed in his father's footsteps, becoming a carpenter and building houses. When he was in his mid-twenties, he enlisted as a private in the Mississippi Infantry and served in the army during World War I. His draft card described him as having a medium build and of medium height, with gray eyes and auburn hair. After the war he worked as a cashier for the Southern Express Company, part of American Express, and later sold cars for local dealers Porter and Claggett. By 1925, though, he was a deputy sheriff, and within five years he became the sheriff of Adams County.[1]

People who knew the sheriff personally called him "Book," a nickname that did not come from booking criminals. Rather, it had been with him since childhood. The story goes that when he was in grade school in the late 1890s,

Duncan Minor (*left*) with Sheriff Clarence "Book" Roberts standing
in front of Glenburnie. (Courtesy of the Thomas H. and Joan W. Gandy
Photograph Collection, Louisiana and Lower Mississippi Valley
Collections, Special Collections, Hill Memorial Library,
Louisiana State University Libraries, Baton Rouge.)

he got into a fight with another boy. In the heat of the moment, the two traded
insults. Clarence called his opponent "Abraham Lincoln," a particularly offen-
sive slur in a region still sensitive about military defeat. But young Clarence
could not have been prepared for the rejoinder: the other boy hit back and
called him "Booker T. Washington," a reference to the black leader who had
ruffled the feathers of many white southerners. Clearly, Clarence's enemy got
the best of him, because the nickname stuck, although in shortened form.[2]

Book finished coordinating search efforts, which included calling George
Allen, a planter from Wisner, Louisiana, who raised bloodhounds, as well as

the state's fingerprint expert in Jackson, then steeled himself for the task ahead: it was time to have a chat with Dick Dana and Octavia Dockery. In Book's mind, they were likely suspects, given their long-running feud with Merrill. Just earlier in the week Octavia and Jennie had gotten into a particularly nasty argument about goats trespassing onto Merrill's estate. And officers had made more visits to speak with Octavia than either of them could count. But had it really come to this?

Along with Deputy Serio, Book drove the short distance to Glenwood along the Kingston Road and then bounced along the gullied driveway that led to the house. The car's headlights provided the only illumination to be found on the property at that hour, which was reflected back to them by the peering eyes of dogs, cats, and goats.

As they approached the house, they had to be careful not to fall through one of the rotting planks of the front porch. The door was unlocked, probably because it would not close properly, so the two men knocked loudly as they entered the front hallway with only their flashlights to guide them. As they did, Book called out for Dick Dana, receiving no response. Again, he called out. Dick refused to come downstairs. As the sheriff looked around, he saw a man's shirt drying out from a recent washing.

Already this was suspicious. Dana notoriously never washed his clothes. Why would a man who locals said had a "singular aversion to water" be washing out a shirt at midnight? It made no sense.

Dana finally came down the stairs and, before the sheriff had an opportunity to explain why he and his deputy were there, blurted out, "I know nothing of the murder." At this point, Jennie was still considered missing. Octavia's fears of Dick saying something when she was not there to supervise him had been realized. The two were arrested and taken to the county jail for questioning.[3]

By the time Dana and Dockery were booked into a cell, George Allen and his bloodhounds had arrived at Glenburnie. The dogs were given a quick sniff of the overcoat found in Jennie's dining room and were off, running first in the direction of the neighboring estate. This made sense, given that the coat originally belonged to John Geiger, who had left it at the Skunk's Nest, the roadhouse he once rented from Dana. It also made sense that the dogs followed the scent in the direction of Glenwood, because Dana had retrieved the coat after Geiger left and brought it back to the main house. As the hounds approached the dividing line of the property, their baying grew louder. The scent led them to a silver coal-oil lamp with a blue china shade. The shade was

Entered N. O. F
Matter Under

Map Shows Scenes Figuring in Merrill Murder

CLUBHOUSE

TO NATCHEZ

DUNCAN PARK

ODELL FERGUSON'S HOUSE. BLOODHOUNDS STOPPED HERE.

KINGSTON HIGHWAY

JANE MERRILL'S HOUSE

TO DUNCAN MINOR'S HOUSE

THICKET WHERE BODY WAS FOUND

WILD'S POND

DEEP RAVINE

"GOAT CASTLE"

MAN IN OVERCOAT SEEN HERE

LAMP

FOOT PATH

WIRE FENCE SEPARATING DANA PROPERTY FROM MERRILL PROPERTY

GATE TO DANA PROPERTY

ROAD TO "GOAT CASTLE"

GATE TO DANA PROPERTY

SKUNK'S REST

KINGSTON HIGHWAY

N
W
S

REPORT ON SLAIN SUSPECT'S PRINTS MAY SOLVE CASE

Disorder, Open Purse in Merrill Home Suggest Robbery Motive

By Gwen Bristow
(The Times-Picayune Staff Representative)
Natchez, Miss., Aug. 14.—If the
fingerprints of the famous "Chicago

ST CATHARINE'S CREEK

BRIDGE

This crime map illustrates the proximity of Glenburnie to Goat Castle, as well as detailed findings from the investigation. (*New Orleans Times-Picayune*, August 15, 1932.)

broken and the lamp tossed into the weeds. Once sheriff's deputies retrieved the items, Duncan Minor recognized it as a lamp that had been taken from Jennie's home.[4]

George Allen and the dogs' handler, S. J. Sturdivant, took the bloodhounds back toward Merrill's house and circled it twice; the dogs then led the men west toward Homochitto Street. The hounds' baying reached a fever pitch as they closed in on Wilds Pond. Allen and Sturdivant felt sure they were on the trail of the criminal or criminals who had been at Jennie's home as the dogs kept circling the pond.

The hounds eventually led the men to the home of twenty-two-year-old Odell Ferguson, the very same person who years earlier encountered Dick Dana swinging from a grapevine. The sheriff knocked on Odell's door and woke him from a deep sleep. The hounds had trailed the scent to Ferguson's property, and the sheriff was there to ask some questions. It could be that Pink and Sister, or even Poe, had traveled in this direction after leaving Glenburnie and tossed the gun in Wilds Pond. But this was just the beginning of the investigation, before Book Roberts knew anything about who was at Merrill's place that evening. For now, the hounds had led him here. Odell would have to account for his whereabouts earlier in the evening, so he was taken in for questioning as well.[5]

As the investigation continued into the early morning hours of Friday, August 5, the search uncovered two of Jennie's hair combs and one of her bed slippers next to a pool of blood at the end of her driveway. Initial reporting hopefully suggested that Merrill had fended off her attackers as she ran into the woods for safety, because this is what local people wanted to believe. Yet this wishful thinking would soon be dispelled.

About an hour before sunrise, at 5:45 A.M., twenty-year-old Alonzo Floyd discovered Jennie Merrill's body in a thicket about one hundred yards from her home. Floyd, described in the newspaper as a "Negro youth," lived and worked on Merrill's estate and had helped Duncan Minor look for Jennie earlier that evening. Duncan had been to the thicket more than once. His intuition told him she was there, so he told Floyd to go there once more that morning. Duncan was right. "Here she is!" Alonzo shouted, as members of the search party ran to where he stood pointing. Her body lay in a thicket resting on a bed of dead moss where she had been tossed—face upward. The bullet wounds to her neck and chest were visible; her clothes were drenched with blood. Miss Jennie had been murdered.[6]

As dawn broke that morning, local officers detained several individuals for questioning. In addition to Dick Dana, Octavia Dockery, and Odell Ferguson, they arrested John Geiger, whose overcoat was found inside Merrill's home. This was the Jim Crow South, so they rounded up local blacks who lived on the estate or near Glenburnie and brought them in for questioning as well. Among them were two men who helped with the investigation—Willie Boyd, who told Duncan Minor about the screams he heard coming from Glenburnie, and Alonzo Floyd, who found the body.[7]

In the early days of the investigation, several more people were brought in for questioning and almost as swiftly released. But Odell Ferguson remained in jail, and John Geiger was kept there for nearly a week. Geiger had to explain how his overcoat ended up inside Jennie Merrill's home. He told authorities he had left it, along with other belongings, back at the Skunk's Nest when he was told to vacate the property by Octavia Dockery for failure to pay his rent. During questioning, she confirmed that Geiger had been sent packing and that the items he left behind—including a filthy mattress—were now on the porch at Glenwood. She maintained that they left the overcoat behind. Dick Dana, too, confirmed this by telling the sheriff that he "sent a Negro to the Skunk's Nest" to gather Geiger's possessions and move them to the main house. In truth, he and Octavia had gone there to drag whatever Geiger left inside back to Glenwood. Leaving anything of value, like the overcoat, did not make sense given what packrats Dana and Dockery were, only adding to their suspicious behavior.[8]

Even after Geiger was released, officers continued to bring him back in from time to time for questioning about what he described as "that pesky overcoat." He became irritated about the number of times deputies called him to come to the Adams County jail to answer questions, because he kept getting called away from work. He even offered to help catch the murderer himself, saying that if this kept up no one would hire him and he'd be "holding a tin cup."[9]

Unlike some whites, Geiger expressed confidence that no one in the local black community was involved in killing Jennie Merrill. "Negroes in Natchez don't do things like that," he said. "They are all good peaceful folks around here," adding, "I don't know a single negro in Natchez that I'd suspect of killing that lady."[10]

Dick Dana and Octavia Dockery, however, were the prime suspects from the beginning. Dana's "nocturnal laundrying," as the *Natchez Democrat* put it, had every appearance of an effort to wash out bloodstains. Deputies also

Chief Deputy Joseph Stone holds the overcoat found inside Glenburnie
during the murder investigation. (Courtesy of the Thomas H. and
Joan W. Gandy Photograph Collection, Louisiana and Lower Mississippi Valley Collections, Special Collections, Hill Memorial Library,
Louisiana State University Libraries, Baton Rouge.)

found fresh drops of blood on the page of an old golf magazine in the parlor of
their home. Dick attributed the blood to butchering a hog earlier that day, but
deputies took it in as evidence nonetheless.

Dana's other statements were also cause for concern. During questioning,
he told police chief Ryan that Jennie and Octavia argued "severely" over trespassing goats earlier in the week. He also provided conflicting statements about

his whereabouts at the time the crime occurred. First, he explained that he was out on a hill at Glenwood "watching the sunset" when he heard a gunshot and a scream, adding that he thought it was "a negro man chastising his wife in a nearby cabin." In another statement he claimed that he was at home when he heard the shots and had intended to go to Duncan Park to phone officers, but Octavia "became hysterical and begged him to remain at the house [because] she was afraid." Then there was his original statement to Sheriff Roberts, "I know nothing of the murder," before Roberts ever mentioned why he had come to Glenwood. He incriminated himself further, while in custody, when he told Chief Ryan, "I did not place the overcoat over her [Merrill's] head."[11]

During this early round of questioning suspects, James Chancellor, the best fingerprint expert in the state, arrived from Jackson to begin his work.[12] That Friday afternoon, Chancellor collected a total of thirty-two prints from furniture, glasses, and a door frame "where a bloody hand had been pressed." He also lifted prints from the silver oil lamp and lampshade discovered on the property. All of these were compared with the ones taken from among those in custody. During a press conference with reporters, Sheriff Roberts said that he was "relying heavily upon fingerprint clues" and confirmed that Chancellor had gathered "a number of almost perfect prints." The sheriff also indicated that there were prints from "a deformed hand," which Dana had. In fact, Dick later told reporters of how his hand had become injured from a fallen window. Still, Chancellor wanted to be sure and refused to commit to any firm results until enlargements of the fingerprints were made. He then returned to Jackson to examine his findings over the weekend, while the sheriff promised the public a report by Monday, August 8.[13]

At 11:00 A.M. that Saturday, August 6, many Natchezeans attended Jennie Merrill's funeral at Trinity Episcopal Church. Generations of her family had been members there, and, of course, Dick Dana's father was once the rector. Now, the rector's son sat in the Adams County jail accused of her murder.

That morning Reverend Joseph Kuehnle, the current rector of Trinity Episcopal, conducted services for the woman whom newspapers continued to refer to—disparagingly, some thought—as the "aged recluse." After, the cortege headed toward the city cemetery, where Jennie was laid to rest in the Merrill family section alongside her parents, grandparents, and siblings.

Only the day before, the editor of the *Natchez Democrat* printed a plea that there be justice for Merrill. "The slaying of this lady in its cold blooded premeditation is the act of a fiend in human form," he wrote, referring to the unknown assailant as a person with "no more compunction on taking lives than the most savage brutes." This person must be made to pay for this crime "on the gallows." In the Jim Crow South, terms like "brute," "fiend," and "savage" were essentially code for black men who whites believed were naturally inclined to engage in this kind of criminality. To use those words amounted to a clarion call for a lynching.[14]

Some in the white community echoed this feeling. As Zaida Wells later recalled, "Without even suspecting negroes of the crime, two white people, Octavia Dockery and Richard Dana, starved, wretched inmates of decaying Glenwood . . . were in the Adams County jail charged with murder."[15] Such rhetoric played out in the local paper, too, and shaped public opinion about the pair's arrest and detention. Only John Geiger, the owner of the overcoat, openly expressed faith in black Natchezeans' essential goodness.

Then Monday came. Chancellor's examination confirmed his initial observations. The first positive fingerprint match was one belonging to Octavia Dockery, found on a washstand in Merrill's home. "Today I picked out a positively identified left forefinger of Miss Dockery as being one of the fingers that touched furniture in the room where Miss Merrill was assailed," Chancellor announced in his report to the sheriff and the newspaper reporters gathered at the Adams County jail. "I believe and still contend as set out in my preliminary report to Sheriff Roberts last night," he continued, "that I have one or more prints that correspond to Dana's." Those prints were collected from the rear door of Merrill's home, an old washstand, a chifferobe, and the lampshade taken from inside the house. But since the original prints collected from Dick were smeared, another set had to be taken and examined. Still, it was enough for the county's district attorney, Joseph Brown, to recommend that the sheriff formally charge the pair with murder.[16]

The evidence was swiftly growing overwhelming, yet Dick and Octavia steadfastly denied any guilt and protested their innocence. Dick even seemed to enjoy the attention, regaling reporters with stories of his youth. But when the conversation turned to the night of the murder, he was unable to recall events, changed the subject, or complained of deafness. His only recollection was of hearing shots and screams coming from Merrill's home. He also denied having told officers there were any recent arguments between Octavia and Jennie over the goats.[17]

Book Roberts felt confident that fingerprint evidence was the key to solving the crime, and Chancellor's findings confirmed his suspicions of Dana and Dockery. Yet he continued his investigation because a third set of prints found at the crime scene did not match up with any of the prints they had taken of suspects in Natchez. He also had reason to keep the case open, because there was pressure to follow up on Duncan Minor's assertion that a "strange negro"—essentially not a local black with whom he was familiar—had come to see Jennie about money or something to eat.[18]

According to Duncan, this same man had also sought him out for work. He had called himself Williams and told him of having recently lived in Detroit or Chicago, that he had "lost several thousand dollars in a bank that failed," and that he had returned to Adams County to look for work. He came to see Minor because he had worked for him when he was a young man. "I did not remember him," Duncan said, "but since his day we have hired and fired so many Negroes it would be easy for me to have forgotten him." At any rate, Minor refused to hire him because, he said, Williams "ruffled my feelings by being insolent."[19]

Based on the evidence, Book Roberts had every reason to believe he had the right people in custody. A third set of prints simply meant there was another person working with Dana and Dockery. He even expressed confidence that the pair might be nearing a confession, as they appeared to be weakening under the intense interrogation by himself, Chief Ryan, and county DA Joe Brown. They must have come close to offering one, as the sheriff suggested that their reason for their fingerprints being inside the house was because they had run over to Merrill's home after hearing shots. After they reached down to touch her "still warm blood" on the floor, they grew afraid and ran back to Glenwood. This, too, contradicted their protestations of innocence.[20]

While the questioning of John Geiger, Odell Ferguson, Dick Dana, and Octavia Dockery continued at the Adams County jail, Book decided to call in additional help. He seems to have been overwhelmed by a case that was already garnering national attention, so he reached out to Maurice O'Neill, a detective with the New Orleans Police Department. Like Chancellor, he was a Bertillon expert. Named for the Frenchman Alphonse Bertillon, such detectives stud-

Maurice O'Neill, chief detective with the
New Orleans Police Department. (Image from
Master Detective, September 1933.)

ied photographs of known criminals, as well as the physical measurements of
their heads and fingers, to develop a physical "roadmap" for tracking suspects.
O'Neill was considered one of the best. He had joined the New Orleans police
force in 1916 and was now the city's chief of investigation and also highly regarded for his ballistics work. He agreed to come to Natchez to assist Sheriff
Roberts, arriving there two days later on the evening of August 11. Bringing
the New Orleans detective to Natchez, it turns out, changed the direction of
the investigation decisively.[21]

　　In the week following Jennie Merrill's murder, James Chancellor worked
tirelessly on developing fingerprint evidence so that Maurice O'Neill might
render his own technical opinion. When New Orleans's chief detective arrived
in Natchez, he met with Sheriff Roberts and his deputies, ostensibly to assist in
the investigation. Before long, however, O'Neill asserted himself and took on
a leading role. He intended to offer his own report on the fingerprint compar-

isons, and in the days ahead, he stood alongside Sheriff Roberts and answered reporters' questions.[22]

Then, in an odd turn of events, Chancellor was said to have "broken under the strain" of spending fifteen-hour days examining fingerprints. It was reported that he returned home to Jackson, where he was "confined to his bed." Coincidentally, it happened within a few days of O'Neill's arrival. Had he been asked to leave? Was he insulted to have his work re-examined by the detective from New Orleans? Or had he honestly "broken under the strain"? These were all possibilities, and yet there was another potential explanation.[23]

Sympathy was growing in Natchez for the "pathetic pair" who sat in the Adams County jail charged with the murder of Jennie Merrill. Despite their conflicting statements and the positive identification Chancellor made of their fingerprints, collected from inside Jennie Merrill's home, locals refused to believe that either Dick Dana or Octavia Dockery was capable of murder. Unnamed advisers declared that if need be, they would appeal to "the friend of the friendless," none other than the American Civil Liberties Union attorney Clarence Darrow, who just seven years earlier earned fame in what was known as the "Scopes Monkey Trial."[24]

The drama that attached itself to Dana and Dockery grew each day the pair stayed in jail. So, after initially allowing Dick and Octavia an opportunity to speak with reporters, Sheriff Roberts changed his mind and decided to keep the pair incommunicado. He did so, in part, because Lee Ratcliff, the son of Ed Ratcliff, who eventually became the pair's attorney, was giving Dana legal advice in jail. The son, himself an attorney, was also in jail on charges of public drunkenness and had been talking to Dana whenever the two were in the "bull room" of the jail and advised him not to answer the sheriff's questions.[25]

Meanwhile, Dana and Dockery received visitors at the jail daily. Young girls from prominent families brought them flowers and petitions for their release. People dropped off books, magazines, bedding, packages of fruit, more bouquets of flowers, and cards of sympathy. After several days, the sympathy even turned to resentment at the thought of the two of them being "bewildered by the relentless questioning."[26]

Trespassing visitors to Glenwood also hastened the call for their release. Press reports of Glenwood's dilapidated condition and unsecured antiques and other potential valuables inside the home drew people from throughout Mississippi and Louisiana and beyond, alarming locals. Hundreds of voyeuristic tourists arrived within days of the pair's arrest. They wanted to see Goat Castle for themselves, and some went so far as to steal items from the house as souvenirs. Dockery used these transgressions to her and Dana's advantage. "Can you wonder that Dick chose to shun the world, when people can be so heartless and cruel?" she asked a reporter. "While we are behind the bars of prison for a crime of which, as God is my bearer, we are innocent, vandals prowl through our house," she continued. "Is there no law, no justice that will protect our property rights—is every one devoid of human feeling?"[27]

Not one to miss an opportunity in the spotlight now that it was upon her, Octavia made her sole newspaper interview count, telling the reporter, "You are a newspaper man! Tell the world! No! I did not kill Miss Merrill." She continued to press her case. "God knows I did not kill her," she said. "True, she was no friend of mine, but had I known her life was threatened on the night I heard screams and gunshots at her home, I would have gone to help her," she asserted. Octavia made the most of her public performance. She certainly had never received this kind of publicity for her poems and stories.[28]

The only people allowed a meeting with Dick and Octavia at the jail, outside of their interrogators, were lawyers. Sophie Friedman, a Memphis attorney, visited with them and offered to represent them pro bono and work alongside either local attorney Laurens Kennedy, who often represented Octavia in her court appearances with Jennie Merrill, or Ed Ratcliff. Friedman, a Hungarian Jew, immigrated to the United States with her family when she was a child. They first lived in Memphis. Then in 1900, her parents, Louis and Mollie Goldberger, relocated to Natchez, where there was a thriving Jewish community and synagogue. The widowed Friedman happened to be in town visiting her mother when she decided to offer Dana and Dockery legal representation.[29]

Yet it was Ed Ratcliff, chief counsel for the Illinois Central Railroad, who stepped in to represent Glenwood's residents. As Dick and Octavia entered into the second week of their incarceration, Ratcliff took charge of their case by filing a writ of habeas corpus claiming that the pair was wrongfully accused of murder and that they had been "unlawfully and illegally confined" since the night of the their arrest. The writ also stated that they had been "deprived of their liberty" by Sheriff Roberts.[30]

Locals considered the writ a good sign. White Natchezeans had practically demanded the release of Glenwood's residents for several days. Now they would be party to the pair's habeas corpus hearing. On August 15, locals crowded into the Adams County Courthouse to witness chancery court judge Richard Cutrer rule on the case and to see Dick Dana and Octavia Dockery, the odd couple who had been held incommunicado for the past several days across the street at the Adams County jail.

It was a dramatic scene as Dick and Octavia entered the spacious courtroom, filled to capacity with their fellow citizens. As they quietly moved through the crowd, people offered them kind words and reached out to grasp their hands in friendship. They then took their seat until their case was called. When it was, Natchez district attorney Clay Tucker stood up and stated that there was insufficient evidence to justify keeping them in jail and asked that they be released. Judge Cutrer agreed and ruled that the two be released on their own recognizance and be allowed to return home — fingerprint evidence be damned.[31]

As Dick and Octavia softly murmured, "Thank you, Judge," the courtroom erupted into cheers and applause. Some in attendance pressed forward to shake Dick and Octavia's hands, while others offered them a place to stay. They politely declined, preferring to return to squalid Glenwood. When asked how she felt about the situation she found herself in, Octavia said only, "No one can tell what turn events will take." The pair then walked out of the courthouse escorted by the Reverend Kuehnle and their attorney, after which their old friend Archibald Dickson drove them home.[32]

Dana and Dockery's brief incarceration may have ended, but the investigation continued, as Sheriff Roberts and Maurice O'Neill worked to piece together the story of the man named Williams. As they did, their investigation took them to Chicago and soon led them to a little shack on the corner of St. Catherine Street and Cedar Alley.[33]

CHAPTER SIX

JIM CROW'S INVESTIGATION

O f all the evidence collected from the crime scene—the overcoat, the broken oil lamp, and the positively identified fingerprints—authorities had yet to find the murder weapon. George Allen's bloodhounds had led them to Wilds Pond and circled it several times, which made him believe the gun was tossed there. Deputy Joe Serio supervised the dragging of the pond in hopes of retrieving the murder weapon but came up empty-handed. Allen sought to vindicate his bloodhounds and even offered twenty-five dollars to anyone who came forward with the weapon. No one claimed the reward.

Based on the coroner's report, the sheriff knew that the murder weapon was a .32 caliber pistol. E. C. Boyt, Jennie Merrill's car mechanic, remembered that she carried such a gun. Her old 1919 Roadster was a rattletrap that needed frequent repairs, and whenever she opened her purse to pay him he noticed what he believed to be a .32 revolver. "I've seen it in her handbag 50 times," Boyt said, adding, "I never really asked her about it, of course. One didn't ask Miss Jennie about her business." When the sheriff entered the house on the night of the murder, Jennie's empty purse was found lying on the floor, and her revolver was missing. Could it be that her own gun caused her death? Even if it had, Book Roberts was under mounting pressure to locate the murder weapon and to identify the suspect who left the third set of fingerprints found inside Merrill's home.[1]

The Sunday after Jennie Merrill was killed, Arkansas police deputy Robert Henslee was making his rounds in Pine Bluff when he spotted a black man he had never noticed in town before. Black men with no clear purpose for being on the street were assumed to be up to no good, so Henslee stopped to question him. The man wore a suit and hat, and his knapsack indicated that he was traveling. According to Henslee, this "suspicious character" refused to answer his questions, so he tried to arrest him. Henslee claimed that the man resisted arrest, and when he reached into the small bundle he was carrying, the deputy shot him—six times—fatally wounding him out of fear that the Negro might be reaching for a gun. Among the man's belongings was a gun, the same caliber of weapon that killed Jennie Merrill, a .32 Colt pistol. There were also papers, including a letter from Austin, Texas, addressed to him in Natchez, which enabled local authorities to determine his identity as George Pearls.[2]

Police chief W. D. Fiveash phoned Sheriff Roberts to share the information he and his deputies collected from Pearls, believing that he may be the figure described in newspaper accounts of the murder. The chief told Roberts that the man killed had resisted arrest and that among his possessions was a letter addressed to him in Natchez and what he believed could be the "murder gun," a .32 Colt revolver. Roberts was appreciative, but the name "George Pearls" was not one of the names he and deputies were pursuing. Book had no idea that he would be calling Chief Fiveash only a few days later.[3]

Within hours of his arrival in Natchez, Maurice O'Neill swiftly took over the investigation. He led the sheriff and deputies into the black community to search for clues. Early on, Duncan Minor mentioned his suspicions about a black man whose last name was Williams and who had asked for work from both him and Miss Jennie. His recollection was that the man was from either Chicago or Detroit. Based on this, O'Neill, the sheriff, and a "slew of deputies" went into black neighborhoods in Natchez and on surrounding plantations.

A major break came on Friday, August 12, when an older man from the black community provided the sheriff a key piece of information. Book Roberts explained to reporters that based on that tip, he and his deputies were able to retrace the steps of a "Chicago-Detroit negro" who had spent time in Natchez under the name of Lawrence Williams. Roberts refused to name his source, saying only that the person had provided the information as "gratitude for a kindness" that the sheriff had shown.[4]

With this break in the investigation, sheriff's deputies swiftly combed the community interviewing local blacks about a person officers assumed was unknown to them. But the man once described in newspapers as a "strange Negro" had actually been born and raised in Natchez. He had left for Chicago nearly twenty years before, like thousands of other southern blacks who migrated north. Williams returned to Natchez, they learned, to "visit with his boyhood friends in the country next to the Merrill and Dana estates." And while in Natchez, he sought work. It was also clear from discussions with people familiar with Williams that he had met Jennie Merrill, Duncan Minor, Dick Dana, and Octavia Dockery. Minor had already confirmed as much, even if he had not recognized the "yard boy" who had worked for him years before.[5]

Several local blacks were brought in for questioning during this stage of the investigation, including Zula Curtis, the owner of a boardinghouse at 33 Beaumont Street, where Williams stayed. They also questioned Louis Winston, a chauffeur for a local white family who, "as a favor to [his] cousin," moved Williams's trunk of belongings to the home of Nellie Black on St. Catherine Street adjacent to Cedar Alley. In Curtis's statement to sheriff's deputies, she described a man she knew as W. C. Williams who had boarded with her for a few weeks in July before he relocated to the house off Cedar Alley. In his statement, Winston confirmed having taken the trunk from Curtis's establishment to Nellie's home. "I moved the trunk, which was very heavy, and placed it inside the door of the Black house," he said, adding, "While I did not know [Williams], I had heard of him from my relatives. He had removed from Natchez when I was a boy."[6]

Zula Curtis's statement to deputies helped them develop a timeline of Williams's activities in Natchez. He boarded with her beginning in July, she said, while he looked for work. This aligned with what Duncan Minor said about Williams coming to him looking for employment. Curtis also mentioned that even after he left her boardinghouse, he came back for a visit and complained that he had been unable to find a job. He had been to Glenwood and spoken with Dick Dana and Octavia Dockery and told Curtis their house was "filthy" and "in dilapidated condition" and that they could not afford to hire him. Williams also told her he had gone to see both Jennie Merrill and Duncan Minor and mentioned that Merrill's home needed painting and repairs but that "they were too stingy to give him work."[7]

Curtis also made the observation that, unbeknownst to her, may have let Dick Dana off the hook. She told officers she noticed that Williams "did not have normal use of his left hand" whenever they played cards. But this was the extent of her description, and she could not discern whether it was deformed, paralyzed, missing a finger, or anything else. Still, officers and reporters seized on this information. A bloody print of a "deformed hand" had been found inside of Glenburnie.[8]

Until now, the sheriff believed the prints found inside Merrill's home to be Dana's. Dick had a damaged hand, but it was his right hand. John Geiger, the owner of the overcoat found in Merrill's home, had a bum hand, too, the result of an injury that had occurred during childhood. It was an odd coincidence that three suspects each had a misshapen hand, but the discrepancies did not seem to matter in Jim Crow's court of public opinion. The deformed left hand of a Negro was guiltier than the deformed right or left hand of any white man, even though Dana's prints had been positively identified from inside of Glenburnie.[9]

Officers traced Williams's whereabouts on the day of the murder, too. He had visited friends and family on the Hedges, Forest, and Beau Pre plantations, just south of Natchez on Highway 61. The Hedges is where he likely grew up; he had Williams cousins there. The last time anyone saw him was around 1:30 P.M. on the afternoon of Jennie's murder as he set out toward Glenwood to see Dick Dana and Octavia Dockery.[10]

In the days following the murder, as sheriff's deputies spread across the black community, Sister likely wondered about Pink. She probably also worried about her own future. While she had grown fond of the man, he had also threatened to kill her if she said anything about that evening. She was also keeping his trunk, because he told her he would send for it once he got back to Chicago. She may have learned by reading the local paper that a man named George Pearls was a suspect in the killing of Jennie Merrill, but she would not have associated that name with the man she knew only as Pink. So, nothing could have prepared her, or her mother, Nellie, for what happened that Saturday, August 13.

Sheriff's deputies rapped their knuckles on the front door. Louis Winston's statement about transporting Williams's trunk to Cedar Alley had led them there. Then in what seemed like the blink of an eye, they confiscated the trunk, arrested both mother and daughter, and whisked them to the Adams County jail.[11]

Inside of Pink's trunk were several items of interest to investigators. Mixed in with some new shirts, a gold watch, and a headlamp "like those used for

Nellie Black stands behind her daughter, Emily Burns.
(Smith family photo, ca. 1913, courtesy of Birdia
Green and Phyliss Morris, Natchez, Miss.)

coon hunting," he had undefined "burglary tools," several .32 caliber bullets like those collected from Jennie Merrill's home, and a number of life insurance policies made out to George Pearls. Sheriff Roberts immediately recognized the name as that of the man shot and killed by police in Pine Bluff and called Chief Fiveash. During their conversation, the sheriff confirmed that Pearls met the description of the man locals knew as Lawrence Williams. Book asked to come there to collect the evidence and photograph the deceased Pearls, but he was too late. George's wife had already been there to claim the body and take him back to Chicago.[12]

Among the papers in his knapsack had been documents identifying Pearls's wife, Meadie, who was in Chicago when her husband headed south. It is unclear whether Chief Fiveash notified Meadie of her husband's demise or if she learned about it from the newspaper or from acquaintances back in Natchez. If the Pine Bluff police chief did not expect to hear back from some poor black woman in Chicago, he was wrong. Meadie Pearls loved her husband. They had a home in Argo and a life together. He also had a daughter, Amelia. So on August 11, Meadie boarded a train on the Illinois Central Railroad and made the long trip to Pine Bluff. When she arrived, she identified and claimed her husband's body so she could accompany him home on a train headed back to Chicago. There, she could plan appropriate funeral services at Peoples' Undertaking Establishment, because George was no "strange Negro" to her.[13]

———

Now, three separate locations held clues to the case—Natchez, Pine Bluff, and Chicago. Book Roberts organized three groups of men to gather the information from those places that would hopefully solve the case. Special Deputies Walter Abbott, the county chancery clerk and former Adams County sheriff, and John R. Junkin, president of the board of supervisors, drove to Pine Bluff to retrieve the gun and Pearls's personal effects. Local deputies, along with district attorney Clay Tucker, remained in Natchez and continued to interrogate local blacks, a process Maurice O'Neill had begun almost as soon as he arrived. Joseph Brown, prosecuting attorney, continued his questioning of Dick and Octavia.

The most crucial task involved determining that George Pearls, alias Lawrence Williams, was the same person who committed the murder and whose fingerprints jibed with those of the third set of prints found in Merrill's home. Sheriff Roberts led this group, which included O'Neill and a local black man named Louis Terrell. Terrell, who was close in age to Pearls, was said to have seen and spoken with the man he knew as Lawrence Williams. Now, he had the unsavory task of identifying the body.

The three men left Natchez on Saturday evening, August 13, headed to Chicago as Meadie Pearls prepared to bury her husband. Their case rested on a positive identification of his body, and they intended to photograph the dead man and collect fingerprints from his corpse. To ensure they could complete those two grisly tasks, the sheriff sent a wire to the Windy City's chief of detectives, William Schumaker, to delay funeral services. It read: "Hold the body of George Pearls alias Lawrence Williams alias Pinkney Williams shipped August 13th from Pine Bluff Arkansas to Peoples' Undertaking Establishment, Chicago. Body accompanied by wife Meadie Williams. Pearls positively identified as murderer [of] Jane Merrill. Signed, C. P. Roberts, Sheriff of Adams County, Miss."[14]

How could he have been positively identified as the murderer even as the sheriff was on his way to Chicago to do just that? Dick Dana and Octavia Dockery were still in jail under murder charges. He continued to believe they were involved, but perhaps he thought George Pearls was the triggerman. There was also the reference to another alias—Pinkney Williams. Most Natchezeans were unfamiliar with that name. But Sister knew.

When Emily Burns and her mother, Nellie Black, were taken to the Adams County jail, they were presumably being held only for questioning about the trunk and how they knew Lawrence Williams, whom Sister called "Pink." No formal charges were filed against either woman. They could not afford an attorney, and none stepped forward to defend them as they had for the residents of Goat Castle. Emily and her mother's race did not afford them such protection.

By now the jail was crowded with suspects and others held for questioning, not to mention the only two people charged with the murder—Dick Dana and Octavia Dockery. Whether Emily saw Dick and Octavia when she was booked into her cell is not known, even though only a few feet separated them. But two days later, when the pair had their habeas corpus proceeding, Emily no doubt heard the roar of the crowd from across the street at the courthouse when the judge allowed the "Wild Man" and the "Goat Woman" to return home on their own recognizance.

Their release came as her incarceration was just beginning.

As officers began their interrogation of Emily and her mother, word came from Walter Abbott and John Junkin in Pine Bluff. Pearls, they were told, had been killed at a railroad crossing on the outskirts of town while resisting arrest. Former sheriff Abbott also believed that the gun he and Junkin retrieved provided "more than sufficient evidence" for solving the crime, noting that it was the same caliber of pistol that had fired the bullets found at Glenburnie.[15]

The men brought the weapon back to Natchez to allow Maurice O'Neill to conduct a ballistics test. Once the gun was returned to the Adams County jail, Chief Deputy Joseph Stone traced its sale using the Colt pistol's serial number. They learned that their deceased suspect, George Pearls, had purchased the gun several years prior, in 1916, at a Sears Roebuck and Co. store in Kiln, Mississippi. The ballistics test, however, would have to wait until the New Orleans detective returned from Chicago.[16]

While Pearls's gun was being retrieved from Pine Bluff, Book Roberts, Maurice O'Neill, and Louis Terrell were en route to Chicago aboard the Illinois Central Railroad, the primary conduit of travel between the Windy City and New Orleans. It was the same railroad that George Pearls used to travel back and forth to Mississippi and along the same line where he met his demise in Pine Bluff. For the three men headed north from Natchez, it was a means to an end, as they sought to confirm Pearls's identity.

While in Chicago the sheriff and O'Neill met with police officials who, as it turned out, were very familiar with George Pearls. He had a long criminal record, and they had mug shots and fingerprints from his previous arrests. Pearls was purportedly a member of a "negro gang." Still, Roberts needed positive identification of the actual body.[17]

It may have been enough that Louis Terrell confirmed that the dead man he saw at Peoples' Undertaking Establishment was the man he knew as Lawrence Williams. But his observations were also confirmed by George Pearls's own daughter, Amelia Garner. And whether or not it was voluntary, she put it in writing so that Book could submit it as evidence in the case he was trying to build. Her note read:

> Argo, Illinois
> August 16, 1932
>
> To Whom It May Concern:
>
> This is to certify that the body of George Pearls is the same man known as Lawrence Williams, also known as Pinkney Williams in the City of Natchez, Miss. He is my own father.
>
> Mrs. Amelia Garner
> 7727 W. 62nd Street
> Argo, Ill.[18]

The address Garner gave was the same as that of her father and stepmother, George and Meadie Pearls.[19]

With photographs, fingerprints, and Garner's letter in hand, the men headed back to Mississippi, making a stop in Jackson to confer with James Chancellor, comparing fingerprints he collected with the ones they brought with them from Chicago. Then it was back to Natchez, where Roberts and O'Neill continued their investigation. While reporters were anxious for details about the latest findings, they were perplexed by the "unusual reticence" both men displayed. "The only thing I can say," Book Roberts explained, "is that we have completed our investigations in Chicago and Pine Bluff and that there are a number of angles that must be looked into in Natchez." And with that, the sheriff, the detective, and Judge Cutrer took a day-long fishing trip to Lake St. John just north of Ferriday, Louisiana, after which O'Neill headed back to New Orleans to conduct the ballistics test on what most believed was the murder weapon.[20]

Although Maurice O'Neill had been called to Natchez to "check and recheck" Chancellor's fingerprint findings, he had yet to verify or contradict that evidence. He went with the sheriff to the crime scene and to Goat Castle, led the investigation into the black community, and accompanied Book to Chicago. While no report was forthcoming, O'Neill fingerprinted additional suspects, including two people who had regular access to Glenburnie. One was Effie Stanton, Jennie's cook, but she was swiftly eliminated as a suspect. The other was Duncan Minor.

Why Minor's fingerprints had never been taken before was surprising because of his own suspicious behavior and because he was the sole beneficiary of Jennie Merrill's will. First, he had failed to report for nearly an hour on the bloody scene he had come upon late on August 4. Then, in the early morning hours of the search for Jennie, he was the person to direct Alonzo Floyd to the area where the body was found. When her will was probated, Duncan inherited everything, including her Glenburnie estate and her two plantations in Concordia Parish—Scotland and St. Genevieve—where her father once owned more than two hundred slaves. There were also her investments in stocks and bonds, as well as the money she had in the bank, which altogether was estimated to be worth between $150,000 and $250,000—no small sum in Depression-era Mississippi. Still, his were not the only fingerprints being gathered.[21]

Sheriff's deputies had rounded up six more blacks from the community, representing an entirely new group of potential witnesses in the case. These included people with whom Williams had interacted on the day of the murder. A few of them were brought in based on information gathered during the interrogation of Emily Burns, now publicly known as the "negress" who operated a rooming house. Some were either family members of Lawrence Williams or friends he associated with while in Natchez, including Percy Perry. Perry was considered an "intimate associate" of the "Chicago-Detroit negro" and a material witness. Sheriff's deputies took Perry into custody and whisked him to an unknown location for questioning before returning him to the less-crowded city jail, where impatient deputies continued their interrogation. Some local citizens said that "they heard the negro [Perry] screaming in the city jail," suggesting that police were likely beating him, though officers "assured reporters that a man was having a fit or being crazy."[22]

Sheriff's deputies interrogated Emily, too, several times a day for several hours at a stretch, but it took more than a week before they wrangled a confession out of her. She may have initially tried to protect Pink from arrest and certain death until she learned that, in fact, he had been killed in Pine Bluff. That news proved devastating in more ways than one, since she had developed feelings for the man and could not know what might become of her now that he was dead. She held out for as long as she could, pretending not to know of events except for what she read in the paper. As intense as the questioning became, however, she did not offer a confession — that is, until the eleventh day of her confinement.

On the evening of Monday, August 22, Special Deputy John Junkin took her in for what became another long and intense round of interrogation. Chief Deputy Joseph Stone was there, along with Hyde Jenkins, who had demanded to be deputized. But this interrogation proved to be different. When Emily entered the room, she saw Junkin place a bullwhip on the table around which deputies had berated her for several days. He told her she had thirty minutes to tell the truth.[23]

There was nothing subtle about placing a bullwhip in full view of a black woman suspect. These deputies knew its history in their community. So did Emily. Her slave ancestors had experienced its brutality, as had countless black men and women in the decades since the Civil War. Now it lay before her, a reminder that this instrument of punishment well known to slaves still existed for those who did not respect the supremacy of white men. The specter of the lash served its purpose. At 12:40 A.M. on August 23, Emily "confessed."[24]

Chief Deputy Stone and his special deputies reported to the press that they had acquired an "authentic" confession from Emily Burns. "After numerous statements in which the woman attempted to avoid a confession," the *Natchez Democrat* reported, "she finally agreed to tell the truth." But a "confession" born of fear did not necessarily represent authenticity or truth. In this instance, Emily stated that the only people involved were Pink (George Pearls), Poe (Ed Newell), and herself. She told them that Pink went into the house to rob Merrill but did not intend to kill her, although he shot her twice. She explained that Poe was with them and that he helped Pink carry the body out of the house. "I carried the lamp," she said. Based on her statement, neither Dana nor Dockery was at the scene of the crime. The only time she mentioned them was to say that Pink "went to [Glenwood]," talked to them, and got the overcoat. Some took this to mean that he simply got it from the Skunk's Nest on the Dana property. Sheriff Roberts, however, did not accept this confession as a solution to the murder and stated he planned to wait until Maurice O'Neill made an official report on the fingerprint evidence collected by James Chancellor.[25]

Book had charged Dick and Octavia with murder based on that fingerprint evidence. He had also offered a compromise during the habeas corpus proceeding—they could go home on their own recognizance, but the murder charges remained. No matter what his own chief deputy believed, the sheriff remained convinced of Dana and Dockery's involvement.

Despite Emily's confession, the sheriff held off on charging either her or Poe with the crime because the investigation was ongoing. Yet by not charging either of them, Book knew that local whites, already upset over the arrest and interrogation of Dick and Octavia, might engage in mob violence. This occurred with some frequency in the Jim Crow South, as whites, impatient with the pace of "justice," seized black suspects from local jails and lynched them. Not long after Burns's and Newell's arrests, a lynching took place in nearby Wisner, Louisiana. A twenty-six-year-old black man named William House, in custody because two white women claimed he insulted them, was taken from the jail and lynched, his body left hanging on a tree by the side of the road where all could see. To avoid this kind of vigilante justice, the sheriff whisked both Emily and Poe to Jackson, where they were held at the Hinds County jail "for safe keeping."[26]

Emily and Poe were not allowed to speak on the ride to Jackson, and once there, interrogations continued. While Poe denied any involvement, Emily repeatedly placed him at Merrill's house on the night of the murder. She also amended the confession she gave in the Adams County jail to now include

Dick Dana and Octavia Dockery at the scene of the crime. She had clearly met them that night, notwithstanding their protestations of innocence.

Despite inconsistencies in Emily's confessions, she always implicated herself, Pink, and Poe—although it was not until later that she explained how Poe came to join them. She maintained that the overcoat found in Merrill's home came from Dana and Dockery. In her confessions, Pink entered the house first as she remained outside as a watch. Now she added that Jennie's neighbors joined them. She also included further details—details that rang true for Book Roberts.

That evening, she said, Pink asked her to go for a walk, and along the way he told her of his plans to "to try and get some money" from Jennie Merrill, adding that "if you tell, I am going to kill you." Their walk led them into the woods near Glenwood, where she waited while Pink got the coat from Dick Dana to be used as a disguise. Poe joined them near Dana's home. "I didn't know we were going to meet him [Poe] until we met him," she said.[27] She then placed everyone at Glenburnie at the same time as they lay in wait under the house until Pink determined the room Jennie was in. Emily allegedly told officers that "there was a struggle from the bedroom to the dining room," adding, "[Pink] shot Miss Merrill," facts she could not have known firsthand if she waited outside. Yet her fingerprints were not found in the house.[28]

It became clear that Pink shot Merrill based on the other details of this confession. Emily heard Merrill screaming and told officers, "It seemed like they broke to her to keep her from hollering." Who were "they"? Pink and Poe. Poe, she said, "came out and threw me the lamp and went back and they carried Miss Merrill down the walk and put her in the bushes." According to her, she accompanied them and then "threw the lamp twenty feet" from the body, but that is not where it was found. Afterward, Pink, Poe, Dick, and Octavia went back through the house searching for money and valuables as she was told "to stay outside and watch." Immediately after, all of them went to the Dana home. Pink and Poe went inside as she again waited outside. Then the three of them left through the woods, crossed the railroad, and "came through Mr. George Kelly's [Melrose] and on home by the back road."[29]

After she and Pink got home, she told officers, Pink "pulled off his clothes and got matches and coal oil and burned them up." He told her he was going to "make [his] way home." On the Monday after the murder, Emily received a letter from him from Pine Bluff telling her he had made it that far and had not been caught. "Don't say nothing," he wrote. "I burned the letter in the stove," she said.[30]

The *Natchez Democrat* published Emily's second confession, but it had been edited from the original that she signed. That document offered additional details but was also written in such a way as to appear coerced and in language that was anything but "authentic." But they were details that aligned with officers' theories about Lawrence Williams's movement that night. While the paper included that part of the statement about the route she and Pink took to get home, it failed to include the detail that Poe was with them for part of that journey until he headed in a different direction on his way into town. Perhaps the route he took went by Odell Ferguson's place, the place the hounds had led officers. The paper also did not include the fact that Dana and Dockery had joined in the ransacking of Merrill's home or that they all went back to Dana's place afterward.[31]

Other parts of Emily's confession appear contrived. The deputy who transcribed her confession repeatedly typed "Poor" for "Poe," seeking to correct what he assumed was black dialect in which "po'" often meant "poor." But it was the final paragraph of her signed confession that rings most false, because it was an obvious attempt by sheriff's deputies to absolve them of any rough treatment of her during questioning, commonly known as the "third degree." When Dick and Octavia were released, Chief Deputy Stone tried to make them sign a similar statement that officers had not subjected them to the third degree. They refused on the advice of their attorneys. But Emily Burns was a poor black woman without any legal option. And she was surrounded by a group of intimidating white officers when she made her confession. She was left with little choice but to sign her name to it.

That final paragraph read:

> While I've been in jail I couldn't have been treated no better if I'd been a white lady. They've been very kind to me. Nobody has promised me anything and nobody has threatened me since I've been in jail. I've told this because I've wanted to and wanted to tell the truth. I'm doing this of my own free will.

A confession under such duress had very little to do with Emily's "free will." That she felt any "better" having implicated herself is questionable. She had simply gone on a walk with Pink when events went horribly wrong, and now she had just signed a confession that absolved deputies of having threatened her with a bullwhip and who knows what other indignities. She had to swallow the lie that they had been "very kind" to her and be reminded, in the most insidious way, of the double standard of southern womanhood. Black women were not thought to be ladies, so she was fortunate to have been treated like a white one.[32]

After Emily's confession in the Hinds County jail, sheriff's deputies returned her to Natchez, while Ed "Poe" Newell remained in custody in Jackson. Book Roberts, who had been keeping quiet about the investigation, opened up to reporters. "We have unquestionably established the fact that George Pearls, alias Pinkney Williams, the 'Chicago-Detroit' negro[,] was the actual slayer of Miss Merrill," he said. "We also have proven that Emily Burns, the negress who conducted the boarding house where Pearls lived[,]is an actual accessory to the murder," he continued. Newell was still being investigated, because Emily had implicated him in each of her "confessions." And while her confessions consistently included Dick Dana and Octavia Dockery, the sheriff claimed that as far as they were concerned, "we are still continuing our investigation," adding, "We have not yet accepted the credibility of either confession." As part of that investigation, officers also arrested Nellie Black's brother and Emily's uncle, George "Doc" Smith. According to Chief Deputy Stone, Smith "spent much time with Emily Burns at her home," so they intended to question him to "determine whether or not he had any knowledge of the plot" that resulted in Jennie Merrill's death. Book also said that Percy Perry and Emily's mother, Nellie Black, were still being held as material witnesses.[33]

While deputies were securing a signed confession from Emily at the Hinds County jail, Maurice O'Neill submitted his ballistics report. The gun found on George Pearls was the same one that fired the bullets found in Jennie Merrill's home, and he concluded that it was the murder weapon. There was still the matter of fingerprint evidence, including those of Dana and Dockery, which the sheriff said would be submitted to the grand jury for its deliberation. James Chancellor, he noted, "is prepared to appear before the grand jury of the Adams County circuit court in November and testify" to the validity of his findings.[34]

Emily Burns had spent nearly two weeks in custody without being formally charged and with no hard evidence to keep her there. But Jim Crow justice meant that there would be no habeas corpus proceeding for her as there had been for Dick and Octavia. And their fingerprints had been found *inside* the Merrill home. Sister had no attorney and could not return home on her own recognizance, as had the two white suspects, because the same rights of citizenship did not belong to black women.

Instead, the sheriff, his deputies, and police offers took Emily back to Glenburnie to reenact the crime. Despite Roberts's attempt to keep this part of the investigation quiet, word got around. Octavia knew something was going on, too. She claimed she was "greatly frightened by the mysterious group" on the neighboring estate, even though she could hardly see them through the overgrown woods surrounding Goat Castle. So she sent her old friend Archibald Dickson into town to inquire about it, knowing intuitively what was taking place.[35]

Octavia was frightened for good reason. Despite being able to leave jail and return home, the murder charges against her and Dick had not been dropped. But on her last night in jail, she believed she might have found an out. While DA Clay Tucker continued his interrogation of her, he asked Octavia about a black man named Lawrence Williams. She knew who he was, she said, and even suspected that he was the murderer. She also confirmed something deputies learned from talking to Emily, who was now in custody, which is that Williams had been by Glenwood on the afternoon of the murder. Octavia claimed that she never mentioned it before because she was "afraid" that Williams would link her and Dana to the murder. There was no reason to make that assumption if they were both innocent.[36]

By asking her about Williams, Tucker provided Octavia the opportunity to speak truthfully about her interaction with a prime suspect in the case and still shift the focus away from her and Dick. The DA must have told her that Williams was dead, and this convenient truth meant she could point her finger at a black man with the confidence of knowing that he would never have the opportunity to incriminate her or her ward.[37]

She never counted on the fact that a black woman might point a finger at her.

———

Book Roberts did not think having Emily Burns retrace her steps on the night of the murder was necessary to solve the crime but claimed that she was "willing" to do so. Joined by other officers, Emily allegedly walked them through the events of that evening, adding new details. According to the published account of the reenactment, officers took her to a clearing on the edge of Glenwood, where she said she waited while Pink went to speak with Dana and Dockery. When Pink returned with the overcoat, she reportedly told officers that they took a shortcut across a bayou on the way to Glenburnie where Poe, who had come from the direction of Duncan Park, met them. Dana and Dockery, whom she first saw as they were standing near Jennie's car, followed them there "to show them how to enter the Merrill home."[38]

In this retelling of the evening's events, Emily Burns added new details. She claimed that Dick Dana assisted Pink and Poe in carrying Jennie Merrill's body out of the house. "They put me in front with the lamp," she said. According to the report, she also pointed out where the body had been thrown and the lamp, too, before the sheriff made her go inside the house to point out other movements.[39]

Yet Emily claimed in all of her confessions that she never entered the house. And, after deputies located the lamp, James Chancellor's test did not find her fingerprints on it, but those of Dick Dana. The sheriff knew, however, that white Natchezeans did not care about the fingerprint evidence even if he found it convincing. So, he had to build a case against the "negress," too, or the murder might not be regarded as solved.

At this point, deputies ceased their interrogation of Odell Ferguson. John Geiger, too, was no longer a suspect. And, after what he had been through, he was not as sympathetic to Octavia Dockery as other white Natchezeans. He filed his own lawsuit against her for the return of the items she took from the Skunk's Nest after forcing him to leave. Geiger claimed that among the missing items were "two cotton mattresses, four feather mattresses, four quilts, three chairs, one lamp, one overcoat, two lumber packs, two tables, one iron bedstead—total value forty-nine dollars and twenty-five cents." He wanted "that pesky overcoat" back.[40]

For most of September, there was little to report as the sheriff worked to put together a case for the November session of the grand jury. John Junkin finally returned Poe to Natchez at the end of August, where he remained in jail until his release on October 6 without any explanation other than that he had been "fully investigated." Emily Burns and Nellie Black continued to be held until the grand jury issued its findings. The only visitor allowed them was the Reverend Charles Anderson from Antioch Baptist Church, where the two women were members. It was the only comfort either of them were afforded.

The grand jury was not scheduled to meet until November 17. All Sister and her mother could do was sit in their dank jail cells and wait.

CHAPTER SEVEN

NATIONAL SCANDAL

I n the fall of 1932, the investigation into the kidnapping and killing of aviator Charles Lindbergh's son was ongoing, Americans elected Franklin Delano Roosevelt president of the United States for the first time, and the Pacific Whaling Company exhibited a fifty-five-foot-long whale encased in a glass-enclosed railway car near the corner of Broadway and Main Street in Natchez. For three days in early November, Natchezeans paid admission to see, on a transcontinental tour of the country, the "the largest mammal ever captured." On Sunday, November 6, "Whalebone Lew" Nichols, a real whaling captain and reverend, also delivered his sermon "God, Jonah, and the Whale."[1]

The fall in Natchez had already been an unusual time in the history of the town. In some ways, neither the Lindbergh kidnapping, nor FDR's election, nor the chance to see a whale compared to what townspeople had going on in their own backyard. Jennie Merrill's murder had captured national attention for weeks. Then came word that a woman in Indiana might contest her will. Goat Castle, of course, garnered the most attention. Its notoriety and that of its residents tarnished the town's reputation but also drew voyeurs seeking what writers described as a drama about an Old South society that was "stranger than fiction." As one Massachusetts newspaper put it, "Novelists have written until their hands were cramped, trying to spin tales of eerie horror, but did they ever invent anything to beat that [story] from Natchez, Miss.?"[2]

During the Great Depression, newspapers were filled with crime stories—bank robberies, child abductions, and murder. These lurid tales sold papers and offered a distraction from the daily economic suffering of millions of

Americans. All the better when the case involved wealthy individuals, because their poor choices — not to mention those of President Herbert Hoover — had helped create that suffering. So, the murder of Jennie Merrill and the salacious details coming out of Natchez that fall provided boundless fodder for newspapers across the country. The aura of a romantic Old South that contrasted with stories of southern decay only added to Americans' interest in the gothic narrative that emerged from Natchez.

It took fewer than forty-eight hours for Jennie Merrill's murder to become national news. The *New York Times* headlined blared "Rich Woman Recluse Slain In Mississippi." Other papers followed suit. Missouri's *Joplin Globe* reported, "Elderly Recluse Is Slain in South." "Army Coat Is Clue to Recluse's Murder," wrote the *Atlanta Journal Constitution*, while the small Georgia paper the *Titusville Herald*'s headline proclaimed "Aged Recluse Slain."[3]

The arrest of Dick Dana and Octavia Dockery made the story even more compelling. Headlines in the days that followed their arrest focused on their curious personalities, the wretched condition of Glenwood, and of course the pair's live-in goats. "Fingerprints and Goats in Murder Case," wrote the *Star-Journal* of Sandusky, Ohio, while the *Charleston Daily Mail* in West Virginia grabbed readers' attention with "Bloody Fingerprints and Goat Herd Link Eccentric with Woman's Death," and the *Salt Lake City Tribune* led with "Hermit Named as Murderer." Newspapers from around the country were more than happy to share the extraordinary details of Goat Castle and its strange residents because the story sold well.[4]

As Sheriff Clarence Roberts and his cohorts worked diligently to solve what was widely described as a "southern mystery," reporters investigated and wrote about the principals. Stories about the lives of Jennie Merrill, Duncan Minor, Dick Dana, Octavia Dockery, and, to a lesser extent, George Pearls and Emily Burns sustained people's interest in the case and in Natchez for weeks. Goat Castle, too, took on a life of its own because the actual conditions of Dana's home and estate defied belief. Pulitzer Prize–winning historian Bruce Catton, a young journalist at the time, asked rhetorically, "Can a novelist have invented a more fascinating, hair-raising tale of decay and morbid gloom than this one from real life?"[5]

The narrative surrounding Jennie Merrill centered on her lineage and the turn her life had taken in the decades that precipitated her death. Accounts of her life always included the fact that she was the daughter of Ayres Merrill, the former Belgian ambassador. An Ohio paper, for example, described her as the "vivacious, charming daughter of the late Ayres Merrill who as friend of President Grant and Ambassador to Belgium saw her presented at the Court of St. James." Despite there being no evidence to support it, the tale of being presented to Queen Victoria at St. James's Palace often found a place in accounts of her life. Papers also described her as a "southern belle" or "belle of the Old South," playing up her relationship to the planter class.[6]

Still, reporters appeared focused on her alleged withdrawal from broader society. The *Natchez Democrat*, Jennie's hometown paper, was the first to call her a recluse and, at nearly sixty-nine years old, an "aged lady." The *New York Times* referred to her as the "envoy's daughter" and described her as a woman who refused to join the modern age. "She lived as nearly as possible in the manner of the ante-bellum South," the *Times* reported and suggested that when she retired from society in the 1890s, her fashion tastes were locked in time. "She dressed always in the manner of a lady of fashion of forty years ago." There were also reports that she had posted a sign on her driveway gate warning visitors to "Keep Out."[7]

There was something peculiar about a woman who had wealth and an aristocratic lineage retreating from the world. With only that to go on, the press repeatedly referred to her as an "aged recluse," a "wealthy recluse," an "elderly recluse," and even a "wealthy eccentric." Her name and money were a reflection of her aristocratic lineage, but her behavior, many believed, was a sign of her social decline as well as that of the Old South.

"Forty years ago Miss Merrill, daughter of a former ambassador and one-time 'belle of the south,' had wealth, position and fame," Bruce Catton wrote, "but something went wrong, somewhere." Not only had the "gay old culture departed" but Merrill, just like her neighbors, had become "eccentric, grim-lipped, [and] mysterious." Catton then pointed to the Old South's decay, where the romantic "culture in the pillared mansions" of both Glenburnie and Glenwood had vanished. "Once these were famous southern plantations," he observed. "Now they are dilapidated, unkempt, weed-grown, their fine manor houses grown decrepit and gloomy, their imposing driveways bordered with rank grasses and undergrowth." Their homes had become a reflection of the people who inhabited them.[8]

Some of Jennie's fellow Natchezeans sought to correct the narrative of the reclusive belle. Zaida Wells, who drove past Glenburnie on the night of the murder, found the phrase "aged recluse" thoughtless and unkind. "People are as old or as young as they make themselves," Wells wrote, "and Miss Jennie was not old." "She was a very alert, healthy little woman who drove her car into town every day attending to her own business," she continued. And while she may have been one of the "charter members of Natchez" and a woman of refinement, she was also well liked by "the busy working element of especially Franklin street," where she did her shopping, and "[exchanged] with them a pleasant word and a smile." In essence, Jennie may not have been social, but she was a nice person to all who interacted with her.[9]

Jennie's cousin Charlotte Surget McKittrick and her husband, David, along with their daughter, Catharine MacRae, offered their own recollections of Jennie to *Times-Picayune* reporter Gwen Bristow, one of a few women writing articles about the case. Sitting on the veranda of their home, Elms Court, where Jennie often returned between her travels, they talked about the woman they knew. Jennie, like her mother, was "very fond of parties and all sorts of social gatherings," Charlotte McKittrick said. Referring to Jennie by her birth name, Jane Merrill, Charlotte spoke of her cousin as "a beautiful woman, a dark brunette, with a tremendous quantity of curly brown hair and long, narrow dark eyes. Her hair never turned gray." She added that Jennie "looked at least 15 years younger than her actual age." What about her being a recluse? David McKittrick answered firmly, "She didn't retire from the world abruptly, like a nun." Like many women do when they grow older, "she gradually went out less and less, and then ceased going to parties at all."[10]

Jennie's relationship with her cousin Duncan Minor also piqued curiosity. Reporters repeatedly referred to him as her "boyhood sweetheart," a man who had courted Merrill in their youth. Rumors abounded as to why they had never married. Some in Natchez heard that "an uncle had threatened to disinherit him if he married [her]," while others believed his mother disliked Jennie. Minor never discussed whether the two were married but told reporters he had lived in the Merrill home for several years. He certainly spent his evenings there and had done so for decades, a ritual that began when his mother was still alive.[11]

Duncan moved into Glenburnie after Jennie was buried and soon refused interviews from reporters. Without a definitive answer from Duncan, newspapers continued to speculate on whether the "boyhood sweetheart" and the "envoy's daughter" ever married. On that, David McKittrick was emphatic. "Yes, I think she was married to Duncan Minor," he said. "I think that for some reason she told him she would marry him if he'd never say that she had, whether she lived or died," McKittrick surmised, "and I think he's keeping his promise." Why would she want it kept secret? He couldn't say.[12]

It was all speculation, of course. Yet the stories of courtship, romance, pa-
rental disapproval, and a secret marriage provided all of the elements of a
melodrama playing out among the last remaining descendants of southern aristocracy. Then, out of nowhere, a woman from the Midwest entered the story.

Nellie Grist added to the mystery surrounding Jennie Merrill's life. The
thirty-year-old woman from Greenfield, Indiana, hinted that she might contest the dead woman's will—which had left everything to Duncan Minor—
because of a visit she had from an attorney in Jackson, Mississippi. One "Mr.
Austin" traveled to her home in Indiana to tell her that Jennie had left instructions to notify her in the event of her death.[13]

While an attorney named H. L. Austin existed in Jackson, he was unknown
to both Nellie Grist and to local Natchezeans. The Indiana woman said she did
not understand why Austin contacted her. She was not personally acquainted
with Jennie, and the only possible connection between the two women was
that Grist's father once had business dealings with Merrill's father. And
yet, given the Depression and the substantial worth of Jennie's estate, Nellie
Grist told her local paper that she intended to visit Natchez to make her own
investigation.[14]

When asked about this latest turn of events, Duncan Minor's attorney, Saul
Laub, laughed it off. Laub, also the mayor of Natchez, told reporters, "It is
ridiculous. We expect no contests from anyone. The Grist woman isn't coming
here and if she does, she will be wasting her time." Even as the mayor scoffed
at the notion of Grist's claim, it did not prevent locals from speculating what
her connection to Jennie Merrill might be. Grist did not come to Natchez,
and while the story subsided that fall, it did not go away and only added to
the circus-like atmosphere being generated by Goat Castle and its residents.

For newspapers whose intended audience was white readers, the descendants
of slaves did not merit the same interest as the descendants of slave owners.
George Pearls and Emily Burns were simply "negroes." Reporters never
sought Emily out for an interview to learn her life story or to give her a chance
to defend her innocence. Emily was presumed guilty because of her race,
whether or not she pulled the trigger on the gun that killed Jennie Merrill.
This was even truer for black men in the South, who were regularly arrested
for petty crimes—much less murder—and made up the vast majority of the
region's prison population.[15]

From the outset, the reports on George Pearls—the man Natchez knew as Lawrence Williams—indicated how southern whites generally regarded the character of black men who behaved independent of white society. Duncan Minor found Williams "insolent" for the way he addressed him when asking for work. For days, the *Natchez Democrat* assumed that Williams was a drifter with no local ties. His outsider status, as a black man who lived in the North, led Sheriff Roberts and reporters to dub Pearls the "Chicago-Detroit negro," even after they determined he had been born in Natchez. There was also the paternalistic reference to Pearls, a fifty-seven-year-old man, as Minor's former "yard boy," not that he had once worked for Minor as a young man. Finally, there was Pine Bluff police deputy Robert Henslee, who referred to Pearls as a "suspicious character" for no other reason than he did not recognize him as a local. And the truth may never be known as to whether Pearls resisted arrest or simply refused to answer questions, because Henslee assumed the former and shot him six times in what the *Times-Picayune* once exaggerated was a "gun duel."[16]

Only African American newspapers gave black suspects like Emily Burns and George Pearls any respect. From the *New York Amsterdam News* to the *Kansas City Plaindealer*, black newspapers referred to Pearls without any qualifiers like "Chicago negro" and used the title "Miss" or "Mrs." when referring to Emily Burns. "Mrs. Emily Burns" offered her respectability not given by whites and suggested that she was a lady. The *Plaindealer* also pointed out what white Natchezeans refused to acknowledge about the case: that despite an investigation that revealed a years-long quarrel between Merrill and the residents of Glenwood, and in the face of the positive identification of Dana's and Dockery's fingerprints from inside Glenburnie, "the police inquiry was pushed among the Negroes of the environs of the state." The paper also expressed doubt of Emily's guilt by reporting that "an alleged confession was obtained from Mrs. Burns."[17]

There was no doubt, however, that what drew America's attention to Natchez for weeks in the fall of 1932 was not so much the mystery of who killed Jennie Merrill but the two people arrested and charged with her murder—Dick Dana and Octavia Dockery. Their personal stories and the life they led on their run-down estate was so shocking that the other principals in the case were nearly forgotten. A woman from Port Gibson, Mississippi, in a letter to her aunt, suggested as much. "It is more weird and exciting than any mystery story I have read in such a long time," she wrote, adding, "and made more tragic because the parties involved came of such high families and have sunk so low."[18]

Local people, both black and white, who lived and worked on estates on or near the Kingston Road had long known about Glenwood and its residents. So did Book Roberts and his deputies, who had been there several times to settle disputes between them and Jennie Merrill. A few, like Odell Ferguson and John Geiger, had logged trees on the estate. They had all experienced what the rest of Natchez, and America, were about to discover — that Dick Dana was odd. Very odd. And his guardian, Octavia Dockery, while self-composed, behaved as if the barnlike state of Glenwood was normal.

Stories of the pair both intrigued and shocked readers, especially the details of Dick Dana's behavior. Dana, they learned, regularly left the house and stayed in the woods around Glenwood for long intervals where hunters or loggers were often the only ones to encounter him. He dashed behind trees to avoid being seen, and when asked, "Dick Dana, why are you hiding?" his reply was, "This is not Dick Dana. Dick Dana has gone to New York to sing in the choir of Christ Church." His wardrobe consisted of gunnysacks — burlap bags with a hole cut out for the head — and he rarely bathed. His hair was long and greasy, and some said his scraggly beard reached a yard in length.[19]

The press homed in on Dana's "wild" nature. The *New York Times* referred to him as an "eccentric woodsman," and the *New Orleans Times-Picayune* called him the "wild eccentric" while the Jackson, Mississippi, paper simply called him a "hermit." Newspapers across the country amped up their stories of Dana with descriptions of his wild appearance, enticing readers by calling him the "bearded and long-haired recluse." Even his hometown newspaper described him as "eccentric and queer."[20]

The press was far kinder to Octavia Dockery, but this was because she controlled the narrative of her life from her jail cell. In early reports, Octavia was simply known as Dana's guardian or housekeeper. She was the foil to Natchez's "wild man." At worst, her link to her ward might elicit a headline like that in a Missouri newspaper: "Eccentric Master and Mistress of 'Goat Castle' Alleged to Have Killed Neighbor Recluse." Then, in a photo of the pair that appeared in newspapers throughout the country, there was the suggestion of some romance between the two as it circulated with the caption that she was Dana's "aged sweetheart."[21]

This photo of Octavia Dockery and Dick Dana, taken within days of their arrest, circulated in newspapers nationwide along with stories of the "Wild Man" and "Goat Woman." (Courtesy of the Earl Norman Photograph Collection, Historic Natchez Foundation, Natchez, Miss.)

The jailhouse photo of the odd couple certainly fueled the bizarre story of their lives. If the sheriff was annoyed by reporters desperate for details in the case, he had only himself to blame. Only a few days following their arrest, Book Roberts allowed Earl Norman, the owner of a successful photo studio in Natchez, to take photographs of Dick and Octavia at the jail, individually and as a pair. The intention, according to the *Natchez Democrat*, was to send the photos "to the large news agencies of the country and large dailies [throughout the South.]"[22]

One photo, in particular, circulated widely because it captured an image of Dana and Dockery that was so well suited to the "Wild Man" and "Goat Woman" storyline. Dana may not have had his long hair and even longer beard, but his unkempt appearance and glassy stare furthered the narrative of the "wild man in the woods." Likewise, the image of Octavia Dockery, who appeared in a floppy straw hat and floral print dress covered with a blue smock, complemented the narrative of a farm woman who not only managed a goat herd but also the mentally ill man sitting next to her.

Certainly the eccentricities of everyone involved in the case provided enough detail to fill more than a few news columns, but what made it all the more fascinating to readers were the contrasts between their lives as young "aristocrats" and what had become of them as they aged. On the one hand, they were descendants "of the flower of old southern aristocracy" and all of the romance that entailed. Both Jennie and Octavia were represented as "belles." Duncan Minor was a "dashing suitor," and even Dick Dana came off as a "gay blade" who, when he played piano in the parlors of Natchez, was a favorite among young society women. Some papers even manufactured the possibility that there had been a romance between Dana and Jennie Merrill. One paper claimed Dick and Octavia had abandoned the life they led "in the days of duels and chivalry." Yet so much of it was fiction, because none of the white principals grew up in the Old South. That world had dissolved long ago. But it did not matter, because it provided the "weird contrast," as one paper described it, to their stories of decay and ruin.[23]

The accounts of Dick and Octavia's lives, more than any others, drove the national story of murder and mystery in Natchez. Jennie Merrill's life story was recreated from secondhand accounts. Duncan Minor refused interviews. But what the national media craved was the story of social decline, wrapped in strange behavior—a story, as one reporter described it, "as dramatic and full of pathos as any ever told by the facile pen of Edgar Allan Poe."[24]

While reporters were intrigued by the eccentricities of the odd couple of Goat Castle, Dick and Octavia's connections to Old South elite—real and imagined—are what made their current circumstances even more peculiar. Much of it unfolded in the interviews Dana and Dockery gave from their jail cells a few days following their arrest. Regional newspapers, as well as those outside of the South, printed all or portions of the interviews, often embellishing the details.

Dick Dana personally provided the particulars of his own life story that helped to explain how he went from being "a scion of one of the South's most distinguished families," as one paper reported, to becoming the "wild man of the woods." He explained his ancestral connections to the Danas of New England that included authors, ministers, and the publisher of the *New York Sun*. He told of being educated at Chamberlain-Hunt Academy in Port Gibson, the Mississippi town where his father once served as rector, and of the two years he spent at Vanderbilt University. Then he went on to tell the story of his music career and its demise. "For a time I studied music in New York and sang in the choir of Christ Church. Before my hand was injured by a fallen window," he explained, "I had a considerable reputation as a pianist." He seemed to be aware of his disheveled state by way of describing himself in younger days. "I was fond of society, prided myself on my appearance, and considered myself a man of parts," he said, continuing, "I did not shun social contacts. . . . I sought them, for it was impressed upon my mind that no true Southern gentleman would be a 'stick.'" He claimed that a failed romance with a woman from the "mountains of New England" and his maimed hand were the reasons he returned to Natchez.[25]

Based on this same interview, a reporter with the *Natchez Democrat* sought to reclaim Dana's aristocratic past and links to Old South elites, describing his life as both "fantastic and weird." In addition to calling Dana a "half-demented musical genius" and a "mental wreck," the writer made sure to include his family connection to the Lees of Virginia, southern royalty if there ever had been. Dana's father, who served as rector of Christ Church in Alexandria, Virginia, for twenty-six years, the reporter explained, had confirmed Robert E. Lee's children. Taking Dana's words as fact, the writer repeated the line that Dana was a "gay, debonair, well-dressed young man, [who was] much liked and very welcome in the best homes of Natchez." In truth, Dana left Natchez as a teen, and when he returned, he did so as a boarder in various homes around town, including that of Richard Forman, Octavia's brother-in-law. He simply was not the "master of Glenwood."[26]

Dana's respectable ancestry, not to mention the reputation of Natchez elites, led the community to look the other way when it came to Dick's peculiar behavior. "Knowing his past, Natchez felt a pitiful interest in Dick Dana, and when stranger fantasies and hallucinations began to people his brain, friends remained close lipped about his affliction," a Natchez reporter wrote. This was followed by the assertion that allowing Octavia Dockery to become his guardian may have been a mistake. Local officials who had dealt "gently with his case" had "allowed [Dana] a freedom that in light of present events has proven a mistaken kindness."[27]

If Dick's story was crafted from his own ramblings and the memories of a few Natchezeans, Octavia Dockery's story was absolutely of her own design. She wanted to be accepted as both an accomplished woman and a sympathetic figure, especially for staying the course at Glenwood. After all, she had remained with Dick Dana "through all his vagaries and cruelties," as one writer put it, "even when he fled from the house like some timorous, frightened beast, and spent days at a time roaming the woods."[28]

Sitting in her cell, Octavia answered reporters' questions and wove a tale that mixed fact with fiction. The story she gave of her life's trajectory was calculated to garner sympathy and perhaps lead to her release from jail. By now, she was well aware of the damning fingerprint evidence found in Jennie Merrill's home. And the prospects of living her last days in prison were very real. But Octavia was cunning and a bit of an actress. She enjoyed the attention and she played her part to perfection.

Reporters were totally taken in. Sitting with this woman "tanned by wind and sun" and whose "work hardened hands [fluttered] nervously . . . to detract attention from her swollen knuckles," it was difficult to imagine that she was once a "proud belle." Regardless of this disconnect, they documented Octavia's telling of her personal history—one that began with promise and distinction but went swiftly downhill. "Her story runs the gamut of human misery," wrote one reporter, and "tells of broken hope, crushed ambition and also an iron determination to follow her own way and drink misery to the very dregs."[29]

Dockery began at the beginning. "I was born on Lamartine plantation in southern Arkansas," she said. Her father, Thomas Dockery, had been a distinguished Confederate officer—a point that likely resonated with southern readers. After the war, she continued, he traveled extensively in the North and South while she and her sister Nydia lived with their mother and a relative in Mississippi. "When I was about twelve years old, we moved to New York City, where we lived fourteen years," she said. While there she attended "the Comstock School on Forty-Second Street, a fashionable school for girls." In truth, Octavia was a few years older when she went to New York, but then she regularly shaved years off of her age. There also was no mention of how her father had died destitute in a New York boardinghouse.[30]

What brought her back to Mississippi was her devotion to her sister, she said, who was like a second mother to her after their mother, Laura, died. When Nydia married Richard Forman, whom Octavia described as "a wealthy plantation owner," she moved to be with her sister in Fayette County, where Forman owned property. Given his "considerable prominence," she explained that she had no cares but "to amuse myself." And how? By traveling frequently to New Orleans and Vicksburg "to attend balls and house parties of friends." In this, she aligned herself with Mississippi's planter elite, even though the details of Forman's actual prominence are quite vague. Octavia even told a story of riding on horseback down Main Street wearing a velvet jacket and feathered bonnet, cutting such a "graceful figure" that she turned men's heads.[31]

Then Octavia came to the part of her life story of which she seemed most proud. Tired of being a lady of leisure, she asserted that she became a professional woman and began writing to make her own money. At best, Dockery had modest success, but this is not how she portrayed it. "My work was enthusiastically received," and, she avowed, "editors praised it for its freshness and originality." She wrote poetry and newspaper articles, and "all were eagerly accepted, printed and paid for." Reporters found her so convincing that they referred to Octavia as a woman of "rare literary ability," not bothering to check the facts.[32]

If she had such a successful writing career, she was asked, why had she turned "from poetry to pigs"? Her answer was a combination of truth and fabrication. Her sister, she said, died not long after the family moved to Natchez, after which Octavia lived briefly with relatives in Mobile. On the one hand, she said she returned to town and took the money she made from selling "magnificent family jewels" to "raise funds to establish a small dairy and chicken farm at Glenwood." On the other, she claimed to have taken what little she earned from writing "to establish a chicken farm on the property of Dick Dana, who was then a prominent planter." With no form of financial support, she asked, "What was I to do?" While her sister did die in Natchez, it occurred more than a decade after they moved there. And it was likely she had to sacrifice family jewelry in the wake of Richard Forman's death, since he was Octavia's sole means of support since marrying her sister decades before. Yet her claim that Dana had been a "prominent planter" was simply untrue. Glenwood may have been his inheritance, but by the time she moved there—along with her sister and brother-in-law—the estate was already in deplorable condition and far from a profitable plantation.[33]

Since people in Natchez barely knew her, Octavia could say what she wanted, and no one could contest it. As she talked, the portrait of her life took on a pathetic tone. "I have stuck it out at lonely, deserted Glenwood with nothing but ceaseless drudgery to fill my days, because I hoped better days would come," she said, adding, "I was almost worked to death." By now the word was out about the appalling conditions of the home she shared with Dana. When asked why goats were free to "roam about neglected rooms and galleries," Dockery returned to explaining her hard life of raising cows and goats to support the pair "without help from anyone." Because Glenwood did not have running water, she told how she transported water over a "distance of three miles" in order to cook meals.[34]

Reporters presumed that since Octavia had been a "belle," she "had not been taught the first principles of housekeeping," which accounted for the accumulation of filth inside her home. "Who ever dreamed that [her] soft white hands should be hardened by such drudgery?" the *Natchez Democrat* reporter declared. Dockery also made excuses for the conditions of Glenwood. "I spend most of my time out of doors," she said, adding, "Dick is unable to help me as everyone knows. It's a dangerous life, I realize, but I must earn my daily bread." She repeated the line of "earn[ing] my daily bread" throughout her interview —a statement she had to know would resonate with so many readers whose own lives involved financial struggle, especially in the depths of the Depression.[35]

If Octavia sought sympathy from readers, she certainly received it. Locals not only stopped by the jail to leave her flowers and a kind word but also soon began to demand that she and Dick be released. And in fact, within a week of her jailhouse interview, the two were able to return home on their own recognizance. But Dockery's story did more than assist in their release. She had now achieved the attention that her writing never brought her. And after she returned to dilapidated Glenwood, the "Goat Woman" decided to take her act on tour.

CHAPTER EIGHT

SIDESHOWS

When the Natchez Garden Club held its first pilgrimage in the spring of 1932, locals were stunned by its success. More than four thousand visitors from thirty-eight states made the journey to their little town on the bluffs of the Mississippi River to tour its magnificent mansions and experience the place "where the Old South still lives."[1]

Perhaps they should not have been surprised given America's fascination with the Old South in the 1930s. Even before the Depression hit, Hollywood was making escapist films set in the Deep South, where, very often, the Mississippi River provided a romantic backdrop. Given the allure of the region's plantation heritage in all forms of popular culture, it is no wonder Americans were drawn to Natchez as the place where this image appeared to come to life.

Plans were already underway to promote the pilgrimage for the coming spring when Jennie Merrill was murdered. Her passing, in many ways, marked the death of the Old South. This alone was a sobering reality for a town so engaged with its antebellum past. Yet it was the publicity surrounding the case, which dominated national headlines for weeks, that gave locals pause. It brought their town the kind of notoriety that both disturbed and embarrassed well-heeled Natchezeans. It was unseemly. And it detracted from the picturesque portrait of the Old South they still clung to.

Yet everything about the case of Jennie Merrill's murder revealed an Old South in ruins, at least where the planter class was concerned. And the news media milked the story until it ran bone-dry.

Glenwood itself became its own story following the arrest of Dick Dana and Octavia Dockery. Its derelict condition, its peculiar residents, and the menagerie of animals that made their home inside its walls shocked locals and outsiders alike and proved an ominous sign of southern decay. Once the respectable abode of Dick's father, the rector of Trinity Episcopal Church, it contained fine furniture and a large library appropriate for such an educated man as Charles Backus Dana. In the decades since his death in 1873, nearly all of it had deteriorated into conditions not fit for human habitation. And yet humans did inhabit it, including the reverend's son. Now thousands of others were eager see it for themselves.

It was clear early on that the story of Goat Castle and the "forlorn pair" arrested for the murder of Jennie Merrill attracted more than general interest. In the days that followed, public curiosity was further piqued by reports about the home and living conditions. News stories ran the gamut of providing realistic descriptions that defied belief to comparisons with Edgar Allan Poe's "Fall of the House of Usher." Yet none of it was fiction, because the world of the "Wild Man" and the "Goat Woman" was nothing short of a southern gothic drama come to life.

Their home, a rambling two-story antebellum structure with four large chimneys, sat atop a rise on the property that faced a deep bayou overgrown with weeds, vines, spiky palm fronds, and a forest of trees draped in Spanish moss. The driveway that approached Glenwood was gully-washed and uneven. Broken furniture, an old horse-drawn carriage, and the ratty mattress dragged over from the Skunk's Nest lay askew along the front porch that was missing planks like Dick Dana was missing teeth. "So weird and ghostly in its appearance," one reporter commented, "that the timid visitor feels a tremor of fear, even in midday. All is desolate, unkempt, and melancholy."[2]

By Sunday, August 7, just three days after Dick and Octavia's arrest, Glenwood was overrun with voyeuristic tourists and more than a few thieves. There were heavy thunderstorms that day, but it did not prevent people from crossing onto the estate and into the house. Archibald Dickson, the pair's good friend whom Octavia later asked to be custodian of the residence in their absence, was not there that Sunday. Yet he was aware that people from Mississippi, Louisiana, and beyond had come there in droves. "I understand that notwithstanding the downpour of rain," Dickson said, "probably a thousand people entered the house." Over the next few weeks, thousands more arrived.[3]

Numerous individuals took personal papers and other items they could carry by hand that Sunday. A few days later in Jonesville, Louisiana, thirty-six miles from Natchez, the local paper announced it was displaying "Dana souvenirs" taken by a man who had "visited" the home. Among the publicly exhibited items were letters written to Dana's father when he was in college, bills for clothing, an 1845 marriage certificate, and a "picture of the celebrated steamboat *Natchez*."[4]

Octavia was in jail when she learned of the theft, but she used it to her advantage to gain sympathy. "While we are behind the bars of prison for a crime of which, as God is my bearer, we are innocent," she said, "vandals prowl through our house. True it is a pitiful place, now, but after all it is ours." She had gotten word from friends, she said, "that fiends in human form have not hesitated to take away the most intimate personal possessions of the father and mother of Dick," adding that among the missing items was "a brooch of mine, one of the few articles of value" she had left.[5]

Speaking on Octavia's behalf, Archibald Dickson went so far as to suggest that the Adams County sheriff was at fault for failing to secure the items stolen from Glenwood. Book Roberts bristled as the implication. Already overwhelmed with the criminal investigation, Roberts now had to deal with the pilfering going on at Goat Castle and called Dickson in to identify the persons who took items. Glenwood's custodian believed that "99 per cent" of the items were taken on the Sunday he was not at the house. Since then, only reporters had been allowed access. Dick Dana had given a few of them permission to remove items to be photographed, but the reporters were always accompanied by officers. Dickson said he had escorted "a woman reporter from Baton Rouge" but vowed she did not take anything.[6]

Ed Ratcliff, Dana and Dockery's attorney, announced that people who had taken items from Glenwood should return them immediately "on pain of prosecution," but even Ratcliff was not immune to the draw of Goat Castle. He provided his wife a pass to go inside the house. "She wanted to inspect the furniture and other valuables," Dickson told the sheriff, "to get a line on what it would bring for sale." Book Roberts asked Dickson if this was for attorney fees. "No," he said, "for the general expense"—likely the huge debt the pair owed on the mortgage. This was the excuse given, but no sale was forthcoming.[7]

The handful of reporters who entered Goat Castle were met with a scene of complete ruin and decay. It defied belief that anyone could live in such filth and neglect. Fleas and other vermin infested the place. Dick Dana himself was not sure whether the papers that were missing from the house were "gone through the ravages of rats and snakes or were carried away by souvenir seekers." Bird droppings and the waste of other animals covered the rotting floors. Old letters and magazines were strewn about, and on one table lay a faded Confederate uniform, likely that of Octavia's father. Rosewood furniture had been cut up for firewood, while cobwebs wafted down from the ceilings. Then there were the goats that fed the residents and gave the home its nickname. They shuffled in and out of rooms, oblivious to visitors, and some of the herd could be spotted on the second-story porch, chewing their cud as they peered down on those entering the house.[8]

Among the reporters covering the case, Gwen Bristow from the *New Orleans Times-Picayune* proved to be a talented investigative journalist. A true reporter who attended Columbia University's school of journalism, she meticulously documented the living conditions at Glenwood. Her investigations in Natchez led to the interview with Jennie's car mechanic, who recalled having seen a gun in her purse. She also interviewed Merrill's relatives the McKittricks at Elms Court. Bristow, a South Carolina native, went on to a successful career as a novelist, writing the best-selling book *Jubilee Trail*, which became a film in 1954. But in the fall of 1932, she attracted national attention with her feature articles on Goat Castle.[9]

Bristow visited the home in the days after Dana and Dockery's arrest and is likely the "woman reporter" whom Archibald Dickson accompanied. She found the house, like Dick and Octavia, to be a study in shocking contrasts, as suggested by Bristow's headline "Damask and Dirt Mingle in Dick Dana's 'Goat Castle.'" She took readers on a tour of the home through vivid descriptions of its condition. "The house from a distance has a look of rickety decay," Bristow wrote, yet the mansion's "crumbling columns" and rotting porch did not compare to what she found inside. "Edgar Allan Poe never described a place such as the 'Goat Castle,' because he never saw its equal," she said, adding, "There are some pictures beyond imagination." Relating what she saw inside, Bristow wrote about the marble fireplaces where the pair cooked,

Interior photos of Goat Castle, including the downstairs library, illustrate the shocking living conditions inside the home. (Courtesy of the Earl Norman Photograph Collection, Historic Natchez Foundation, Natchez, Miss.)

using bedsprings to smoke goat meat—some of the same goats they lived with. "Chickens and ducks run in and out of the doorway and flutter over the furniture in the hall with easy familiarity. Cats scramble over the sofa in the front parlor," she wrote, and the dust that covered everything inside was so thick "that even the titles of some of the magazines could not be read."[10]

The magnificence of this southern mansion, Bristow noted, was lost in the filth and ankle-deep debris. She described the library where Octavia Dockery did her cooking. The hearth contained a "half burnt . . . greasy frying pan," kettles and pans rested on a once lovely carved table, and the floor was covered with "straw, gunny sacks, old shoes, cans [and] sticks." The mirror above the black marble mantel was blackened with age, and an odd assortment of items rested on the mantel's edge—burned matches, empty tobacco bags, an old calendar, a pipe, and a bust of Charles Dickens. Adjacent to the mirror was a portrait of Dick's father in his vestments, his stern gaze still casting a pall across the room.[11]

The library had long ago ceased to function as a space of gathering and repose. Over the course of its decline, "the scholarly books of the Rev. Dr. Dana," Dick's father, had "been shoved back on their shelves to make room for lard buckets and coffee cans and black cooking pots." Books written in Latin and Greek served as a resting place for a can of nails. Pinecones and kindling lay on top of a rosewood sofa, while fragile chairs were covered in hen feathers. Just off the library was another room, which Bristow surmised had once been a dining room but was now "used by Dana and Miss Dockery as a pen for their goats."[12]

At the top of the wobbly staircase, traveled by both humans and animals, were the bedrooms. Octavia's room contained a grand four-poster mahogany bed, a relic of the antebellum era, but that was not where she slept. Her bed "was an old mattress laid across a series of [shaky] supports," which consisted of "two broken chairs, a drawer from a dresser, a box, and two sticks of wood." It was covered with "an old carriage robe." Dick slept in an adjacent room. He placed his mattress on the bare floor covered with "a pile that presumably was once sheets and blankets." Above his bed was a tattered mosquito net that no longer served its purpose.[13]

Octavia cooked upstairs, too. In what had been another bedroom across the hall from where the odd couple slept, she had taken the bedsprings from one of the four-poster beds and used them to smoke goat meat. Bristow knew this because Octavia had left a large piece of meat from a recently slaughtered goat lying on the springs. In this same room were trunks of books, Reverend Dana's sermons, letters, and antique clothing—hoopskirts and men's dress suits. Here, Bristow ran into other vermin. "On the lid of these trunks . . . are five wasp nests, the occupants of which buzz dangerously around your head when you approach," she wrote.[14]

Faulkner had imagined southern degradation, but this was no imaginary place. When a local reporter in Natchez said that nothing about the home suggested that "someone lived here," Octavia agreed. It looked this way "because nobody did stay there," she said. Then she repeated the line about Dick staying out in the woods for days and how she "didn't have time to clean up" or was so worn out from work she could "scarcely move."[15]

In the weeks ahead, though, Octavia discovered energy she did not know she had.

Octavia Dockery fashioned a bed out of an old mattress supported by chairs and dresser drawers, which lay adjacent to the once-grand bed from which the mattress came. (Courtesy of the Earl Norman Photograph Collection, Historic Natchez Foundation, Natchez, Miss.)

Dick Dana slept beneath tattered mosquito netting when he was not otherwise occupied in the woods around Glenwood. (Courtesy of the Earl Norman Photograph Collection, Historic Natchez Foundation, Natchez, Miss.)

Regardless of what they were called—"visitors," "souvenir seekers," or "tourists"—it was more than one guard could handle. Hundreds of people crossed onto the estate and managed to gain entrance to the home. Dickson described at least a thousand visitors the first Sunday after Dick and Octavia's arrest. And on the following weekend, just before the two were released, hundreds more beat the same path to Goat Castle. "Cars poured into Natchez from Mississippi and Louisiana and far distant states to seek out Glenwood," the *Natchez Democrat* reported. Automobiles were lined up along the Kingston Road near the entrance to Dana's estate, and the city's restaurants were crowded. No one was allowed inside the house, but they freely entered the grounds. People were so bold as to trespass onto the grounds of Elms Court, too, just across the road from Glenwood. On one occasion, the McKittricks returned to their home to find a family had spread a picnic on the grounds, which they graciously allowed them to finish.[16]

Octavia Dockery thought that when she and Dana were released from jail, the two of them would return to the life of quiet they had known before their arrest. What she had not counted on was that the story of their lives, and that of Goat Castle, had generated a public interest they could not escape—though she would find ways to make her sudden fame serve a purpose.

Even before Dick and Octavia were freed, "sympathizers" reached out to their attorney about charging admission to Glenwood. According to the *Natchez Democrat*, just two days before the two were released, "cars from Texas, Oklahoma, Louisiana and Illinois" were "blocking the highway on the Kingston road" in front of Glenwood. "All day curiosity seekers poured into the city," all for the chance to see "Goat Castle." Local residents, too, were eager to see what they apparently had no idea existed in their own town. It is no surprise, then, that the pair ultimately decided to charge for the opportunity.[17]

The dramatic descriptions of their home, which had circulated on both the Associated Press and United Press International wires, had sparked a daily barrage of visitors. Now that they could see the estate not as trespassers but as tourists, they willingly paid the twenty-five-cent fee just to visit the grounds of Goat Castle. Dick told a reporter that given the Depression, he thought the fee was too high and suggested that it should be ten cents, but he was "overruled." It did not matter. The desire to see Goat Castle was so intense, people did not balk at paying a quarter for admission. As soon they opened their estate, in fact, "scores of sightseers, many of them residing in Natchez, but others coming from distant points, took advantage of their first opportunity . . . to visit the grounds of 'Goat Castle.'"[18]

Perhaps with the Reverend Joseph Kuehnle's admonition not to "capitalize on human misery" ringing in their ears, the admission to the grounds of Goat Castle was presented to the public as a means of rehabilitating the house. Receipts from the Natchez Pilgrimage had gone for a similar purpose, so why not Goat Castle? And just as the residents of Melrose and Greenleaves and other homes greeted their visitors, so too did Dick Dana. He seemed to enjoy the attention and the company. Tourists "were surprised as well as impressed with [his] Chesterfieldian mannerisms," a reference to how elegant and refined he appeared. Dick also seemed "ready and willing to talk of art, science, politics or any current affairs—except the Merrill murder mystery."[19]

Octavia, on the other hand, "seldom put in her appearance to the curious," at least early on. Visitors frequently referred to her "quiet dignity." She may have enjoyed the opportunity to tell her story in jail, but being a public spectacle was not likely part of her agenda. The descriptions of the condition of their home and questions of why it had been so long ignored were said to have "brought them more humiliation than even their arrest and formal charge of murder"—though Octavia, more than her ward, felt that humiliation.[20]

For the time being, entry to the house was still off limits. So while Dana made daily appearances to play piano "before an enthusiastic, if strange, audience" at nearby Duncan Park, Octavia was "busily engaged in assisting two young men in the arduous task of cleaning Goat Castle." As the *Times-Picayune* reported, "Rakes, brooms, brushes and the vapor from vermin-killing spraying machines were to be seen through the downstairs window" of the house. Octavia knew as well as anyone that it was the interior that people were eager to see. As one local report put it, thousands of visitors had come to Natchez "curious to view the fantastic dwelling place . . . which in itself tells a tragic story of thwarted lives and crushed ambitions."[21]

The goats were also a draw, even if the crowds who came to see Glenwood were unable to get in the house. They could be seen resting on the front porch and peeping from broken windows on the second floor, but sometimes the crowds were simply too much. As one reporter noted, the herd's patriarch, "Old Ball," led the flock of goats away from the house, "and [they] showed their disapproval of publicity by remaining in retirement in a nearby bayou."[22]

Once Octavia had cleared a path for the onslaught of tourists, Dick began offering weekend performances at Goat Castle. There was an old dust-covered piano in the house on which he tried to pluck out a few songs to entertain guests. He seemed to delight in the attention and the opportunity to play. But the piano was so out of tune and for so long had been a roosting place for

After being provided a new suit, Dick Dana offered piano concerts,
first at Duncan Park (shown), then at Goat Castle, and finally when he was
on tour as the "Wild Man." (Courtesy of the Earl Norman Photograph
Collection, Historic Natchez Foundation, Natchez, Miss.)

chickens and geese that it made for a pitiful spectacle. When word got out, an
anonymous donor had a new upright piano delivered to Glenwood. Dick could
now play and sing to his heart's content and to the enjoyment of tourists.[23]

On Saturdays and Sundays, he held morning concerts at ten and eleven
o'clock and again at three and four o'clock in the afternoon. And while Dick
would have performed for nothing more than people's attention, Octavia had
not been working to clean the house just to let the gawkers in for free. Entry
into the house required a separate admission fee of twenty-five cents. This
was no small sum in the Depression, but it did not prove to be a deterrent. On

Sunday, September 4, more than five hundred people—from as far away as Texas and Illinois—paid to go on the grounds, several of whom also paid the additional fee to hear Dana play piano and sing.[24]

Train companies also saw an opportunity to make money by providing excursions to Natchez to exploit the vast public interest in Goat Castle. The Mississippi Central Railroad offered a special trip from Hattiesburg and Brookhaven the first weekend in September on which an estimated 250 people paid the fare to visit Glenwood and for the chance to meet Dana and Dockery in person. Those who purchased tickets were afforded access to the property but had to pay the additional fee to enter the house for one of Dana's concerts. The Yazoo and Mississippi Valley Railroad also offered train trips in late September originating from three separate starting points—Jackson, Vicksburg, and New Orleans. Similarly, ticket buyers were promised the chance to see the "Wild Man" and "Goat Woman" in person. While some locals may have been horrified by the voyeurism, their town benefited economically from these excursions since after their tour of Goat Castle, visitors went into town to have meals and tour other historic sites.[25]

The opportunity to make money off of Dick and Octavia's national notoriety did not end with tours of Goat Castle. In late August a man named Sam Abbott, who claimed to be the "public relations counsel" for the pair, announced that he had arranged for Dana to offer a radio concert to be broadcast on WSMB in New Orleans, then affiliated with the National Broadcasting Company. Abbott stated that he had coordinated with the local manager of Southern Bell Telephone, who assured him that he could provide a remote connection to have Dana offer his performance from the clubhouse of Duncan Park.[26]

The pair's attorney Ed Ratcliff, however, ended all talk of a radio broadcast. While it was true that he did not advise against charging admission to Goat Castle, he seems to have balked at the radio broadcast. The murder charges against Dick and Octavia were still in effect, so perhaps he believed that a radio performance that had the potential of reaching a national audience was unwise. Publicly, however, Ratcliff stated that the reason for not permitting the broadcast had to do with Dana's poor physical condition. He suggested that such a performance would be "injurious to his general health," given "the strain of the past few weeks together with the nervous condition caused by the hundreds of people who visited his house." Still, Ratcliff promised to "build up the physical condition of Mr. Dana" so that perhaps at some future date a radio broadcast could be offered. Given the steady flow of people coming to

Glenwood, it seems unlikely that either Dana's physical or his nervous condition would improve. More than five hundred people visited Goat Castle the day Ratcliff made his announcement. It is more likely that the couple's attorney was buying time until he believed the charges against them were dropped.[27]

Sam Abbott was undeterred, as were other "friends." And tourism was a two-way street. So, acting as Dana and Dockery's booking agent, he set up several engagements for the couple. Now, the curious could purchase tickets to see Goat Castle's residents in person. Initially, nearby towns sought Dana out for piano concerts. He performed for a crowd of two hundred people in nearby Woodville and later to an audience in Vicksburg following an invitation by that city's Thomas Pantoliano, described as a man of "experience in the amusement business."[28]

By October, Octavia and Dick were being booked as an "act." "Dana-Dockery Entertainment Makes a Big Hit" read the headline after the pair appeared before a capacity crowd at the St. Joseph Theatre in Tensas Parish, Louisiana. The two told stories of their life, some "humorous," after which Dana, who was said to have a nice tenor voice, sang songs and played the piano, including a performance of Stephen Foster's "Old Black Joe." The act also expanded. Instead of simply holding a piano concert, the two were actually introduced to the audience as "the wild man and goat woman of Goat Castle." Dick also appeared before the crowd in the coveralls he was wearing when he was arrested, the same ones he wore in the photograph that circulated nationally.[29]

The "Wild Man" and the "Goat Woman" went on to give other programs in Louisiana, including at Sicily Island High School, where they displayed old papers, books, and magazine articles written by Dockery, among other "relics" from the home. Dick and Octavia also took their show to Jonesville, Louisiana, where weeks before there had been an exhibit of items taken from their home.[30]

After performing and displaying Goat Castle relics in Port Gibson, the pair was booked for a two-day engagement, on October 27 and 28, at the Jackson Auditorium in the state's capital. To spur additional interest in the event, sponsored by a branch of the Disabled Veterans of America, antiques from Dana's home were exhibited in the street windows of the Emporium, a major department store in the city. The organization's efforts paid off, and the pair's performance was a "hit." An "immense crowd" greeted the two, and after the program they received a standing ovation. Octavia, who regaled crowds with stories of the Old South, was given several bouquets of flowers. While in Jackson, the pair also gave an interview to a local radio station in front of a live audience that included the wife of former governor Earl Brewer.[31]

The tour of towns throughout Mississippi and Louisiana may have come because of the "possibility of dwindling receipts" from Goat Castle. Advisers of the pair, who were at once described as "friends" and "the committee," helped to determine their next moves. In addition to Sam Abbott, their public relations counsel, it appears that their pro bono attorney Sophie Friedman was also involved, especially when it came to escorting them to various events. They also outfitted Dana with clothing for his performances — on- and off-stage. Onstage, he wore the dirty coveralls. When not performing, he was dressed in a "frock coat, a slouch hat and string tie . . . to take on the appearance of a professional Southerner." After being groomed and given a clean shave following his release from jail, by mid-September he was "sporting a 'Buffalo Bill' mustache and goatee," which complemented his attire and led some to refer to him as "Colonel" Dana.[32]

Dick had his own opinions on his appearance. He was convinced that "hair and artistic ability [were] analogous" and wanted to let his hair and beard grow long again. There were other matters of concern, too. Dick, who was toothless, declared that "until he has been provided with some new store teeth," he refused to offer musical recitals to the public, except for at Goat Castle. Apparently, the many women visitors "made him insistent on the question of teeth," although he "vigorously denied it." Still, it was true that he had attracted the attention of female visitors and received fan mail from women, too.[33]

Despite Dana's misgivings about his hair and teeth, he and Octavia continued to tour and host the daily droves of sightseers to Glenwood throughout September and October. There seemed to be no end to people's interest in this southern gothic spectacle. For now, the strange pair entertained, even as they stood charged with the murder of Jennie Merrill.

Yet November was just around the corner, and with it came the meeting of the Adams County grand jury. Octavia knew as well as anyone that Sheriff Book Roberts remained convinced of their guilt. So she placed bets that her role as the downtrodden southern belle and Dick's obvious mental deficiencies had won them not only the sympathy of the local community but also their freedom.

CHAPTER NINE

COLD JUSTICE

As mid-November approached, frigid air swept through the Deep South, bringing freezing temperatures across the Mississippi River and over the bluffs into Natchez.[1] Adams County jail cells were stark and miserable, so the bitter weather must have seemed like an added cruelty to Emily Burns and her mother, Nellie Black. They had been there since their arrest in mid-August. During those three months the seasons had changed, but no formal charges had been filed against either woman, and neither was afforded legal counsel. It was a clear violation of their civil rights, but not in the Jim Crow South, where Negroes were second-class citizens. Unlike Octavia Dockery, who awaited her legal fate while collecting receipts at Goat Castle, Emily and Nellie languished in their cold cells, weighed down by the memory of generations of southern black women before them who had never known justice.

Book Roberts and his team of officers had been working the Merrill murder case since late in the evening of August 4, but by mid-September the sheriff had decided to keep relatively quiet about the case. The national publicity and public speculation had only made his job more difficult, and people gave him unsolicited advice. One person wrote him to say, "You and all the law force are on the wrong track about the murder of Jane Merrill. . . . It seems like you should arrest and question to the fullest extent the man named Duncan Minor." It was signed "an old resident of Natchez." An individual from New Orleans also wrote to tell him she was certain that the "guilty party" was Duncan Minor, who had "a tall black negro man" help him. The letter writer was very specific about the details, saying Minor "fired the shots with her [Jennie

Merrill's] 32 cal pistol" and that he hid the gun near his home. "If you search you'll find it and if you put Mr. Minor through the 3rd degree . . . he'll admit to this," the woman wrote, then added, "I am quite an unusual psychologist and am really able to do these things." Such letters added to the tense climate, a reminder to the sheriff and his deputies to maintain their silence until trial.[2]

The term of the Adams County Circuit Court finally arrived on Monday, November 14. Sixty-seven-year-old Robert Corban, the presiding judge, in-structed the grand jury to fully investigate the cases before them, which in-cluded the Merrill murder. It was time to review all of the evidence that had been gathered, including the fingerprint evidence, the ballistic report, material collected from Pine Bluff and Chicago, the notes from interrogations and in-terviews, and, of course, Emily Burns's signed confession.[3]

The work of the grand jury began in the early morning and went late into the day. Attorneys first called Sheriff Roberts in for questioning and to pro-vide a list of the people he had interviewed during his investigation. "A steady stream of witnesses" was called, most of them deputies but also special officers hired for the case, like Hyde Jenkins and John Junkin. The sheriff told report-ers he had provided the jurors with "every scintilla of evidence" and expressed confidence that they would return "a number of indictments." Without saying so, he meant the deceased George Pearls, who all agreed had murdered Jennie Merrill, as well as individuals whom Book considered accessories. This in-cluded Emily Burns and Edgar "Poe" Newell, even though the latter had been released from jail a month before. But Book also trusted that the evidence he submitted would "substantiate the drafting of murder charges against Miss Octavia Dockery and Richard H. C. Dana."[4]

While the county prosecutor, Joe Brown, shared the sheriff's confidence, he knew that District Attorney Clay Tucker had different ideas about indicting Dana and Dockery. The two men had shared terse exchanges about the guilt or innocence of Jennie's neighbors. Tucker had been responsible for helping set the couple free on their own recognizance during their habeas corpus proceeding because he did not believe there was sufficient evidence to keep them in jail. Given this, many locals believed he would not seek indictments against the pair.[5]

Yet Joe Brown, and not Clay Tucker, had been involved in the investiga-tion throughout its entirety and believed Dick and Octavia were involved. There was the fingerprint evidence. There was Dick's statement that he knew "nothing of the murder" before Merrill's body had even been found. There was also the timing of it all, which Jennie's cousin David McKittrick alluded to in an interview following her death. "Whoever killed [her] timed the crime so perfectly that he was evidently well acquainted with her habits," he said. McKittrick, who assumed the murderer was male, added, "He staged it so as to arrive after dark, but before Duncan Minor would arrive," which was "always . . . between 8:30 and 9 o'clock." The only other people who had any knowledge of her evening habits were blacks who lived and worked at Glenburnie and her neighbors, Octavia Dockery and Dick Dana—not the man who had left Natchez for Chicago nearly twenty years earlier.[6]

None of it mattered. After three days of reviewing evidence, there was just one indictment. On November 17, the jury returned a true bill against "Lawrence Pinkney Williams, alias George Pearls," for the murder of Jennie Merrill. The true bill meant that even though Pearls was now deceased, he could still be held accountable, setting the stage for a postmortem conviction. Emily Burns was indicted on two counts—accessory to murder and aiding a murderer to escape. In Mississippi, an accessory to murder was considered the same as having committed the murder in the eyes of the law. So, the indictment read that "Lawrence (Pinkney) Williams alias George Pearls and Emily Burns . . . did willfully, unlawfully, feloniously and of *their* malice aforethought kill and murder one Jane Surget Merrill, a human being."[7] Neither Ed Newell nor Dick Dana nor Octavia Dockery—the three individuals Emily consistently included in her confessions—was indicted.[8]

The following day Emily Burns was arraigned before Judge Corban in circuit court. She felt weak in both body and spirit. The anxiety of the past three months had caused her to lose twenty pounds, and knowing that she alone would be put on trial for the murder of Jennie Merrill was beyond comprehension. When called upon, all she had to tell the judge was that she had no attorney. Neither could she afford one. Judge Corban appointed Wilfred A. Geisenberger, Gerard Brandon, and William E. Logan to represent her and then set her trial date for November 25, leaving them barely a week to prepare Emily's defense.[9]

On Thursday, November 24, the court was adjourned for Thanksgiving, but Sister had little to be thankful for. Although she had not pulled the trigger that resulted in Jennie Merrill's death, the local white community wanted justice.

And since the man who committed the crime was also dead, killed by an Arkansas deputy during an unrelated incident, her conviction would have to do. Emily had every reason to fear the worst possible outcome. Her attorneys likely advised her that DA Clay Tucker, who would present the state's case, planned to seek the death penalty. In Mississippi, this meant hanging. So if this became Sister's fate, she would be moved to death row on the jail's second floor in a cell that overlooked the gallows, where she would meet her fate.[10]

At forty years old, Wilfred Geisenberger was only a few years older than his client. He was a World War I veteran who had attended the University of Mississippi Law School and was a member of Temple B'Nai Israel. His father, Abraham Geisenberger, had also been an attorney, including for Jennie Merrill during one of her trespassing cases over Octavia Dockery's hogs. Wilfred maintained a successful law practice in Natchez and eventually went on to serve as the president of the Mississippi Bar Association. For now, though, he had the challenge of defending a black woman in a case in which the person murdered belonged to the last generation of the town's antebellum elite. Although two young attorneys in their mid-thirties, Gerard Brandon and William Logan, were also assigned to the case, Brandon bowed out. With very little assistance, Geisenberger was faced with a nearly impossible task.[11]

On the morning of Friday, November 25, Emily Burns, accompanied by officers and her attorneys, made the short walk from the jail across State Street to the Adams County Courthouse, which was filled to capacity to observe the trial. *The State v. Emily Burns*, case number 4708, began at 8:30 A.M. with the selection of jurors. A special venire of fifty white men had been subpoenaed for jury duty, but it took quite awhile to select jurors because several of the men admitted to having fixed opinions in the case. After twelve jurors were finally seated, the trial began with Judge Corban presiding.[12]

Before Emily Burns could be tried, the deceased Lawrence (Pinkney) Williams, alias George Pearls, received a postmortem conviction for murdering Jennie Merrill. Then the state's attorney, Clay Tucker, moved swiftly to try Emily Burns, and the first witness was Chief Deputy Joseph Stone of the

sheriff's department. Tucker began the questioning with Stone because the
deputy had been involved in the investigation since the night of August 4 and
was credited with securing Emily Burns's confession. Stone testified that she
made her statement on the evening of August 22, although it had come after
midnight on August 23, when she was taken to the "residence part of the jail"
for questioning. He claimed that she "fell on her knees" and said, "I want to
tell the truth." The deputy then relayed how she told him that Pink, who he
referred to as George Pearls, along with Ed Newell, Dick Dana, and Octavia
Dockery were all at Glenburnie when Pearls shot Merrill. Her original confession, Stone said, was made to him alone, but she repeated it to former sheriff
Walter Abbott and Special Deputies John Junkin and Hyde Jenkins. The next
day "a written confession was made in Jackson."[13]

Stone then testified that Burns confessed that Pearls had asked her to go for
a walk, during which time he told her of his plans to rob Jennie Merrill. He
said she confessed to the timeline of details — that they went through Duncan
Park and stopped at Glenwood, where Dick Dana gave Pearls the overcoat,
after which they walked through the woods until they arrived at Glenburnie.
Stone then testified that Emily confessed to hiding with Pearls under the
house until he went inside, after which she heard a scuffle and the shots. Then,
Stone said, "they all went into the house." This was untrue. Emily had never
confessed to having gone inside the house. For her, "they" had always meant
Pink, Poe, Dana, and Dockery. Stone then said she told him how Pearls and
Newell took the body out of the home and that "she was given a lamp, which
she threw away in the yard," which suggests she had remained outside.[14]

Stone continued, claiming that Burns told him that all five people were in
Merrill's house after Jennie was shot — Pearls, Newell, Dana, Dockery, and the
defendant. Initially, everyone she implicated went back to the Dana property
— a detail not provided in her signed confession, though she had made several
confessions and Stone may have been referring to a particular answer she gave
during one of her many interrogations. He concluded his testimony by relay-
ing Burns's description of how she and Pearls made their way home from the
crime scene, to her place on St. Catherine Street, where he burned his bloody
clothing, changed into clean clothes, and said he was leaving for Chicago.[15]

Wilfred Geisenberger cross-examined Deputy Stone for the defense. His
first question was meant to determine the length of time and frequency with
which Emily Burns had been questioned. The deputy responded that officers
questioned her daily, usually for two hours at a time. Geisenberger then asked

pointedly, "Was Emily Burns questioned in a room with a whip on the table in clear view and told to tell the truth?" Stone denied it and testified that even Emily Burns said she had been treated "fine." It is true that Emily signed a confession that read, in part, "While I've been in jail I couldn't have been treated no better if I'd been a white lady . . . and nobody has threatened me since I've been in jail." Yet such a statement absolving officers raises the question of why it would need to be included if, in fact, they had not threatened her. It was particularly unlikely that a black woman would willingly use language comparing herself to a "white lady," especially in the Jim Crow South.[16]

Several other members of the "sheriff's posse" testified about their search during the night of August 4. All stated that they began their search as soon as Merrill was reported missing. They each described evidence of bullet marks in the door facing of Merrill's dining room, a bloody slipper on the dining room floor, and bloody fingerprints on the walls. Each testified to the trail of blood that continued out and around the porch and then down the front stairs. They all attested to finding a second slipper and hair combs in a large pool of blood near the driveway, noted that Jennie Merrill's body was found about three hundred feet from her home, and told of the use of bloodhounds in the search that led to locating the lamp "some distance from the house" and yet on her property. Dr. E. E. Benoist, the physician summoned for the coroner's inquest, was called next. He testified that Merrill was shot twice—once in the breast and a second time through the neck, adding that he "couldn't be certain but she could have been shot from behind."[17]

The state's next three witnesses were local black citizens, all of whom could identify the man who went by Lawrence Williams and place him as having been in Natchez since July. Barney Johnson was the first called to the stand. He testified that he drove Williams to Zula Curtis's boardinghouse on Beaumont Street. He also testified that the trunk Williams had with him was the same one he saw at the county jail. The state then called Zula Curtis. Her testimony confirmed that a man named W. C. Williams stayed with her for one week in July before moving away. She testified that after seeing his photo in the paper, she recognized him as the man who had stayed at her house. Louis Winston, who picked up the trunk from Curtis's home and delivered it to Nellie Black's place, also testified that the photo of George Pearls in the paper was the man he knew to call himself Williams.[18]

The state planned to call Maurice O'Neill, the New Orleans detective, to the witness stand, but he had a bad case of the flu and had yet to make it to

Natchez. Clay Tucker did, however, call Dr. W. E. Clark to the stand. Tucker had anticipated that Geisenberger might employ an insanity defense. Clark was an "alienist," the contemporary term for a psychologist, and the assistant superintendent of the state's insane asylum. He testified that Emily Burns was sane and had never been to the state asylum.[19]

Testimony lasted until 9:30 in the evening. The state had subpoenaed several witnesses, many of whom had not testified. Witnesses for the defense had yet to be called. And Clay Tucker's intuition about an insanity defense was correct. But it was late, and Judge Corban ordered the trial to be adjourned until the following morning, a Saturday, beginning at 8:30 A.M.

When morning came, the Adams County Courthouse was again packed with spectators. The state continued its case against Emily Burns by calling former sheriff Walter Abbott to the stand. Abbott testified that Burns had implicated herself, Pearls, Newell, Dana, and Dockery but that during the reenactment of the crime at Merrill's home she "failed to include Newell, Dana and Dockery." He also emphasized that she had not been "coached or aided" and had been given plenty of time to reenact the crime.[20]

Maurice O'Neill felt well enough by this time to return to Natchez from New Orleans and take the witness stand. He first testified that he had conducted the ballistics test proving that the bullets found at the crime scene matched those fired from the gun found on Pearls in Arkansas. Then, in dramatic fashion, he "brought with him a small machine for comparing bullets and gave a demonstration for the jury in the courtroom." O'Neill also presented the bullets fired at the test range as well as those found at Merrill's home. Last, he testified to having gone to Chicago with Sheriff Roberts along with Louis Terrell to identify Pearls's body "along with members of Pearls['s] family." He then showed a photograph he had taken of Pearls's body at the Chicago funeral home, which was then introduced into evidence. Despite many objections to O'Neill's testimony, all were overruled.[21]

To confirm O'Neill's testimony, Louis Terrell and Sheriff Roberts were called to the stand. Terrell testified that he had gone to Chicago with the sheriff and identified the body, while Book Roberts testified that he gave the bullets to O'Neill for comparison and that the New Orleans detective had accompanied him to Chicago.

Officer Robert Henslee, the Pine Bluff police deputy, and John Junkin, who had been sworn in as a special sheriff's deputy, were also called to the stand. Henslee, who later filed a claim for the $100 reward for capturing George Pearls, testified that he shot and killed Pearls for resisting arrest and then removed his gun and the bundle of clothes he was carrying. Junkin, who happened to be a close personal friend of Sheriff Roberts, testified next. He confirmed that he had gone to Pine Bluff to collect Pearls's gun and his clothing, adding that Emily Burns had identified the clothes as belonging to the man she new as Pinkney Williams. Junkin also testified that Emily had given several confessions in his presence, but when cross-examined he denied making any threats with a bullwhip.[22]

The final witnesses for the prosecution did little to help Emily's case. First, A. E. Sims, a mail carrier, testified that he delivered a letter postmarked from Pine Bluff, Arkansas, to Emily Burns. His testimony was then followed by that of Herbert Kingsberry, described as the "Negro trusty at the county jail." Kingsberry said that Emily had given him a letter to give to a man named Ben Johnson to be taken to Annie Reed, one of her neighbors on St. Catherine Street. There was a reason Kingsberry was called a "trusty," because rather than deliver Emily's letter to Johnson, he gave it to the jailer, Laurin Farris. Farris and Special Deputy Hyde Jenkins both testified to the contents of the letter addressed to Annie Reed in which Emily urged Reed to go to her house and "get out of it a pistol, rifle, overcoat, and hat and some letters from [Pink]" and either "destroy or hide them." With this damning testimony, the prosecution rested its case.[23]

Wilfred Geisenberger faced an uphill battle in his defense of Emily Burns. Her association with Lawrence Williams was clear — he had boarded at her home, and there were the letters from Pine Bluff indicating that their relationship had been more personal. She had kept quiet to protect him until the day the bullwhip became part of the interrogation, and she had written an incriminating letter asking Annie Reed to remove Williams's belongings. Emily's attorney knew that she was likely to be convicted, so just as Clay Tucker predicted, he did what he could to save her life by making the case that she was mentally unstable.

Geisenberger first called Sheriff Roberts to the stand to establish a simple point of fact: did he hear Emily Burns make a confession to the Reverend

Charles Anderson, her minister at Antioch Baptist Church? Roberts claimed he was in the cell but did not hear a confession. This set the stage for Pastor Anderson, as Sister knew him, to be called to the stand. And when he testified, it was the most detailed account of what happened after the murder that anyone had yet heard.

Charles Anderson described what Emily told him in her cell, confirming much of what sheriff's deputies had testified to regarding what had happened at the Merrill home. Anderson then testified to what came next. She told him that after she and Pink returned home, "he took off his bloody clothes and she put them in a tub with some stain remover and water." He then grabbed a bundle of clothes, and the two of them "went down Reynolds Street to the railroad, [then] up the railroad to Aldrich Street." Poe was waiting for them with his car. "[We] got in the car," she told Anderson, then "drove out Pine Street to Oak Street, down Oak to Cemetery [Road], out Cemetery to a hill where [Pink] left." Sister and Poe then returned to Natchez.[24]

Emily's minister had just confirmed the details of her confession about who was there the night of the murder. She had implicated herself, but she was also caught up in a bad situation with no simple way out. He reaffirmed that Poe was involved, as Emily had always said. Anderson's testimony also demonstrated Sister's loyalty to Pink, which she maintained even at her own peril. While Reverend Anderson did not say anything about her state of mind, Geisenberger seems to have used his testimony to suggest that given the events of that night, no one in her right mind would have become willingly involved.

The defense next called Mrs. H. L. Baker to the stand, whose testimony would suggest that Emily was not at the crime scene that evening. Mrs. Baker and her husband had been walking near the Merrill home near dusk on the night of August 4. She testified that she saw a man with a black hat and overcoat walking toward the Merrill home but was unsure "if he was white or colored." She said no one was with him. If this man had been the murderer, then the implication was he acted alone or could have been white.[25]

Geisenberger was planting seeds of doubt, and with the next few witnesses he pressed not necessarily an insanity defense but a defense that demonstrated that his defendant's mental state left her incapable of making anything but poor decisions. Along those lines, the defense called Dr. A. W. Dumas to the stand. Dumas, a black physician at the Natchez Sanitarium, testified that he had treated Emily Burns and "did not consider her perfectly sane." He believed her to be "abnormal," and it was his opinion that "she was suffering from dementia praecox," a condition that many contemporary psychiatrists had begun to diagnose as schizophrenia.[26]

Dr. Dumas's testimony set the stage for the next witnesses—people who knew Emily Burns personally. Sarah Elmore, who ran the East End Beer Parlor on St. Catherine Street near Emily's home, testified, as did Edward Sims, a neighbor who lived around the corner from her on Cedar Avenue. Both of them attested to her strange behavior and claimed that she had "fits" and "spasms," during which time she "foamed at the mouth." Then, in what had to be a difficult experience for both mother and daughter, Nellie Black testified that her own child "was not well or normal and had fits during which she acted crazy."[27]

After their testimony, the state called Book Roberts, Chief Deputy Joseph Stone, and Special Deputy John Junkin back to the stand to dispute the previous testimony by testifying that Emily Burns was "perfectly sane" while she was in jail. Months before, Stone was quoted in the *Natchez Democrat* describing Emily Burns as "bright" and "smart," but then he seemed to contradict himself by saying, "She must be telling us the truth, because no sane person would hang herself like she has in her confession." If only Emily's defense team had been given a little longer to prepare, Stone's public statement could have been used to dispute his own testimony.[28]

There was one person mysteriously missing from the entire proceedings—James Chancellor, the fingerprint expert from Jackson. Book Roberts had been quoted as saying that Chancellor stood firm by his findings and would testify at trial. But the prosecution never called him. Roberts also claimed to have brought Maurice O'Neill to Natchez to "check and re-check" Chancellor's work and that all would be revealed at the time of trial. O'Neill did testify, but as Zaida Wells later wrote, "He talked bullets, but never fingerprints." So where was the Bertillon expert from Jackson?

James Chancellor was subpoenaed as a defense witness but never appeared in court. On November 22, just three days before Emily Burns's trial, Clifford Fields, the circuit clerk of Adams County, sent a letter and subpoena to the sheriff of Hinds County to summon Chancellor to Natchez. "The attorneys requesting this subpoena could not recall Mr. Chancellor's first name," he wrote, "but he is the gentleman who took fingerprints in the 'Miss Merrill Murder

Case.'" How was it that Emily's attorneys did not know Chancellor's first name given the publicity surrounding his visit? Better yet, why had they not simply made a phone call to Sheriff Roberts and ask?[29]

The trial began three days later and there was no sign of Chancellor, so Emily's attorneys filed an affidavit to continue the trial at a later date. Emily was sworn in to defend the motion for continuance. The motion stated that her court-appointed attorney Wilfred Geisenberger had requested that the circuit clerk of Adams County issue a subpoena for "Mr. _____ Chancellor, a fingerprint expert of Jackson, Mississippi." As far as she knew, the "subpoena was issued . . . but never returned," but her attorneys believed he "can be found and required to attend this trial as a witness in her behalf."[30]

The prosecution claimed that the lamp found on Merrill's property was the same lamp taken from her home and the same one the defendant had carried. But since Chancellor had developed fingerprints from the lamp, Geisenberger wanted him there. He considered him a critical defense witness, because his testimony would show "that fingerprints he discovered and identified" on the lamp "bore no fingerprints of the defendant." Rather, "he obtained fingerprints and positively identified them as Richard Dana's, [based on] certain other articles in the Merrill home."[31]

The affidavit concluded that Emily Burns "is without any means whereby to obtain the presence of witnesses in her behalf and has done all that she could to have the process of this Court produce them in her behalf at this trial, and that she has used every diligence and means at her command to obtain the presence of this witness." Emily's motion for continuance was denied. Yet her affidavit made it clear why the state's attorneys never called Chancellor to testify. They were there to convict Emily Burns, not Dick Dana or Octavia Dockery.[32]

The last witness in the trial was Emily Burns, who took the stand in her own defense. She declared that she was not guilty of murder and that the story she told was based on what she had read in the newspapers. She repudiated all of her confessions and said she made them because she was "afraid." She told jurors how she was "questioned continually by two, three," and sometimes "five persons," and it made her so nervous, she said, "I did not know what I was saying." She testified that on the night of her original confession, "Mr. John Junkin took me in a room where I saw a whip and he told me he was going to give me thirty minutes to tell the truth," after which she said, "I did not want to be whipped." This, she said, is when she "confessed" to being at the Merrill home and implicated Pinkney Williams, Ed Newell, Dick Dana, and Octavia Dockery.[33]

While on the stand, Emily also denied ever leaving the home she shared with her mother on the day of the murder. She stated that "[Pink] left her home on Monday morning before the murder" and that "he left town before the murder." She then testified that after reading the newspaper detailing Dana and Dockery's arrest, she "put them in the story" when she told officers. She added Ed Newell to it "because the officers wanted him in it, and she was afraid not to do what they wanted." When asked about the details of her conversation with Reverend Anderson, she replied that since the sheriff was present at the time, "she thought she had better do what the officers wanted her to do."[34]

On cross-examination, she cast doubt on her reenactment of the crime. She claimed that she was "guided" by what she had read in the newspapers and "by talk of the men present who led the way from place to place." Those present included not only Sheriff Roberts and former sheriff Abbott but also Duncan Minor, all of whom were present the evening the investigation began. Finally, she reiterated that she was not at the Merrill home on the night of the murder and that she made up her statements to officers.[35]

What becomes clear in Emily Burns's testimony is the absolute terror she felt during the previous three months of her life, from the time Pink left town, to her arrest ten days later, to her incarceration, interrogation, and indictment for murder. As she took the stand in her own defense, all she could see were white faces. The jury, the judge, the attorneys, and the stream of officers who took the stand were all white men. And throughout the courtroom were the faces of local whites who came in part for the spectacle, but also to see her convicted.

Nearly four months had led to this—a trial to determine her guilt or innocence and whether she lived or died, and it concluded in less than a day and a half. The jury left the courtroom with its instructions a little before 11:00 A.M. while Emily waited on its decision with her attorneys.

———

Zaida Wells, who attended the trial, had mounting doubts about the outcome. Her interest in the case began the night she walked out of the Baker-Grand

Theatre and saw the frenzy of activity outside the Adams County jail. It bothered her and others in the community that the case rested on only parts of Emily Burns's confession while it ignored those parts that implicated Dick Dana, Octavia Dockery, and even Edgar Newell. "Common sense seems to dictate that it was either all true," she wrote, "or else if part of it was lies, the whole of it was lies."[36]

The state provided the jury with several instructions, most of which required jurors to "believe from the evidence in this case beyond a reasonable doubt that Lawrence (Pinckney) [sic] Williams alias George Pearls and Emily Burns conspired together to rob or burglarize the home of Jane Surget Merrill" and that Pearls killed Merrill. The instructions further asked that even if the jurors believed the evidence proved "that Emily Burns was on the outside of the house and not actually in the immediate presence of the deceased when [she] was shot," they should find her guilty of being an accessory to the murder.[37]

Jurors were also instructed to determine, beyond a reasonable doubt, if she conspired with Pearls to rob Jennie Merrill prior to their going to Glenburnie. If so, the instructions read, "Emily Burns is guilty of the crime of murder as a principal the same as though she had actually fired the shot which killed and murdered the said Jane Surget Merrill." If they believed she "aided, assisted and encouraged George Pearls or any other person or persons in murdering Jane Surget Merrill," then she should be found guilty "as such other person or persons." If it "was her intent to aid and abet" Pearls, then, once again, she should be found "as guilty as the one who did the killing."[38]

The state submitted two other instructions intended to offset any doubts jurors might have regarding Emily's guilt or innocence. One advised the jury "that the law does not require you to know that the defendant is guilty, before you return a verdict of guilty as charged, but only that you should believe her guilty, beyond all reasonable doubt arising out of the evidence." The other dealt directly with the defense Wilfred Geisenberger had presented. It read that "in the prosecution for a homicide, where the defense is insanity, total or partial, the test of the Defendant's criminal responsibility, is her ability, at the time she is proved to have committed the act, to recognize her ability to distinguish right from wrong."[39]

Geisenberger submitted a number of jury instructions as well, intending to remind jurors of Emily Burns's legal rights and protections if the state had not proven her guilty beyond a reasonable doubt. In other words, the state had the

burden of proof, and the defendant "is at no time required to prove her innocence . . . [because] the presumption of innocence is a protection, which the
law gives this defendant." If the state failed, then the jury must return a verdict
of "not guilty." The defense also instructed the jury not to disregard Emily
Burns's testimony "because she is the defendant," that it was their duty to
consider her testimony among all the other evidence, and that, based on her testimony, if there was a "probability of her innocence," they should acquit her.[40]

Based on his line of questioning in the case, Geisenberger also instructed
the jury to consider "whether or not the confessions of the defendant were
freely and voluntarily made by her, without fear of punishment . . . by any of
the officers to whom or in whose presence they were made." In doing so, he
reminded them that Emily Burns testified to confessing out of her fear of being
whipped. If they believed her, then they should find her "not guilty." In addition, he asked the jury to acquit his client if there was a reasonable doubt that
she was there when Pearls killed Jennie Merrill, as she testified to being home
that evening. Finally, he reminded the men that if "a single member of the jury
[who] entertains in his mind a reasonable doubt as to the defendant's guilt, then
it is the duty of such juror to vote for the acquittal" of Emily Burns. Geisenberger also asked the jury to "disregard and ignore the alleged confessions of
the defendant" and not take them into consideration as part of the evidence in
the case. It was the one instruction Judge Corban refused.[41]

The jurors also received instructions about their verdict, too. If they found
her "guilty as charged," which the state called for, then Emily would be sentenced to hang. The jurors could also reach a verdict of manslaughter, in which
case she would be sentenced to the state penitentiary "for a term of years, not
to exceed twenty years." They might also find her guilty and "fix her punishment at life in the State penitentiary." And, should they find her not guilty on
the grounds of insanity, then Judge Corban would determine whether she was
a danger to the community and could have her "confined in one of the State
asylums for the insane."[42]

In the end, the attorneys spent more time drafting instructions than the
jury spent deliberating. The men returned to the courtroom after less than
thirty minutes.

When Judge Corban asked for the jury's decision, the foreman returned to
the judge a small piece of paper with the jury's verdict written in pencil. Corban read the decision in quiet before telling Emily Burns to stand and face the
jury. By all accounts, she remained calm as she received her sentence, which
she knew could be death. Then the foreman spoke. "We, the Jury, find the

Defendant Emily Burns, guilty as charged, but certify that we cannot agree on the punishment." They could neither agree to sentence her to death nor to the state penitentiary. Some of them may have wanted the death penalty while others had been swayed by Wilfred Geisenberger's pleas for mercy. In the event of a verdict where jurors were unable to determine punishment, Mississippi law fixed the punishment at life at the state penitentiary.[43]

Sheriff's deputies escorted Emily back across the street to her cell in the Adams County jail to await her sentencing, which was set for Monday, just two days later.[44]

Newspapers across the country reported on Emily Burns's conviction, but the *Times-Picayune* made clear the tragedy that had befallen her. "For an alleged conspiracy to rob an aristocratic old lady recluse who hardly kept a dollar in money at her house," the paper reported, "Emily Burns, a negro rooming house keeper of Natchez, must go to the penitentiary for life." That the paper used the word "alleged" signaled what many throughout the area were coming to believe: Emily Burns was headed to prison for a crime that she had not conspired to commit.[45]

On Monday, November 28, Emily Burns was once again escorted across the street to the Adams County Courthouse, where she and nine others whose trials were held during this term of the circuit court were to be sentenced. Before imposing her sentence, Judge Corban told Emily that he believed she "had committed the crime through bad company" and then asked if she wished to make a statement. She did. "I am not guilty," she said, "but so long as the jury has found this verdict, I ask the mercy of the court." And with that, the next words she heard were "Emily Burns, you are hereby sentenced to serve the rest of your natural life in the state penitentiary."[46]

The woman whom friends and family called "Sister" had been in the Adams County jail since mid-August. Her trial moved so swiftly she barely had a chance to process what was happening to her. She did not kill Jennie Merrill, but she was convicted as if she had. Dick Dana and Octavia Dockery were just as guilty, if not more so, and yet they were set free. They were there the night when it all went wrong. But having grown up in Natchez, Sister understood that the life of a Negro was dispensable. Now she knew it firsthand, as she sat in her cell bearing the weight of a life sentence.

In her one last week there before beginning her incarceration at the Mississippi State Penitentiary, known as Parchman, no evidence exists to suggest that she had any visitors. The following Monday, December 5, the prison's traveling sergeant, Chester Tullos, arrived in Natchez to escort her and seven others to the penitentiary. In addition to Emily Burns, one other woman and six men, only two of whom were white, had also been sentenced to prison. After being shackled in leg cuffs and linked by the long chain that kept prisoners together, Sister and the others shuffled slowly out of the Adams County jail and stepped up into the paddy wagon. As traveling sergeant, Tullos drove to local jails to pick up prisoners headed to Sunflower County. It was a fairly routine job, but it was not without its risks. Five months after he made the trip to Adams County, two prisoners he picked up in Hattiesburg overpowered a fellow officer, took his gun, and shot and killed Tullos, escaping with the paddy wagon. Their desire to avoid Parchman's brutality was that strong.[47]

Sister had probably never been outside of Adams County, having lived her entire life to that point in Natchez, much of it at the corner of St. Catherine Street and Cedar Alley. She was just thirty-seven years old. A widow, she was a poor woman by any definition. She had worked hard as a laundress for much of her life—a life that had dealt her a tough hand. Now as she sat in the back of the paddy wagon bouncing along rough roads on her way to the prison farm in the Delta, Sister knew it was only going to get worse.

CHAPTER TEN

HOLLOW VICTORY

E mily Burns's conviction and life prison sentence did not satisfy every white Natchezean, least of all Book Roberts and Octavia Dockery. The sheriff had spent countless hours collecting evidence that he was sure would return indictments against her and Dick Dana. Yet not only had the pair been allowed to leave jail on their own recognizance and earn money from their notoriety, but District Attorney Clay Tucker refused to indict either of them for alleged lack of evidence. On the other hand, Octavia felt certain that the sheriff had besmirched her name by arresting her and then charging both Dick and her with murder.

Emily's conviction proved to be a hollow victory for both the sheriff and the Goat Woman. In Book Roberts's mind, the murder of Jennie Merrill remained an open case until Octavia Dockery stood trial for the role she played. And as far as Octavia Dockery was concerned, her reputation had been injured by the whole affair, and she held the sheriff responsible. Their disdain for one another simmered for months following the trial. Then, almost a year to the day Jennie Merrill was found dead, those frustrations boiled over.

Life in Natchez slowly returned to normal in the months following the trial. While people continued to discuss the case, most were relieved that the tragedy of Jennie Merrill's murder, the circus-like atmosphere surrounding the investigation, and the revelations stemming from Goat Castle were behind them. Or so they thought.

Locals busied themselves preparing for the second annual pilgrimage of homes. The Natchez Garden Club, buoyed by the success of the first pilgrim-

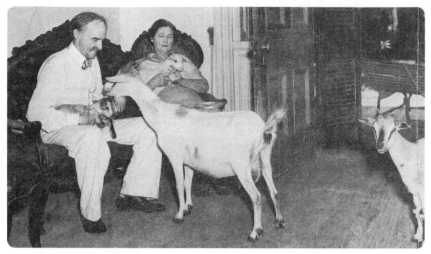

Dick Dana and Octavia Dockery inside Glenwood
with their goats, ca. 1933. This and other images of the pair
and their goats circulated in newspapers nationwide.

age, was steadily working with homeowners in anticipation of the onslaught
of visitors from around the country eager to experience antebellum grandeur.
The nation's leading newspaper, the *New York Times*, advised visitors to set
aside at least two days to see all of the twenty-two homes scheduled to be
open, while *Better Homes and Gardens* planned an illustrated feature story
with Katherine Miller, the garden club's publicity chair. Black Natchezeans
were instrumental to the success of the pilgrimage, too. Several of the women
planned to dress as mammies and serve food, while men in top hats and tails
intended to work as carriage drivers taking tourists from home to home. A
blended choir from several black churches also spent hours practicing for a
concert of Negro spirituals called "Heaven Bound" to raise money for their
schools.[1]

The people advising Dick Dana and Octavia Dockery assisted them in pro-
moting their ruinous home and estate among pilgrimage visitors, too, taking advantage of the groundwork laid by the garden club. In the months following their release from jail, the pair regularly welcomed paying tourists to
Glenwood. Twenty-five cents allowed people to see the grounds, and an extra
twenty-five cents gained them admission to the house.

In anticipation of the thousands of visitors who were expected to be in Nat-

Goat Castle flyer advertising tours and promises of restoration, ca. 1933.
(Courtesy of the Thomas H. and Joan W. Gandy Photograph Collection,
Louisiana and Lower Mississippi Valley Collections, Special Collections,
Hill Memorial Library, Louisiana State University Libraries, Baton Rouge.)

chez for the annual pilgrimage, Dick and Octavia's advisers, the group known
as "the committee," printed and distributed flyers inviting those same tourists to visit "beautiful historic Glenwood." At least that was the caption that
accompanied the photo of the run-down house on the leaflet. In even larger
letters, it advertised "GOAT CASTLE" as "Internationally Famous." And because
they showcased family heirlooms, the two listed their home as the "Dana and
Dockery Museum." The flyer was marketed directly to pilgrimage visitors
who were promised entertainment, namely one of Dick's piano recitals. There
was also their plea to "Help the 'Old Folks' Restore Glenwood."[2]

Of course, little restoration took place at Glenwood. It was too far gone. Dick and Octavia, in fact, could not even afford to pay taxes on the place and had not done so for years. Charles Zerkowsky's heirs, who owned quite a bit of dilapidated property in town, including the home Emily and her mother had rented on St. Catherine Street, held title to Glenwood. Yet collecting admissions is how Dick and Octavia survived for years following the trial, not one cent of which went to paying their debts.

Members of the Natchez Garden Club never publicly mentioned Goat Castle, since their goal was to promote the splendor of the Old South. They tried ignoring it, but the media would not let them. Several years of successful pilgrimages did not prevent the *Saturday Evening Post* from mentioning the unmentionable in a lengthy article intended to promote the now nationally famous tourist event. "There is [an] independent Pilgrimage, so to speak, of which Natchez would just as [well] not talk," the article stated. "For twenty-five cents the visitor may see another old mansion, Glenwood, better known since 1932 as Goat Castle, a side show which might have been plagiarized from a story by William Faulkner." Tucked in between beautiful photographs of Natchez, the article referenced the murder of Jennie Merrill, and the magazine reminded its readers that while Dick Dana "was absolved of the crime," it did not happen "before squalorous Goat Castle had been described in word and photograph in every paper in America."[3]

While Dick and Octavia made money off of their notoriety, Book Roberts decided to tell his side of the story to a crime writer from Memphis named Homer G. Wells. Wells, a former coroner and detective, regularly wrote for crime magazines and offered to write about the by-now nationally famous Merrill murder for *Master Detective*. In a five-part series that began in May 1933, Wells offered a dramatic retelling of what he called "The Crimson Crime at Glenburney Manor."[4]

Several details that were public knowledge made it into the *Master Detective* series, as well as behind-the-scenes revelations. The sheriff's story "as told to" Wells provided details and dialogue that may or may not have occurred but helped to dramatize an already vivid tale of intrigue. In newspaper coverage, for example, the public learned very little about Emily's mother, Nellie Black. In Wells's account, though, she comes to life. Nellie is described as a "typical 'old mammy' whose portly figure was topped by a gingham bonnet that covered graying hair braided close to the scalp." Readers also "hear" from Nellie in this retelling as she discusses her daughter's relationship with George Pearls. "My gal and dat scampish nigger from the No'th lef' de house befo' dark dat evening and dey didn't come back 'til late dat night," she allegedly told Sheriff Roberts, who believed that "her voice had the ring of truth." Whether she looked as Wells described her, said those words, or spoke in the dialect that he used may never be known. But it was in keeping with the stereotypes people believed about southern black women of the time.[5]

If the story is to be believed in its entirety, readers learn why Edgar Allan Poe Newell was not charged as an accessory in the murder of Jennie Merrill. Emily Burns made several confessions implicating him. Deputies arrested Newell and went so far as to take him to Jackson to secure a confession. Yet in Book's retelling of the story to Wells, Ed Newell claimed to be in downtown Natchez at the time the crime occurred and provided the names of "several reputable citizens" who could testify to his whereabouts.[6]

While Homer Wells freely used the real names of nearly everyone associated with the crime and investigation, the names and relationship of Dick Dana and Octavia Dockery are changed, even though photographs of the pair and their home illustrate the story. Anyone familiar with the case, however, would know that "Mr. Jack and his wife" are Dana and Dockery. Yet Book Roberts, who vowed to continue the investigation after Emily Burns's trial, needed to be careful not to use their real names in the event the pair was eventually indicted for murder.[7]

Octavia may have heard about, or even read, the *Master Detective* series. Even if she had not, she remained convinced that the sheriff was responsible for exposing the life she once led in the shadows of Glenwood. Aside from him and the deputies who frequented the estate to settle disputes between her and Jennie Merrill, and the local blacks who lived and worked nearby, most people in Natchez had no idea that Octavia lived in such filth and decay. Neither were they aware of Dick's mental state and his "wild" habits. It had all remained hidden from public view until their arrest. As the anniversary of that day approached, her anger reached a tipping point.

That August, against the advice of "the committee," Octavia Dockery filed a civil lawsuit against Book Roberts on her own and a separate one on Dick Dana's behalf seeking damages in the total amount of $32,000 for their false arrest, mistreatment, and the humiliating publicity that followed. She named

Octavia Dockery in front of Goat Castle, 1933.
(Courtesy of the Sophia Smith Collection, Smith
College, Northampton, Mass.)

the National Surety Company of New York as a codefendant since it provided
the official bond on the sheriff and insured him against such lawsuits. The firm
of Brandon and Brandon in Natchez, and very likely Gerard Brandon himself,
drafted the documents, but she personally filed both cases without hiring any
attorney to represent her.[8]

In her civil suit, Octavia claimed that Sheriff Roberts came to Glenwood
"late at night, being early in the morning of the 5th day of August," and entered the house and the "bedroom to which she had retired for the night" and
falsely arrested her "without any warrant, without just cause, and without

reasonable ground to suspect that [she] had committed a felony." Her suit also alleged that the sheriff did not inform her of why he was there and "at no time during her false arrest and imprisonment did [he] make any formal charge against her."[9]

The suit went even further in its allegations by complaining that Sheriff Roberts and his deputies also subjected her "to cruel and humiliating questionings, examinations and inquisitions, and to humiliating associations with criminals and persons charged with the crime." The latter part of Octavia's accusation revealed her anger for having her name associated with the two black persons held responsible for Merrill's murder—George Pearls and Emily Burns. Her lawsuit also alleged that the sheriff and his deputies "did brow-beat and threaten [her] with physical violence," something Emily Burns experienced though without any recourse of the law. These same men, Octavia believed, used "unlawful means and trickery" in an attempt to "extort" a confession from her for a crime of which, she adamantly declared, she was innocent. Octavia also claimed that they took her fingerprints "forcibly" and then "subjected her to being photographed, viewed, and interviewed under humiliating circumstances," even though she posed for the camera and spoke freely of her life with reporters. All of it, she claimed, caused her "to suffer great mental anguish, humiliation, shame, and physical suffering," not to mention the "loss of sleep and rest."[10]

In addition to her alleged personal suffering, Dockery held Roberts responsible for the items that went missing from Glenwood in the days following the pair's arrest. Not only had he not kept away trespassers, but she also claimed that by failing to provide a custodian for the property he was responsible for the personal property removed from their home, which she valued at $1,000. That amount, along with the $10,000 in damages she sought for false arrest and imprisonment and the $5,000 in punitive damages, brought the total to $16,000—the very same amount she sought on Dick's behalf.[11]

Book Roberts once told a reporter, "I hope I never see Dana and Miss Dockery again."[12] Together they had made a spectacle not only of themselves but also of the murder investigation. A year after the case seemed to run its course, there was still no relief. Octavia had filed a civil suit and another one on Dick's behalf seeking damages against him and the company that insured his work as an officer of the law. But through his attorneys he answered back and filed a "notice under the general issue" detailing the evidence he intended to produce at trial.[13]

According to Sheriff Roberts, it was while he was in the process of investigating the whereabouts of Jennie Merrill that "he was informed [she] had been killed" prior to the time he arrested Dockery, a clear reference to Dick Dana's unsolicited statement "I know nothing of the murder." Book had first arrested Dick, who then rambled on about what had happened earlier that evening and subsequently implicated Octavia, which is why the sheriff went back inside Glenwood and arrested her, too. In response to Dockery's allegations, Roberts also referred to the "conduct and statements" she had made to him and his deputies, which gave them "just and reasonable cause to believe" that she was "connected with [the murder] either as a principal or as an accessory before or after the fact." Given this, he regarded it as his duty to arrest her without a warrant and that he was legally justified in entering her residence and taking her into custody so he could question her about the "facts and circumstances surrounding the killing [of] Miss Jane Merrill." He did not even mention the numerous visits he and his deputies had made to Glenburnie and Glenwood to settle arguments between Merrill and Dockery over trespassing animals, including a particularly vicious exchange in the days before Merrill's murder.[14]

Book Roberts's response to the civil suit made it clear that he believed Octavia acted "either as a principal or as an accessory" in the murder of Jennie Merrill. He also maintained that keeping her in jail was "reasonable and proper" and replied to her allegations of physical threats and browbeating by arguing that she had never been mistreated and that interrogations of her were made legally and during "reasonable hours." Octavia knew very well why she was in jail because he had "fully advised" her of the reasons for her arrest "and of the crime then being investigated."[15]

Dick and Octavia's claims of humiliation did not go unanswered. Here, Roberts finally got in his licks. Not only had they not suffered from embarrassing publicity, his attorneys countered, but also both of them "made capital thereof, and by written advertisements and publication . . . created much additional publicity." Dockery distributed flyers "throughout the State of Mississippi and the State of Louisiana and elsewhere." She even "took unto herself the stage name of 'Goat Woman'" and called her home with Dana "Goat Castle." Under their advertised names of "Wild Man" and "Goat Woman," the pair traveled throughout Mississippi and Louisiana and made public appearances "in alleged concerts and performances." While doing so, they "greatly benefited financially" and "made large profits" based on the circumstances surrounding their arrest, an arrest the lawsuits against him claimed to have caused them both great injury.[16]

Last, and in response to the allegation of "humiliating associations" with those who were subsequently charged with the crime, Roberts's attorneys were clear. In the advertising and publicity of Dana and Dockery's public performances, they made "unmistakable reference" to their connection with the crime and its principals by the use of "Goat Woman," "Wild Man," and "Goat Castle"—nicknames given to the pair and their home "through newspapers and magazines" that covered the crime and by which the story circulated throughout the country. In sum, Dick and Octavia had capitalized on their arrest and confinement.[17]

———————

For over a year, Book Roberts had demonstrated the patience of Job where it concerned the couple from Glenwood. The civil lawsuit, however, was the last straw. As the November term of the Adams County Circuit Court approached, little did Dick and Octavia know that Roberts had been busy securing evidence needed to indict the pair for Jennie Merrill's murder. Octavia, who filed her civil suit in August, was ready for her face-off with the sheriff when Deputies Joseph Stone and Pat Mulvihill showed up at her door on Wednesday, November 15. Both she and Dick assumed the men were there about the matter of their civil suit. Instead, the deputies were there to arrest them—again—for the murder of Jennie Merrill. They vigorously protested to no avail as the deputies took them into custody and straight to the Adams County jail, where they were held under a bond of $1,000 each. Later that day, they were arraigned before Judge Robert Corban, where District Attorney Clay Tucker read aloud the joint indictment of the pair as accessories in Merrill's murder.[18]

Dick and Octavia's indictment for murder came on the very day that their civil suit against Sheriff Roberts was to be heard. Gerard Brandon, Ed Ratcliff, and Everett Truly from Truly and Truly in Fayette had just signed onto the civil suit, since Octavia had filed it without an attorney. So, when they went into court that day, they had not counted on representing her and Dick Dana in the murder charge, too, even though they subsequently requested to be their court-appointed attorneys. Given the short timeline, their first action was to request a continuance in the civil suit while they dealt with the murder charge. Ratcliff then stated that he planned to file a motion for the couple's release.[19]

Book Roberts was ready. His attorneys, Laurens Kennedy—who had previously defended Octavia Dockery in her cases with Jennie Merrill—and C. F. Engle, objected to a delay in the civil suit, arguing they were prepared for the case. For his part, the sheriff ordered his deputies at the jail "not to release the two without his personal sanction of the bond." Judge Corban, the same judge who had presided over Emily Burns's trial, declared the entire proceeding "the most peculiar [I've] ever known since being on the bench." But he gave lead attorney Gerard Brandon only until the following morning to make the case for a continuance, adding that Book Roberts, as the chief officer of the county, could not perform his duties with "a civil suit pending against him indefinitely."[20]

The following morning, attorneys for Glenwood's residents lost their bid for a continuance. Certainly, the reasons for their motion were legitimate. They had only just entered the civil case and needed simultaneously to prepare to defend Dana and Dockery on the murder charge. They also argued that they would not let their clients testify in the civil suit because "it might be prejudicial to their interests in the forthcoming murder trial."[21]

Attorneys on both sides clashed bitterly during the hearing, and one particular exchange proved revelatory. In the midst of their arguments, attorneys for the sheriff disclosed that "not only had the grand jury of the present term of court indicted Dana and Miss Dockery on charges of murder" but a previous grand jury had as well. This was an explicit reference to the November 1932 term of court when Emily Burns was indicted. That grand jury had voted 11–8 to indict Dick Dana and Octavia Dockery as accessories in the murder of Jennie Merrill. And they would have indeed been indicted, if only District Attorney Clay Tucker had not felt there was insufficient evidence to try the case. Book had grudgingly agreed with Tucker not to indict the pair at that time, which he likely regretted, given the present circumstances.[22]

Judge Corban had heard enough. He dismissed the civil suit against Sheriff Roberts and then set the date for *The State v. Octavia Dockery and Richard Dana* for the following Wednesday.

Goat Castle's residents had to spend only one night in jail as two men stepped forward to pay their bond—William Logan and Isaac Zerkowsky. It was an odd coincidence that these particular men lent their assistance. A year earlier, Logan was one of Emily Burns's court-appointed attorneys. And Zerkowsky? He was one of Glenwood's mortgage holders. This was an interesting development, since Dick and Octavia were already indebted to him. They had been, and continued to be, squatters on the run-down estate, even while they collected admissions. Perhaps he helped pay their bond in order to legally protect his title to the property. Either way, Dick and Octavia walked out of jail a day after their arrest and promptly went to lunch at a "restaurant in a leading hotel," very likely the Hotel Eola. This time they were reluctant to speak to journalists except to say that they had been well treated while in jail and that the sheriff had sent a physician to see about Octavia, "who was slightly ill from the nervous reaction" to her arrest.[23]

Criminal cases were on the docket of the next week's circuit court. In an odd coincidence, another familiar face from the Merrill murder investigation was on trial the same week as Dick and Octavia. That Monday John Geiger, the man who had rented the Skunk's Nest from them and whose overcoat made him the subject of intense interrogation, was scheduled to go before Judge Corban for "desertion of children." His bad luck, and association with Goat Castle, seemed to never end.[24]

As Wednesday approached, there was already speculation that the court would have difficulty seating a jury to try the case against Dana and Dockery. DA Clay Tucker hinted that he planned on bringing in a "witness from the state penitentiary," an obvious reference to Emily Burns. Surprisingly, Octavia had nothing to say. But Dick Dana, who loved to chat with the press, made a surprisingly lucid statement. "Our case is in the hands of our attorneys and . . . we will abide by whatever they think best," he said. "We are anxious for the trial to be held and to get it over with."[25]

When Wednesday arrived, Dick and Octavia's attorneys filed, and received, a motion for severance to allow the two to be tried separately. Octavia's trial was scheduled first, for the following Monday. Her attorneys also succeeded in having Book Roberts temporarily removed from his duties as sheriff, citing his personal interest in the case. Because the sheriff issued subpoenas for trial witnesses, there was concern that his "bias and prejudice" against the defendant might be damaging to her case. Judge Corban appointed Ned Smith, the county coroner, to serve as acting sheriff for the duration of the trial.[26]

While those motions were successful, Octavia's attorneys failed in their motion to strike the names of George Pearls and Emily Burns from the indictment against her. They argued that since Pearls was now dead and Emily had already been convicted as an accessory and sent to prison, "no good can be accomplished" by the inclusion of their names and that doing so was "highly and improperly prejudicial" to their client. It went without saying that Octavia did not want her name associated with two guilty "negroes." Nonetheless, the indictment remained as written for her upcoming trial.[27]

Sheriff Roberts reopened the case, he said, because of "secret new evidence" that he had acquired since the fall of 1932. But it was not that simple. Dick and Octavia's attorneys were probably right to suggest that he had a personal interest in the outcome of the case, especially on the heels of their civil suit. "I'm anxious to have the case reopened," he told a New Orleans reporter, adding, "I'm tired of those people making money and getting all this publicity at my expense."[28]

Natchez, the *Times Picayune* reported, awaited Roberts's revelations "with a sort of exasperated eagerness," because they thought the "airing of skeletons in the 'Goat Castle' imbroglio was over." People in town, it seemed, had grown weary of the whole affair. They were "never fond of the sensational publicity" and wanted it all to go away. Yet, a woman was murdered, and members of her family—it was never disclosed who—still sought justice, enough that they retained former district attorney Bob Bennett, known as a relentless prosecutor, to assist the state's attorneys.[29]

Several of the witnesses from Emily Burns's trial were subpoenaed to return for Dockery's trial, including Maurice O'Neill, Duncan Minor, Edgar "Poe" Newell, Zula Curtis, and several officers. Emily Burns, too, was brought back from Parchman to serve as a witness for both the state and the defense. There was an additional black witness, Richard Blanton, whose name was never mentioned until this trial but whom the defense planned to call to offer Octavia an alibi. According to her, the two were engaged in an argument that lasted until well after the time of Jennie Merrill's murder, even though in her civil suit she alleged she had retired to Glenwood for the evening when shots were fired.[30]

On the day of her trial, Octavia headed into town two hours early to confer with her attorneys. She wore a black coat with a fur collar, a navy-blue felt hat, a blue dress with a blue and white matching scarf, and brown shoes. Dick showed up later, closer to the time of the trial, wearing a gray suit, a striped shirt, and a "peacock-blue silk tie." In his pocket appeared to be a new pen and pencil set. His hair was neatly cut, and his "wild man" whiskers had been traded in for a "Vandyke" beard. He refused offers for a ride into town, he said, and called a taxi because he "had plenty of money now that people were paying to look [at] Goat Castle."[31]

The courtroom was packed for *The State v. Octavia Dockery*. Acting sheriff Ned Smith even "placed extra seats in the courtroom for women attending the trial" whose constitutions were clearly strong enough to hear the grotesque details of not only the murder but also Goat Castle. Many of them remained curious as to how Octavia Dockery went from the "charmed, cultured girl" to the "Goat Woman." Dick Dana's appearance and behavior could be dismissed, but "no one has ever suggested that her mind went to pieces with the years," a reporter noted.[32]

Octavia and Dick both gave statements to the press as they headed into court. "It's ridiculous to charge us with this murder," she said. "I worked hard that day and was awakened by the shots, but I paid no attention as I thought some of our Negro neighbors were having domestic troubles," she said, declaring, "We feel confident we will be acquitted." Dana, too, felt that they would be "free of charges for this murder." He told reporters, "Of course, I heard the shots, and started to go out, but Miss Dockery told me it was probably just some Negroes fighting, so we didn't need to leave home." She may have coached him on what to say, but then Dick, always the performer, improvised. "My only regret," he said, "is that our lawyers refuse to allow us to be photographed, but I suppose they know what's best."[33]

Given the enormous publicity surrounding the case, defense attorneys had requested a special venire of two hundred men to be summoned for possible jury service. Dick sat next to Octavia during jury selection, occasionally stroking his beard and putting on his horn-rimmed glasses to read the newspaper. From time to time, Octavia chatted with "stylishly dressed women who pressed closer to be near her."[34]

One by one the men called to jury duty were dismissed. When court adjourned at 6:30 P.M., Judge Corban ordered an additional venire of one hundred men be summoned. Once again, man after man was dismissed. Many of them claimed to have fixed opinions about the case, while others claimed that they were opposed to the death penalty. The latter may have been true, since not even Emily Burns received that sentence. A third reason potential jurors were dismissed was a defense strategy that Dockery's attorneys hoped would lead to a mistrial—they eliminated men who were delinquent in paying their poll taxes. So often, failure to pay this tax was used to the detriment of black citizenship—to prevent them from voting—but in this case it was applied to poor white men to prevent them from jury service.[35]

On Tuesday afternoon, after a second day of failing to secure twelve male jurors, Judge Corban called a "cessat" to the proceedings. "As I see it, it is impossible to get a jury in Adams County for the trial in this case," he said. "The ends of justice must be served," Corban continued, and "in a murder case it is essential that there be a fair and impartial jury. So much publicity has been given this case, it has been joked about so much and discussed, not only here, but all over the country, that I see no chance of it to go to trial at the present term of circuit court." The same scenario applied to the case against Dick Dana, so he, too, avoided trial. While a cessat meant that a future court could take up the case, it was very unlikely.[36]

When the judge declared a mistrial, the court erupted. The *Natchez Democrat* described it as a "short demonstration on the part of some of the spectators," but the *Times Picayune* correspondent Gwen Bristow, who had always provided more detailed accounts of the case, described it differently. "Thunderous applause greeted [Judge Corban's] announcement," which, she noted, "court officials tried in vain to stop." After the announcement, moreover, a "throng pressed around Dana and Miss Dockery to offer congratulations, making it impossible for some minutes for persons in the front of the courtroom to leave their places."[37]

As Octavia Dockery left the Adams County Courthouse and headed back to Glenwood, she called the trial a "farce" and asked that she and Dick be left in peace. Book Roberts did not speak to the press. His "secret new evidence" would never be heard. Not to be outdone, Octavia had one more surprise for him. Less than ten days after the mistrial, she appealed the dismissal of her civil suit against the sheriff to the Mississippi Supreme Court.[38]

CHAPTER ELEVEN

LONGING FOR HOME

E mily Burns arrived at the Mississippi State Penitentiary on the afternoon
of December 5, 1932. Nervous and afraid, she was taken from the paddy
wagon to a room where she waited for a white woman named Ola Mae
Spickard, the prison registrar, to call her name. Spickard had registered
thousands of convicts since she began working at Parchman in 1907, a year
after it opened. Emily Burns would be one of her last before retirement, and
yet hers was just another face whose humanity went unnoticed as Spickard
filled out the cards for the more than one hundred men and women who entered prison that day.[1]

When Sister stepped forward, Spickard jotted down her crime and sentence:
Murder. Life. County of conviction: Adams. Then she filled in the blanks that
detailed Sister's identity, appearance, and background. Name: Emily Burns.
Age: 37. Height and weight: 5'1" and 105 lbs. Hair: Black. Eyes: Black. Com-
plexion: Brown. Face: Oval. Mouth: Large. Teeth: Good. Nose: Small. Eye-
brows: Medium. Education in years: 5th grade. Her closest living relative was
her mother, Nellie Black. Her most recent occupation was listed as "maid."
Spickard also recorded her religion—Baptist. Sister and her family were longtime members of Antioch Baptist Church, but on this day she joined a different
kind of congregation, becoming Convict No. 7290.[2]

The overwhelming majority of prisoners at Parchman were black men, and
the majority of women who were incarcerated there were also black. On the
same day Emily Burns entered the penitentiary, Ethel Reed, a twenty-three-
year-old black farm laborer, also from Natchez, began her one-year sentence
for robbery. They joined other women, black and white, who only recently arrived to serve their sentences. They included Pearly Love, a seventeen-year-old
black housemaid sentenced to seven months for burglary, and Mary Jernigan,

a twenty-seven-year-old white woman who received a five-year sentence as an accessory to murder, as opposed to Emily's life sentence for the same conviction. There was also a forty-three-year-old white housekeeper named Mary Bowers, who willingly pled guilty to killing her husband and brother-in-law. She fed them both poisoned biscuits because the latter had "paid too much attention to her daughter from a previous marriage." All told, sixty-six women were incarcerated that year—a number that fluctuated to as high as eighty over the next decade. All of them, except for the white women assigned to the superintendent's home or perhaps a sergeant's home, were placed in Camp 13—the Women's Camp.[3]

———

Parchman. Just the name conjured images of a wretched place. Nearly sixteen thousand acres in size, it functioned like the antebellum plantations of a century earlier. This was the plan. Governor James K. Vardaman regarded the penal farm in the Mississippi Delta as the perfect place to discipline black criminals and teach them to respect white authority. It had opened in 1906, and he kept his promise by sending prisoners there from the old state penitentiary in Jackson, where they were put to work like their slave ancestors. Thousands of acres were given to planting cotton. They raised cattle and hogs, which were then slaughtered and used to feed prisoners. There was a small canning factory for putting up the vegetables—mostly peas and corn—and a sewing room, where female prisoners made the striped convict clothing known as the "ring arounds" and the "up and downs."[4]

Women like Sister did it all—picked cotton, slaughtered hogs, canned food, and sewed stripes, bed ticking, and cotton sacks. She worked six days a week. Her day began at 4:30 when Rubin Sledge, the sergeant for the women's camp, rapped a stick on the iron bed she slept in to wake her. The days were twelve hours long, and the lights went out at 8:30 P.M. It was hard labor, day in and day out, and there was no rest but Sunday rest. Some women worked that day, too, in a desperate effort to shorten their sentences, because even though it was the Lord's Day, Parchman was a godforsaken place.[5]

Entering the penitentiary at any time in the Jim Crow era would have been difficult, but Emily Burns's incarceration began during one of the prison's most troubled periods. The Great Depression wreaked havoc on the prison budget at a time when the number of prisoners was growing exponentially.

Emily Burns worked long hours in the Parchman prison sewing room during the
eight years of her incarceration. This photo was taken in the 1930s during the time
she served. (Courtesy of the Archives and Records Services Division,
Mississippi Department of Archives & History, Jackson.)

O. G. Tann, the prison superintendent, tried desperately to convince the penitentiary board that conditions on the farm were dire. In the midst of the
economic downturn, the prison population had grown, on average, 20 percent
each year. But even with this growth, the state cut the prison budget in 1932
by 40 percent. Tann warned not only of overcrowding but also of the poor
condition of the wooden dormitories that were "old" and "hard to keep clean
and sanitary." He described one of the camps as a "regular firetrap." The one
physician assigned to look after thousands of prisoners' health expressed concern over a malaria outbreak that had also caused overcrowding in the prison
hospital.[6]

From its inception, Parchman was intended to be a self-sustaining operation
through sales of cotton and growing the food necessary to feed prisoners. The
fact that thousands of African Americans were sick and dying did not seem to
matter much to the state legislature. Tann's efforts to restore the budget fell
on deaf ears, so conditions in the camps got a lot worse before they got better. The little shacks that Sister knew along St. Catherine Street in Natchez
might have been poorly maintained, but they were far better than her new
accommodations.

Eight months after she arrived, Emily Burns got word that she was needed back in Natchez, but it was no homecoming. She would have to stay in a cell at the same Adams County jail where she had spent nearly four months before going to the penitentiary. Attorneys wanted her as a witness in the trial of Octavia Dockery. What could she say beyond what she had said at her own trial? Miss Dockery was there when Jennie Merrill was murdered. So was Mr. Dana. Yet she never got to testify in 1933 and tell the court once more what she knew to be true. There would be no trial, and the Goat Woman remained free.

Sister returned to Parchman, where the women had the blues as bad as the men. They sang about them, too. They had the "Long Line Blues," from working what seemed like unending rows of cotton they were forced to pick. Their blues spoke of homesickness, of being separated from their mothers, of feeling alone and friendless. No doubt Sister felt all of it. One of the women she knew from the Women's Camp, Fanny Walden, wrote a blues poem called "My Prison Life" that was close to her own experience in Adams County. Walden had also been convicted of murder, and her poem told a story that Sister knew all too well—about a swift trial, longing for home and family, and the awful day she left for prison when "the Long Chain Man appeared," shackled her, and took her to the penitentiary. Then there was the fear she felt that day she first saw the place where she was sentenced to spend the rest of her life.

> Arriving at Parchman just before night
> Oh, dear me: what an awful sight
> Convicts like Zebras, dressed in stripes
> Kerosine [*sic*] lanterns were used for lights.

The loneliness of prison was all too real, even among the group of women at camp. "Reluctant I sit on my bed tonight," Walden wrote,

> Looking up at the prison's gray walls
> No hope of release, no friend to cheer
> Ah, an Unseen Friend is never near.[7]

Women like Sister also prayed for mercy, hoping that one day they might be released from prison and allowed to go home. During her sentencing, Emily had asked for the court's mercy but received none. She left Natchez believing that she would never see her family or home again. But when she arrived at the prison, she learned that the governor occasionally came there and held what he called "mercy courts," where he sometimes set prisoners free. So she held onto this sliver of hope and prayed that she might be shown the mercy she never got in Adams County.

Governor Mike Connor started the tradition of holding mercy courts the year Sister began serving her time. Occasionally throughout the year he traveled to the state penitentiary, where he interviewed convicts, reviewed their files, and read petitions from citizens who vouched for prisoners they believed should be set free. And Connor did pardon some convicts and suspended their sentences. But not Sister's. A word from a sheriff or a prosecutor generally prevented any commutation of a prisoner's sentence. Had Sheriff Roberts or District Attorney Clay Tucker warned against her release? Perhaps. But this did not keep Emily Burns from seeking mercy, because she was innocent. So, she clung to hope in a hopeless place.[8]

Year after year she went before the governor's mercy court to plead for her release. She had no success with Governor Connor or his successor, Hugh White. But there came another governor, one who saw her case differently than the others had.

———————

Paul B. Johnson Sr. was sworn in as governor of Mississippi in January 1940. A former attorney, judge, and U.S. congressman from Hattiesburg, he had also grown up poor and identified with the plight of tenant farmers and sharecroppers. In his previous campaigns for governor, he called himself the "Champion for the Runt Pig People," and when he finally won he did so on the promise of instituting Franklin D. Roosevelt's New Deal reforms to help the poor and working class.[9]

Governor Johnson was no doubt familiar with the Merrill murder and the conviction of Emily Burns when he held what was called his "Christmastime mercy court" toward the end of his first year in office. He went to Parchman expecting to pardon or suspend the sentences of prisoners with records of good behavior. There, on December 18, 1940, he met Emily Burns.[10]

Dressed in her striped prison uniform, Sister got down on her knees and through her tears told the governor that she was "as innocent as a newborn babe." "I was convicted of something for which I was not guilty," she said. Governor Johnson carefully examined her record. Emily had proven her trustworthiness while in prison. She received a suspension of fifteen days in November 1938 and returned to prison a day early. This was followed by a ten-day suspension that December. It is unclear why she was offered these brief respites from the penitentiary — perhaps there had been a death in the family — but her good behavior made it possible.

Previous attempts to secure her release had been blocked by unnamed Adams County officials, and another group of Adams County citizens entered their own protest against granting her clemency during Governor Hugh White's term of office. Sister had gone before that governor and been rejected. Now she stood before a third governor, and what came next made Sister believe that her prayers had finally been heard.

Governor Johnson suspended Emily Burns's sentence indefinitely. As long as she maintained good behavior, she was free to go home and never return to Parchman. In suspending her sentence, he remarked that he did so "at the request of a large number of reputable citizens of Adams County." He also stated that he was "thoroughly convinced of [her] innocence" and that "she convinced him that she had been convicted on circumstantial evidence." In making his announcement, the governor also dismissed previous petitions against her release, saying, "When I am convinced that I am right, no man or a group of men can put pressure on me to make me change my mind."[11]

Emily Burns was free.

Sister was probably still in shock when she left Parchman the following day. She had labored there for eight solid years, from December 1932 to December 1940, doing backbreaking work, especially in the steamy heat of the prison sewing room. She had begged for mercy at every opportunity, from every governor, since she arrived. Year after year, her prayers went unanswered, but her faith was strong. Now she was free and headed home.

When Sister returned to Natchez, not much had changed in her old neighborhood. St. Catherine Street was still bustling with activity, even though the Rhythm Club that hosted jazz bands had burned down the April before her release. More than two hundred men and women had died in the fire, including several former friends and neighbors, devastating the black community. Her cousin Alfred Smith pulled several people to safety before the club was engulfed in flames.[12] The home she shared with her mother, on the corner of St.

Catherine and Cedar Alley, was still standing. It was also where she returned to live, despite its memories of Pink and her arrest there eight years before.

Sister learned that Dick Dana and Octavia Dockery, who went free while she lost eight years of her life to a prison sentence, were still making money on tours of their disgusting house out on the Kingston Road. But she had no desire to ever set eyes on them again. She also had to earn a living, and her time in Parchman's sewing room had provided her with a new skill. She no longer had to take in boarders or wash clothes; rather, Sister became a seamstress.

She was now forty-five years old. While St. Catherine Street had not changed much, she was changed forever. She might tell friends, family, and neighbors about what it was like on that prison farm, but only she knew its brutality. It was probably best to try and forget, if she could. She did that, in part, by returning to her home church, Antioch Baptist, where she could worship with her family, give thanks to her Lord, and replenish her spirit.

Sister knew all too well that freedom could be fleeting, especially for black men and women in Natchez. It could be taken from them in the blink of an eye. So she silently cherished it and put her faith in God to help her make a way forward.

EPILOGUE

Natchez was unable to escape the southern gothic narrative of Goat Castle for decades following Jennie Merrill's murder. Americans remained captivated by the spectacle of a dilapidated antebellum mansion teaming with animals, the quirky ramblings of Dick Dana, and the social decline of once respected southern families. Some may have also concluded that William Faulkner had been telling the truth.

White Natchezeans, especially members of the garden club, did their best to ignore this story of southern degradation. Their annual pilgrimage of homes celebrated Old South romance. It, too, garnered national media attention. Year in and year out, thousands of tourists traveled to their small town on the bluffs of the Mississippi River to see the mansions of another era. Nonetheless, the specter of Goat Castle continued to cast its eerie shadow over the pageantry of antebellum splendor. And the touring public found both fascinating.

———————

After escaping a murder trial in 1933, Octavia Dockery and Dick Dana went back to their lives at Glenwood and continued to offer tours, making money under the guise of restoring their shell of a home to its former glory. Yet they didn't own the house. Charles Zerkowsky had held the mortgage to the property since the 1920s. He died without taking complete ownership, so his heirs now had the burden of what to do with a ruinous estate and two well-known squatters who refused to leave.

Years passed and Dick, Octavia, and the goats remained at Glenwood. From time to time, one of Zerkowsky's heirs went to the estate to try to convince them to leave. After one of these visits, Octavia and Dick staged a "sit-down strike" to avoid eviction. She fought, tooth and nail, any attempts at foreclosure.

In 1937, likely at Octavia's behest, journalists reported that she and Dick were being threatened with eviction. Isaac Zerkowsky, one of the men who helped pay the $1,000 bond that set her free in 1933, reassured the press this was not the case. "I am no Simon Legree," he said. "I did try to persuade them to leave, but they refused," he stated, adding, "Many of my friends have almost stopped speaking to me on account of this 'Goat Castle' business. I am not going to throw those old people out."[1]

Octavia Dockery repeatedly proved herself to be a formidable adversary, and a litigious one at that, all in an effort to hold onto Glenwood. When another heir, Seaman Zerkowsky, succeeded in getting the Adams County Chancery Court to foreclose on the property, Octavia filed an appeal to the Mississippi Supreme Court, which later upheld the lower court's decision. She may have lost the battle but not the war. She and Dick held on to Glenwood for another decade, even as the house was literally falling down around them.[2]

During that time, in 1939, Duncan Minor died. He spent three years fending off Nellie Grist's claim to Jennie's estate until she finally withdrew her lawsuit in 1935. She once said she had no idea why she was told of Merrill's death but later claimed that she was Jennie's illegitimate daughter. Her attorney, Ed Jackson, the former governor of Indiana, told reporters that Merrill traveled to his state in 1902, where she had a baby girl. Minor pronounced the story "preposterous" and Grist's challenge to Jennie's will an attempt at blackmail. Still, it took three years of litigation before Grist finally dropped her suit, eventually saying that it was a case of mistaken identity. By then, the story had generated even more rumors about Duncan's relationship with Jennie.[3]

Dick Dana, like Octavia, was growing old and frail. On October 10, 1948, at the age of seventy-seven, he died of pneumonia and other complications, still a resident of Glenwood. The *New York Times* recounted the life of the "Master of Goat Castle" in an obituary that recalled the details of his arrest in the murder of the "ambassador's daughter" as well as his Dana ancestry. His funeral was held at the church his father once served, Trinity Episcopal, before he was laid to rest in the family plot in the Natchez City Cemetery. The *Times* also referred to Goat Castle by saying, "Most of the goats have died, and Miss Dockery continues to live there alone."[4]

The Zerkowskys likely believed they could now assume control of the estate. Because public sympathy had long rested with Dick and Octavia, they never forced an eviction, even though they had legal title to the property and could have done so. They had paid property taxes for years with no hope of recovering their money from the impoverished and aged pair. Certainly, in the wake of Dick's death, the Zerkowskys thought they could move forward. They were wrong.

At eighty-three, and in failing health in the months following Dick's death, Octavia had one more card to play. In February 1949, she filed a bill of complaint asserting that she now owned the estate because she and Dick had been man and wife. Her suit claimed the two were wed in a ceremony in 1902 and had lived at Glenwood as man and wife since that time. Octavia also claimed she and Dick were "generally recognized as man and wife and assumed all the duties and relationships of husband and wife to each other." She named Isaac, Sam, and Seaman Zerkowsky in her suit, along with Jeanette Habas, all of whom now co-owned the property. In it, she asserted that as Dick's widow, she was entitled to the property that had been left to him in his mother's will. The Zerkowskys answered that she had never been known as "Mrs. R. H. C. Dana" and that her claims to the property were "wholly fictitious, false and pretended," which they were.[5]

Only a few weeks after filing this lawsuit, Octavia Dockery died. The news of her death, like that of Dick Dana, made national headlines. The *New York Times* carried her obituary, as well as the story of her connection to the Merrill murder and, of course, her herd of goats. Yet it was the headline in the *Delta Times-Democrat* (Greenville, Miss.) that captured her resolve to keep Glenwood. It read "Death Won Case for Miss Dockery." This was not hyperbole. She had literally maintained a death grip on Goat Castle.[6]

In June, the children of her paternal uncle filed a claim to her personal belongings and came to Natchez, where they held an auction on-site at Glenwood. The Zerkowskys immediately dispensed with the estate, selling it to a developer. Then in 1955, Goat Castle was razed and a modern housing development of ranch homes took its place. They named the new neighborhood "Glenwood," so that today "Goat Castle" is nothing more than a memory.

───────────

Events in Natchez in 1932 demonstrated how little progress had been made between former masters and former slaves since emancipation. There, as it was throughout the South during the era of Jim Crow, the lives of blacks and whites remained intertwined even with laws meant to segregate them. And, in many ways, race relations looked as they had a century before. Jennie Merrill, whose ancestors had been wealthy slave owners, was still wealthy, and she maintained a relationship with African Americans similar to that of her parents in that she saw them as a servant class of people. She had a live-in cook and black families who worked and lived on her estate. On the other hand, black women like Emily Burns and her mother, Nellie Black, whose ancestors were slaves on plantations in Adams County and Concordia Parish, may not have had to pick cotton, but in town they were relegated to domestic work for white families as their maids, cooks, and laundresses.

In truth, opportunities to work independent of whites were few and far between in Jim Crow Mississippi. Ed "Poe" Newell had such a job, as an embalmer for a black funeral home. Others, like Lawrence "Pink" Williams, left Natchez for Chicago, where he changed his name, to escape the "southern way of life." He found work in a corn refinery only to lose it during the Depression, which forced him back to Mississippi in hopes of finding work with his former employer, Duncan Minor, whose parents owned slaves—perhaps even Pink's own parents.

Dick and Octavia, poor whites believed to have a respectable lineage, frequently interacted with local blacks, too. From time to time, they hired men to help them with farming, livestock, and, later, to collect admission from tourists at the front gate of Goat Castle. Sheriff Clarence Roberts, too, relied on his relationship with local blacks. He hired a trusty at the jail, for example, because he knew very well that African American men and women had good reason not to put their faith in white men who upheld laws that held them down. So, what appeared to be willing assistance from members of the black community was very often predicated on fear, since they, too, could find themselves in jail.

Jennie Merrill, Duncan Minor, Dick Dana, Octavia Dockery, Lawrence Williams/George Pearls, and Emily Burns—white and black—are forever connected by a crime. But it was one that revealed the everyday interactions between the races in a place like Natchez, where the majority of the population was African American. Williams had interacted with all of them. Sister, much to her regret, had accompanied him on an evening stroll that placed her at Jennie Merrill's home along with Dick Dana and Octavia Dockery. Then there were Octavia's dealings with Williams. They met and talked and plotted together. She probably planted the seed of robbing Jennie Merrill—a neighbor she despised and whom she knew was wealthy. She may have pretended later not to know Emily Burns, but she could afford to plead ignorance because her word as a white woman trumped anything a black woman might say. And yet,

Octavia knew who Emily Burns was and carried with her the memory of that evening at Glenburnie whether or not she ever admitted to it. Sister carried that memory, too, as well as the injustice she endured. She was the other victim in this crime, wronged not simply because of her interaction with Octavia Dockery, but by merely being born black in a place and at a time when black women were particularly vulnerable to the dictates of white society.

Emily Burns and Octavia Dockery lived far different lives in the aftermath of the Merrill murder. Aside from the double standard of justice that sent one home and the other to prison, Octavia Dockery, and not Emily Burns, is the woman who never escaped her ties to the murder of Jennie Merrill. Whites in Natchez swiftly forgot about the woman who was punished, but have yet to forget Octavia Dockery and the fact that she and Dick Dana were implicated. Even her headstone reads "Mistress of Goat Castle," which would lead the curious to ask, "Why?"

Within the black community, the memory of Sister's involvement and incarceration seems to have vanished except among family and a few others. Duncan Morgan, a respected member of the African American community and of Holy Family Catholic Church, recalled knowing Emily Burns from when he was a young boy in the 1950s. She lived across the street from him. Children from the neighborhood, he remembered, sometimes made cruel comments to her about the crime, and she defended herself, he said, by saying, "All I did was carry the lamp."[7] Several of Emily's second cousins, including Birdia Green, learned very little about the case other than that "Cousin Sister," as she knew her, was "in the wrong place at the wrong time."[8]

While Octavia Dockery engaged in one legal battle after another, Emily Burns served eight years in prison. She might have spent the rest of her life there if not for Governor Johnson's suspension of her sentence, so it is a testament to her inner strength that she survived Parchman and returned to Natchez to carry on with her life in light of what she had been through.

The signs of her reentry into society after her incarceration appear in Natchez city directories. Sister first returned to 228 St. Catherine Street, the home she shared with her mother before her arrest, where she lived at least until 1947. Public records of Emily's mother, Nellie Black, stop in 1939, but it is likely that the two women lived together when Sister returned from prison. Whereas city directories documented Emily's occupation prior to her trial as "laundress," she was now listed as one of the city's dressmakers. By 1950, Sister, now fifty-five years old, had moved to Liberty Road, where she was listed as a "householder," which meant that whether she owned or rented her home, she was the head of her household.[9]

She had been a widow for over twenty years by now, eight of which had been taken from her. But some time between 1950 and 1955, Sister remarried, this time to a man who attended her church. Lee Randolph, described as a tall and very large man, was her same age. He had been married before and had children. And he was one of Antioch's deacons. Sister left her home on Liberty Road and moved into a house on Concord Avenue with her new husband, where she lived until her death in September 1969.[10]

The *Natchez Democrat* did not record her obituary. Sister had health issues that required family members to rotate in and out of her house to care for her in the last years of her life, but her life cannot be measured by her illness or her incarceration. She carried the strength of her slave ancestors with her, a strength that willed her to survive prison and life under Jim Crow. She also lived long enough to witness the determination of the black community to fight for civil rights in Natchez. And she lived long enough to become a mother of the church at Antioch—a position of respectability. Given the personal struggle that had been her life, it was respectability well deserved.[11]

Regardless of the name given to what happened that night in August 1932— the Merrill murder or the Goat Castle murder—it is important to understand that the case involved more than two eccentrics and their goats. A woman was murdered. A man lost a woman he loved. Another woman served hard labor in prison. And several members of the black community were rounded up for interrogation. Natchez, too, was thrown into the spotlight, and what the media exposed was not flattering. Pilgrimage tours aside, this was a society in flux. Old South romance simply served as a cover for Jim Crow ugliness.

Previous writers have been taken with the southern gothic overtones of this story, which is why they have focused their pens on Dick Dana and Octavia Dockery and the spectacle of Goat Castle. Yet there is another gothic South, one that speaks to the devastation of black lives in a society that did not value their lives. It is important, therefore, to restore Emily "Sister" Burns's experience in its retelling so that her suffering, and return to Natchez, is not lost to history.

The tragedy of what happened in Natchez in 1932 has largely faded from community memory. Americans, who followed the story for months that fall, moved on to the excitement of other tales of true crime. And yet Goat Castle is worth remembering for what it tells us about America in the 1930s. It reveals the public's fascination with the gothic South alongside the romance of the Old South. It provides a window onto crime stories of the decade, as well as onto southern race relations, Jim Crow, and the narrative of southern civilization in decline. Finally, it reminds us of the importance of Natchez, a town older than the nation itself and a place whose history runs as deep as the Mississippi River along which it sits.

ACKNOWLEDGMENTS

Years ago, while working at the Mississippi Division of Archives and History in Jackson, I was in search of material that might offer insight as to why the Natchez Pilgrimage—a tour of antebellum mansions—had drawn thousands of American tourists to this little town on the bluffs of the Mississippi River during the 1930s. This is when I first met Clinton Bagley, a longtime historian at the state archives and a Natchez expert. When I told him why I was there, his eyes widened and he said, "What you should really be looking at is Goat Castle. Goat Castle put Natchez on the map." I asked him to repeat himself. "Did you say 'Goat Castle'?" He had. I was intrigued. He pointed me to a vertical file that held the contents of newspaper articles about a murder that had taken place in Natchez in 1932—the very year the Natchez Pilgrimage began. Goat Castle, I learned, was the nickname of a derelict antebellum mansion where its occupants—Dick Dana and Octavia Dockery—lived with several goats. The two eccentrics once stood accused of the murder of their neighbor in a case that received national attention. I was hooked. I photocopied everything in that file because I instinctively knew that this was going to become my next book project.

So the person responsible for setting me on this journey is Clinton Bagley. All kidding aside, I am forever grateful to him, because this story has been a real gift to me as a historian and a writer. It introduced me to the world that is Natchez, historical and contemporary, the many lovely people I have met there, and the amazing sunsets from its bluffs overlooking the Mississippi River.

After Clinton, my thanks must begin in Natchez. Mimi Miller, the executive director of the Historic Natchez Foundation (HNF), is an absolute treasure. Her knowledge and her local contacts were invaluable. She and her husband, Ron Miller, have also been generous hosts during my many research trips there. I learned early on not to be in a hurry to get up from the breakfast table, because Mimi is telling stories. Plus, research doesn't begin until she's at the foundation. Being on Natchez time is not so bad. I cannot thank her and Ron enough for their insights into Natchez history and society, to say nothing of their hospitality.

Many of the people I have met in Natchez provided information that proved critical to completing this book. Among them was Duncan Morgan, a member of the African American community whose historical memory can be taken to the bank. If it were not for him, the story of Emily Burns would still be lost to history. During my several research visits, he provided information and introductions that allowed me to flesh out her role as a principal and the only person to be held accountable for Jennie Merrill's murder. I am forever grateful to him.

Among Duncan's introductions were Doris Maynard and her mother, Daisy Green, members of Antioch Baptist Church, where Emily's family has worshipped for several generations. Ms. Green has since passed, but I appreciate the time she and Doris gave me. They were the first to share with me the fact that Emily Burns was known as "Sister," and they invited me to attend their church. In October 2015 I finally made that visit. There, for the first time, I met Emily's second cousins—Birdia Green, Phyliss Morris, Linda Griffin, and Felice Davis—who knew her as "Cousin Sister." On the following day, Birdia messaged me to meet at her sister's home. It was during that visit, sitting around the kitchen table with Phyliss, Birdia, and Linda, where I first saw a photograph of Emily Burns. It is the only one that exists and is used in the book. The photo and the generosity of these sisters have meant the world to me. Since that time, Birdia and I have remained in touch, for which I am thankful. I owe all of these women a debt of gratitude.

At the HNF, there are several people to thank. Early in my research, Catherine Prince bravely accompanied me to a warehouse where hundreds of ledgers from the Adams County Courthouse were being held for safekeeping. The warehouse had once been a pie factory, and the records were being held in what had been the freezer that held the piecrusts. Navigating the dark and dingy room required us to wear gloves and masks and to carry flashlights, but that visit proved to be a success when I located the witness docket for Emily Burns's trial, and a case number, which proved invaluable. Thank you, Catherine.

Thanks also go to Patricia Catchings, who expressed interest in my research from the beginning and pulled many of the archival boxes I needed. She also graciously offered her lovely home so that I could introduce a group of adventurous friends to the wonders of Natchez. Madeleine Iles, who was fulfilling a history internship with the HNF, helped me by photocopying materials. Her curiosity about this project was refreshing, and she has a bright future as a historian should she decide to take it on as a career. Trevor Brown and Anna Rife have also made my time working at the HNF more interesting.

Elsewhere in Natchez I want to thank Jeff Mansell, historian with the Natchez National Historical Park, who shared some of his own research on the Surgets and Minors, as well as on Civil War–era Natchez. Thanks go to Carolyn Guido, the current owner of Glenburnie, for inviting me to her home and sharing her personal archive of material on the house and the murder. Elizabeth Boggess and Anne MacNeil, sisters and owners of Elms Court, have also shared their time and knowledge, not to mention their hospitality. I will never forget having dinner at their home, my first beneath a punkah.

Native Natchezeans Sallie Ballard and Kathie Blankenstein were also generous. Their mothers were founding members of the Natchez Garden Club, and the two of them shared fascinating stories of its origins. During an early visit to Natchez, both women came to the HNF to be interviewed, and each of them proved to be a wonderful storyteller. During one trip, Sallie opened her home to me and a friend, while Kathie gave me access to the archives at Magnolia Hall. Kathie and I have exchanged e-mails, and she's been wonderful to meet me for lunch or dinner when I'm in town. On one of my last research visits, she told me a story about Zaida Wells, who is featured in this book, which had Mimi and me in stitches. I also owe her a huge thank you for introducing me to Old Fashioneds.

Last but not least in Natchez, I want to thank Joan McLemore, who let me interview her about local history and lore, and Ben Hillyer with the *Natchez Democrat*. He sent a reporter to interview me about my research in hopes of bringing me one step closer to the story of Emily Burns.

The Louisiana State University Special Collections held material that was critical to the writing of this book. Natchez-related archival collections, including the Thomas H. and Joan W. Gandy Photograph Collection, helped bring this story to life. Thanks go to Mark Martin for his assistance in helping me navigate the photo collection and to Tara Laver for her assistance with use and permissions.

At the University of North Carolina at Charlotte, I am very grateful to Dean Nancy Gutierrez, who provided a research fund that made this book and scholarly presentations on my findings possible. She has also expressed a personal interest in the book. Her support, along with a senior research leave provided by the College of Liberal Arts and Sciences, as well as a fellowship from the UNC Charlotte Department of History Cotlow Endowment, meant that I had a year to focus on writing. Ask any scholar what she or he wants most, and the answer is almost always "time to write." I am grateful for the time, and this book is the result.

Talented colleagues and former students have also been supportive. In the UNC Charlotte history department office, I especially want to thank Linda Smith, who steered me through the travel bureaucracy of the university and who has shown genuine excitement about the project. Thanks also go to Catherine Forbes, in our college IT office, who took on the challenge of scanning images I needed. My colleague Ritika Prasad not only is one of the smartest people I've ever met but has also been a wonderful friend to me. She was one among that adventurous group who accompanied me on a trip to see Natchez and is an all-around great gal. Former students who've expressed interest in this story and who are fine historians in their own right include Nicole Moore, Brandon Lunsford, Bill Jeffers, Boyd Harris, and Emily Taylor. Thanks for keeping up with my progress.

I must also offer a huge thanks to Christopher Geissler, whom I met when he worked for UNC Charlotte's special collections. He went with me to Natchez one weekend and helped me go through that dark and dingy place that housed ledgers from the Adams County Courthouse. I needed to be sure I had not missed something, even if it felt like searching for a needle in a haystack. While there, he became a fan of the town and got to meet Sallie Ballard, who regaled us with stories that made us laugh. Love you, Brother Man.

In Charlotte, I want to thank Mary McLaughlin, a good friend and my wine tasting companion. She's listened to me yammer on about this project for months on end, showing tremendous patience but also a sincere interest. I also wish to thank Carann Brown for the pet care she provided during numerous research trips.

Thanks, too, go to the women who thought a trip to Natchez sounded exciting. In addition to Ritika Prasad, our group included Minoa Uffelman, Louise LeBourgeois, and Andrea Hewitt. I barely knew them before the trip, but all were enthusiastic and eager to learn, and we came away as friends.

The people at the University of North Carolina Press are the best, and I've been fortunate to work with them on this book. Mark Simpson-Vos initially tried to convince me to go with the press, but I demurred. I wanted to let my agent, Geri Thoma, shop the book around, only to find that UNC Press was best suited to handle the project. By then, I had met the very talented Brandon Proia. I recall very well the phone conversation with him in which I expressed how important it was that I be able to write the book I wanted to write. He reassured me I could, and with that I signed on and offered a mea culpa to Mark. Thank you, Geri, for guiding me back to UNC Press.

I can't say enough good things about Brandon Proia. He's been the editor I needed. He's talented and encouraging and has been very responsive to my e-mails and phone calls. He's helped me to streamline the narrative without changing my intent or even my writing style. All historians should be so lucky.

There are so many academic friends to thank that I could not possibly thank them all, so I just want to offer a shout-out to all of you on Facebook who cheered me along the way as I posted numerous updates on the writing. I have appreciated your interest and your encouragement. There is one person, however, who deserves special recognition, and that's Sarah Gardner. She joined me on my first visit to Natchez on a fall break in 2012. I don't think either of us will ever forget the tour we had at Dunleith, one of Natchez's most outstanding examples of antebellum architecture. We were first told we could not get a tour, so we asked to walk the grounds. That's when we met David Grimsley, who gave us a tour anyway. It is, by far, one of the best house tours I've ever taken, and we enjoyed his sense of humor, even when he took the opportunity to make fun of history professors, not knowing he was giving two of them a tour.

There are academics, and there are those who show you the meaning of true friendship. They are the ones who always have your back. In this, I am most fortunate to claim a group of women friends who not only are outstanding historians but also have given me tremendous love and support in ways only we will know. They are my "girls' weekend" crew. Shannon Frystak, Alecia Long, Danielle McGuire, and Heather Thompson, I love you gals. Thank you for getting me through the tough times and cheering me on in better days.

I also have family members to thank. My mother, Flora Carter, has been excited about this book from the beginning. She read a chapter but refused to read others because she didn't want it to "ruin" her experience of reading the book in its entirety. Now she can. My aunt Wilma Smith, the original historian in the family, has also been enthusiastic. Thank you, both. I love you more than you know. Thanks, also, go to my cousin Katura Crum, an avid reader who has been a cheerleader for this project from the very beginning.

Now, my most faithful supporters, the ones who give me unconditional love on a daily basis, are my pets. The cat, well, is a cat. Her name is Halen, and while she has a poor reputation with *some* guests, there is no doubt she loves me, especially when it suits her. Then there's my heart, Phoebe. I adopted her at the end of my first year of teaching in Charlotte. A lab mix, she is always the sweetest pea in the room. I often look at her and ask, "How did I get so lucky to get you?" Because honestly, she's the best girlfriend I've ever had. She kept me company while writing and hung out with me in the room where I worked to make this book a reality. Her snores and sighs provided comfort, while her nudges to go for a walk reminded me it was time to take a break and get some fresh air. She's the one who has always greeted me with love and excitement and the one who has been steadfast and true. This book is dedicated to her.

NOTES

ABBREVIATIONS

HNF   Historic Natchez Foundation, Natchez, Miss.

LLMVC Louisiana and Lower Mississippi Valley Collections, Special Collections, Hill Memorial Library, Louisiana State University Libraries, Baton Rouge

MDAH Mississippi Division of Archives and History, Jackson, Miss.

ND   *Natchez Democrat*

NYT   *New York Times*

TP   *New Orleans Times-Picayune*

PROLOGUE

1. "Neighbor Pair Held in Natchez Murder," *New York Times*, August 9, 1932.

2. The last name is spelled in newspapers and documents as both Pearles and Pearls. This book uses the latter.

3. "Rich Woman Recluse Slain in Mississippi," *New York Times*, August 6, 1932; "Elderly Recluse Slain in South," *Joplin (Mo.) Globe*, August 6, 1932; "Weird Mississippi Murder Traced to Row over Goats," *Helena (Mont.) Independent August 8, 1932*; "Southern Goat Castle Scene of a Tragedy," *Lebanon (Pa.) Semi-Weekly News*, August 15, 1932.

4. Cox, "Revisiting the Natchez Pilgrimage," 356–57.

5. Jenkins, "Melrose, a Multifaceted Jewel in the NPS Crown," 372.

6. Quitman's tour is described in Scarborough, *Masters of the Big House*, 40.

7. Johnson, *River of Dark Dreams*, 6–12, 84–87.

8. Discussion of the Forks of the Road and Natchez slave traders is drawn from Barnett and Burkett, "Forks of the Road Slave Market at Natchez"; and Ingraham, *The South-West by a Yankee*, 192–97.

9. W. Anderson, *Life and Narrative of William J. Anderson*, 14.

10. The name of the home is written as "Elmscourt" and "Elms Court." This book uses the latter. "Natchez, The First Town on the River, Gen. Grant on a Visit, Runaway Negroes in the Contraband Camp, Secesh in Despair, etc.," *NYT*, August 16, 1863.

11. Figures on slave population are drawn from "Spread of U.S. Slavery, 1790–1860," accessed June 10, 2014.

12. Jennifer Moses, "The Lost Tribe of Natchez," *NYT*, September 20, 1998.

13. Cox, *Dreaming of Dixie*, 81–105.

14. H. Wells, "Crimson Crime at Glenburney Manor"; Z. Wells, *Merrill Murder Mystery*; Charles East, "Natchez Gothic," in East Papers, LLMVC; Tidwell and Sanders, *Sterling A. Brown's "A Negro Looks at the South,"* 358; Kane, *Natchez on the Mississippi*, 312–33; Callon and Smith, *Goat Castle Murder*; Llewelyn, *Goat Castle Murder*.

CHAPTER ONE

1. Cook, "Growing Up White, Genteel, and Female," 312–20. Cook's work focuses specifically on Natchez.

2. Details on Surgets and Merrills are from various sources including *Biographical and Historical Memoirs of Mississippi*, 430–31; Scarborough, *Masters of the Big House*, 11–12, 100; and Mansell, "Elms Court."

3. According to the 1900 U.S. Federal Census, Jennie was born in August 1863. Regarding Merrill's slaveholdings, see U.S. Federal Census 1860—Slave Schedules, Adams County; and Mansell, "Elms Court."

4. Merrill's visit is described in Mansell, "Elms Court."

5. Marszalek, *Papers of Ulysses S. Grant*, 9:216.

6. "Letter from Natchez," *Milwaukee Daily Sentinel*, February 17, 1864. The letter itself was written January 25, 1864.

7. The Merrills lived at 29 W. Washington Square in New York City. The firm of Goodman and Merrill is discussed in Scarborough, *Masters of the Big House*, 342. An 1866 advertisement for the firm of Goodman and Merrill is in *Commercial and Financial Chronicle*, 285. Walter Goodman's father married Ayres Merrill Jr.'s aunt Anna Merrill. The dates of marriage and of Walter Goodman Jr.'s death in 1883 are located on the Find a Grave website, http://www.findagrave.com/cgi-bin/fg.cgi?page=gr&GSln=GOO&GSpartial=1&GSbyrel=all&GSst=45&GScntry=4&GSsr=3161&GRid=38977971&, accessed May 29, 2016.

8. The Newport, Rhode Island, City Directory lists Ayres Merrill for 1867–68; details on Harbor View are available from Miller, *Lost Newport*, 123.

9. St. Mary's Hall is now the Doane Academy. Historical information on the Doane Academy can be found at "Doane Academy—Our History," accessed May 29, 2016.

10. Several newspapers noted Merrill's nomination, including, for example, the *Washington (D.C.) Evening Star*, which reported his confirmation as Belgian ambassador on January 7, 1876.

11. Miscellaneous news clippings, October 11, 1877, Dicks Family Collection, HNF.

12. "The Beauties of America," *New York Sun*, October 11, 1877.

13. Clippings on President and Mrs. Grant's visit, Dicks Family Collection, HNF. See also Simon, *Personal Memoirs of Julia Dent Grant*, 193, 209–10.

14. Pennsylvania, Passenger and Crew Lists, Passenger Lists of Vessels Arriving at Philadelphia, Pennsylvania, 1800–1882, Roll M425, Line 7.

15. Notice of Merrill's stroke appears in the *Memphis Commercial Appeal*, April 19, 1877. Boltwood, *The History of Pittsfield*, 23; New Jersey, Death and Burials Index, 1798–1971.

16. "King's Daughters — History," accessed July 14, 2015.

17. "125,000 King's Daughters," *New York Sun*, January 26, 1890, 1.

18. Clippings on Jennie Merrill's reform work are found in Dicks Family Collection, HNF; Riis, *How the Other Half Lives*.

19. Miscellaneous newspapers clippings describe Merrill's work on behalf of tenement reform in New York, found in Dicks Family Collection, HNF. There were also notices in the *New York Evening World*, March 1892, and the *Pittsburgh Dispatch*, March 24, 1892.

20. "A King's Daughter Confers with Cardinal Gibbons about the Slums of New York," *Baltimore American* (n.d.), in Dicks Family Collection, HNF.

21. Scarborough, *Masters of the Big House*, 22–26.

22. Walter Goodman to Jennie Merrill, letters dated October and December 1884 and January 1885, Dicks Family Collection, HNF.

23. Oakland, Adams County Historic Sites Subject Files, HNF.

24. The U.S. Federal Census for 1900 shows Duncan Minor was born in July 1863 and Jennie Merrill in August 1863.

25. Kate Minor's testimony as well as that of Thomas Spain can be found in Petition of Katherine S. Minor, August 30, 1871, Records of the Southern Claims Commission, Records of the General Accounting Office, Record Group 217, National Archives and Records Administration, Washington, D.C. See also Joyce Broussard, "Occupied Natchez, Elite Women, and the Feminization of the Civil War."

26. Oakland, Adams County Historic Sites Subject Files, HNF; Mansell, "Oakland."

27. Mansell, "Oakland."

28. U.S. Federal Census data, 1860, 1880, 1900.

29. Duncan Minor to Jennie Merrill, 1883, Dicks Family Collection, HNF.

30. Ibid., letters dated 1883, 1885.

31. Ibid., November 3, 1889.

32. Ibid., April 24, 1900.

33. On details of the home and Merrill's ownership, see "Glenburnie," *National Register of Historic Places Inventory*.

34. E. C. Boyt, Jennie's car mechanic, was quoted as saying that Natchez police knew of her penchant for running through stoplights but never gave her a ticket. "Slain Spinster's Own Gun Sought as Death Weapon," *TP*, August 11, 1932.

35. L. T. Kennedy to Duncan Minor, August 25, 1915, in Adams County Chancery Court Records, Case File 3195, HNF.

36. *R. H. C. Dana by His Next Friend Miss Octavia Dockery, Complainant vs. Duncan Minor, Defendant*, in ibid.

37. "R. H. C. Dana — An Alleged Lunatic, Final Decree," February 6, 1917, Adams County Chancery Court Records, Book E, p. 470, HNF. According to the summary,

a jury of six men concluded that Dana was "incapable of taking care of his property" and recommended the appointment of a guardian.

38. Details of her estate are drawn from testimony in *Miss J. S. Merrill v. Miss Octavia Dockery*, Mississippi Supreme Court, Series 208: Case Files, Case No. 21416, January 10, 1921, MDAH; and, "Glenburnie," *National Register of Historic Places Inventory*.

39. Sheriff Mike Ryan's testimony is found in *Miss J. S. Merrill v. Miss Octavia Dockery*, Mississippi Supreme Court, Case No. 21416. Ryan is the same man who served as Natchez's chief of police during the Merrill murder investigation.

40. Ibid.

41. Ibid.

42. *Miss J. S. Merrill v. Miss Octavia Dockery*, Mississippi Supreme Court, Case No. 21416.

43. Ibid.

44. Ibid.

45. Ibid.

46. Ibid.

47. Ibid. Quotation about Merrill holding a gun on hired hands is from Charles East's interview notes with Natchez chief of police Charlie Bahin, March 17, 1977, East Papers, LLMVC.

48. *Miss J. S. Merrill v. Miss Octavia Dockery*, Mississippi Supreme Court, Case No. 21416.

CHAPTER TWO

1. Based on handwritten notes from East's January 1974 interview with Odell Ferguson in Natchez, East Papers, LLMVC. The 1920 U.S. Federal Census confirms Odell Ferguson's age.

2. On Charles A. Dana, see J. Wilson, *Life of Charles A. Dana*. Quote from Charles B. Dana to Richard H. C. Dana, May 27, 1890, Dana and Family Papers, LLMVC.

3. Information on Charles Backus Dana is found in *General Catalogue of Dartmouth College*, 12.

4. Copy of Charles B. Dana and Elvira Close marriage certificate, East Papers, LLMVC.

5. Dana's report appears in *Journal of the Thirty-Fifth Convention of the Protestant Episcopal Church*, 76.

6. "Battle of Port Gibson," accessed August 26, 2014.

7. *Journal of the Proceedings of the Protestant Episcopal Church, Mississippi Diocese*, 26.

8. Elvira Dana died in February 1886; see Mississippi Wills and Probate Records. Her will shows that her son Richard was enrolled at Chamberlain-Hunt Academy in Port Gibson, Mississippi. Her executor was attorney T. Otis Baker, and, at her death, the estate was valued at $15,000. Charles B. Dana to Richard H. C. Dana, May 27, 1890, Dana and Family Papers, LLMVC.

9. Charles Dana, New York, Spanish-American War Military and Naval Service Records, 1898–1902.

10. Dana told a reporter that his finger was injured by a falling window in "Dana's Life Filled with Tragedy and Futility," *TP*, August 9, 1932.

11. R. H. C. Dana is listed as a boarder with Duncan Baker in the 1900 U.S. Federal Census. This is the same Baker of Baker-Grand Theatre. According to Charles East's interview notes with Charlie Bahin, East Papers, LLMVC, Dana sometimes played piano to accompany silent films at the Baker-Grand Theatre.

12. Dick Dana's handwritten diary speaks of Mr. Forman, Sadie, Nydia, and Octavia. Diary, 1906–1907, Dana and Family Papers, LLMVC.

13. Details on Thomas Dockery and family are found in the 1850 and 1860 U.S. Federal Censuses. See also Arey, "Thomas Pleasant Dockery, 1833–1898," accessed May 29, 2016. Regarding the number of slaves Ann Dockery and Thomas Dockery owned, see U.S. Federal Census—Slave Schedules, 1860.

14. According to the website Measuring Worth, the amount of $75,000 in 1860 had a relative value of $2,170,000 in 2013.

15. U.S. Federal Census—Slave Schedules, 1860, Lamartine, Arkansas.

16. U.S. Federal Census, 1850 and 1860. Marriage to Laura West occurred in 1859, Coahoma County, Mississippi. The U.S. Census of 1860 shows Nydia was just five months old.

17. On Dockery's role in the Civil War, see Arey, "Thomas Pleasant Dockery, 1833–1898," accessed May 29, 2016.

18. Ibid. Laura Dockery's death was recorded in the *Daily Arkansas Democrat*, September 15, 1880.

19. U.S. Federal Census, 1880, Coahoma County.

20. New York City Directory, 1888, lists Thomas Dockery's occupation as a broker.

21. New England, United Methodist Church Records, 1787–1922, documents their marriage at Colchester Methodist Episcopal Church in New London, Connecticut, on April 25, 1883.

22. "Gen. Dockery on the War-Path," *NYT*, March 22, 1884.

23. "Accused by His Wife," ibid., March 23, 1884; "Mrs. Dockery in Hysterics," ibid., March 24, 1884.

24. Octavia would later claim that her father was one of Grant's pallbearers. There is no evidence this was the case.

25. "An Incident in Grant's Career," *New York Evening World*, August 7, 1885.

26. Letter to Thomas Dockery regarding Richard Forman's appearance, Dockery Papers, MDAH.

27. Richard Reed to Octavia Dockery, May 9, 1889, ibid. Reed is listed as a lawyer on the U.S. Federal Census of 1900 for Adams County. By then, he had married someone else.

28. Richard Reed to Octavia Dockery, 1892, Dockery Papers, MDAH.

29. Ibid. Reed recognized his romantic efforts were not paying off, and he married the very next year.

30. Thomas Bulger to Octavia Dockery, June 23, 1896, and November 11, 1896, ibid.

31. Dockery, "Held by the Enemy."

32. Dmitri, "So Red the Rose," 19.

33. U.S. Census 1900 and 1910, Adams County.

34. U.S. Census 1910.

35. "Mrs. Richard H. Forman Buried," *ND*, February 21, 1911, 6.

36. Sadie Foreman is shown as a renter at a house on Rankin Street in the Natchez, Mississippi, City Directory, 1912.

37. Diary, 1906–1907, Dana and Family Papers, LLMVC.

38. Octavia Dockery is listed as a boarder at a home on Pine Street in the Natchez, Mississippi, City Directory, 1912, 109.

39. Descriptions are drawn from Gwen Bristow's reporting with the *Times-Picayune* in August 1932.

40. Re: Guardianship of R. H. C. Dana to the Chancery Court of Adams County, Mississippi, January term, 1919, Adams County Chancery Court Records, HNF. Chancellor R. W. Cutrer approved Mulvihill's request to lease Glenwood to Dockery on March 29, 1919.

41. Ibid.

42. Dana's beating of Octavia is discussed in "Inquiry in Natchez Shifted to Skunk's Nest Area," *TP*, August 14, 1932.

43. There were several accounts of Dana spending time outside on the estate. See, for example, "New Fingerprints of Dick Dana Are Being Compared," *ND*, August 9, 1932.

44. Details of the history of the "Skunk's Nest" are from "Will of Murdered Natchez Eccentric Gives All to Minor," *TP*, August 12, 1932.

CHAPTER THREE

1. U.S. Federal Census, 1930, Summit Township, Chicago, records George Pearls's birthplace as Mississippi and both parents as from Louisiana. On the Great Migration, see Wilkerson, *Warmth of Other Suns*.

2. On the domestic slave trade, see Deyle, *Carry Me Back*; Johnson, *River of Dark Dreams*; and Baptist, *The Half Has Never Been Told*.

3. Johnson, *River of Dark Dreams*, 40–41; Scarborough, *Masters of the Big House*, 3–9.

4. The names of Nellie's mother and grandmother were revealed in a conversation with Emily Burns's second cousins, specifically with Linda Griffin, Natchez, Miss., October 9, 2015.

5. U.S. Federal Census, 1900, 1910, 1920, 1930; Natchez, Mississippi, City Directories, 1912, 1922, 1925, 1928. The names of Emily's grandmother and great-grandmother are contained in the Smith family Bible.

6. On the movement of former slaves to urban areas, see Rabinowitz, *Race Relations in the Urban South*, 4–30.

7. Members of Emily's family continue to worship at Antioch Baptist Church.

8. Sanborn Fire Insurance Maps tell the story of St. Catherine Strcct, as do details from Natchez City Directories and U.S. Federal Census records.

9. Ibid.

10. Dolensky, "Natchez in 1920," 24.

11. Sharpless, *Cooking in Other Women's Kitchens*, 65–88.

12. Emily's marriage and address were culled from U.S. Federal Census data for 1920 and 1930, as well as from Natchez City Directories. Edward Burns is listed as her husband in the 1925 Natchez City Directory, 59.

13. The U.S. Federal Census of 1930 shows Newell as a boarder and an embalmer. The Natchez City Directory for 1928 lists him as employed by Bluff City Undertaking.

14. Emily's name for Williams is confirmed in her signed confession, in which she refers to him as "Pink," short for Pinkney. Burns Signed Confession, August 23,1932, East Papers, LLMVC.

15. Williams/Pearls's height and weight are based on Maurice O'Neill's notes on the case, which were transcribed by Charles East during his visit with O'Neill's daughter, Marion Prevost. East Papers, LLMVC.

16. While Wells's *Master Detective* series on the crime embellished some details about George Pearls, including that he was a "big burly Negro," it accurately described many known details of the crime. According to the September 1933 issue, some of the items found in his trunk of belongings were letters from several women with whom there was romantic familiarity. H. Wells, "Crimson Crime at Glenburney Manor," September 1933, 57.

17. Phillips, "Reconstruction in Mississippi," accessed June 8, 2015; Blackmon, *Slavery By Another Name*, 27.

18. As quoted in McMillen, *Dark Journey*, 125.

19. "Samuel Thomas, Testimony before Congress, 1865," https://chnm.gmu.edu/courses/122/recon/thomas.htm, accessed July 8, 2015.

20. Ibid.

21. Ibid.

22. Quote from Duncan Morgan, interview with author, Natchez, Mississippi, July 21, 2013.

23. Schroeder, "Summit, IL"; and M. Wilson, "Food Processing," accessed August 11, 2015.

24. U.S. Federal Census of 1930 lists "George Pearls," Summit Township, Cook County, Illinois. See also Schroeder, "Summit, IL."

25. "Coroner Abandons Attempt to Reopen Inquest in Murder," *TP*, August 11, 1932, reveals Pearls used to work for Minor.

26. Pearls's letter to his wife transcribed by Charles East from Maurice O'Neill's investigative notes, East Papers, LLMVC.

27. Minor quote from "Coroner Abandons Attempt to Reopen Inquest in Murder," *TP*, August 11, 1932.

CHAPTER FOUR

1. Evidence, including Emily Burns's confession and a countersuit from Sheriff C. P. Roberts, places George Pearls at Glenwood earlier in the day of August 2, 1932.

2. Details of their movement that evening are drawn from Emily Burns's confession, August 23, 1932, East Papers, LLMVC.

3. Details of that evening are drawn from Burns's confession, as well as from newspaper accounts from both the *Natchez Democrat* and the *Times-Picayune*. The two papers covered the event very differently. The *Times-Picayune* reporters offered more detailed information, perhaps because the Natchez paper had to be careful in how it reported given the individuals involved. See "Woman Mysteriously Missing, Atrocious Murder Indicated," *ND*, August 5, 1932, and "Bullet Riddled Body of Woman Found in Thicket," *ND*, August 6, 1932; "Natchez Recluse Shot to Death in Natchez Home," *TP*, August 6, 1932, and "Slaying Mystery Suspects Held Incommunicado While Fingerprints Are Studied," *TP*, August 7, 1932. See also Burns confession, East Papers, LLMVC; and last, H. Wells, "Crimson Crime at Glenburney Manor," September 1933, 57–58. Here, the story is told that they ran into Ed "Poe" Newell and that Pink convinced him to join them.

4. The *Times-Picayune* reported that local blacks who "still cling to their African voodoo belief" were the ones who had nicknamed Glenwood the "spooky mansion" and Dana and Dockery as the "Wild Man" and the "Goat Woman." See "Natchez Recluse Shot to Death in Natchez Home," *TP*, August 6, 1932. Regional and national media subsequently adopted these nicknames and perpetuated them in stories about Dana and Dockery.

5. Emily Burns's formal confession statement, as entered into the court proceedings at her trial, speaks of Pink's threat. East Papers, LLMVC.

6. The detail about Pink listening for Jennie's humming appears in H. Wells, "Crimson Crime at Glenburney Manor," September 1933, 57.

7. "Deformed Hand Again to Fore in Murder Case," *ND*, August 16, 1932.

8. "Slain Spinster's Own Gun Sought as Death Weapon," *TP*, August 11, 1932; Charles East interview with Chief of Police Robinson, March 17, 1977, East Papers, LLMVC.

9. Burns's confession and news accounts were consistent in saying there were three shots fired. While it was reported that Merrill was hit three times by bullets, the autopsy report listed only two wounds—to the neck and the left chest. Jane Surget Merrill, Standard Certificate of Death, Adams County Certificates of Death, State File 10970 (32–10970), MDAH.

10. Sheriff Roberts suggested that a tall man carried her body out of the house. Dana was tall. "Bridge Near 'Skunk's Nest' Yields Clue in Merrill Murder," *TP*, August 13, 1932.

11. Jennie's body was reported as being found "face up" in the *ND*. The details of the lamp are important. Emily always claimed to have tossed the lamp twenty feet from Merrill's body, and yet the lamp was found nearly one hundred yards away near

the dividing line between Glenburnie and Glenwood. According to the account in the *Master Detective*, Pink was the one who carried it back to the house. This left the door open for Dana or Dockery to retrieve it to light their path back to Glenwood and then smash it before they crossed the property line. H. Wells, "Crimson Crime in Glenburney Manor," September 1933, 57.

12. The details of what happened are drawn mostly from Emily Burns's formal confession. She gave more than one, but her last gave these details and was entered into her trial with her signature. Burns confession, East Papers, LLMVC.

13. Under questioning, Dick Dana made reference to this argument. "Dana's Life Filled with Tragedy and Futility," *TP*, August 9, 1932.

14. "Woman Mysteriously Missing, Atrocious Murder Indicated," *ND*, August 5, 1932, and "Bullet Riddled Body of Woman Found in Thicket," *ND*, August 6, 1932. While the Natchez paper identified only Willie Boyd, the New Orleans paper reported that both Boyd and Hacher heard the shots. And, indeed, both were brought in for questioning. "Slaying Mystery Suspects Held Incommunicado While Fingerprints Are Studied," *TP*, August 7, 1932; "Murder Suspect's Identity Certain, Declares Sheriff," *TP*, August 15, 1932. Black men in the Jim Crow South could be, and were, arrested for the slightest offense or hint of disturbing a white woman. Even worse, they could be lynched. See McMillen, *Dark Journey*; and Oshinsky, *"Worse Than Slavery."*

15. "Bullet Riddled Body of Woman Found in Thicket," *ND*, August 6, 1932

16. Z. Wells, *Merrill Murder Mystery*, 9. Zaida Wells recalls "he sent the negro boy to a store to telephone for the sheriff." In new accounts, Minor is said to have "called" the sheriff. The *Times-Picayune* reporting was more detailed and explained that Minor sent one of his "negro search party" to call the sheriff. "Bridge Near 'Skunk's Nest' Yields Clue in Merrill Murder," *TP*, August 13, 1932. In a 1979 interview with the *Natchez Democrat*, Laurin Farris claimed that he was sitting on the porch of the Adams County jail when Duncan Minor "came loping up" to say something had happened to Merrill. Farris claims that he was the first one to go to the crime scene. He may have been part of the search party. Photocopy of undated article from private file of Carolyn Guido, Natchez, Mississippi.

17. Notes from East's interview with Charlie Bahin, chief of detectives in Natchez, October 21, 1976, East Papers, LLMVC.

18. Ibid.

19. Z. Wells, *Merrill Murder Mystery*, 9; East interview with Charlie Bahin, October 21, 1976, East Papers, LLMVC.

CHAPTER FIVE

1. Information on Roberts's life is derived from U.S. Federal Census of 1910, 1920, and 1930, along with the Natchez City Directory for the years 1922 and 1925 and U.S. World War I Draft Registration Cards, 1917–1918, for Adams County, Mississippi, no. 331.

2. The story of Roberts getting the nickname "Book" is told in "Bridge Near 'Skunk's Nest' Yields Clue in Merrill Murder," *TP, August 13, 1932.*

3. "Bullet Riddled Body of Woman Found in Thicket," *ND*, August 6, 1932; "Natchez Recluse Shot to Death in Natchez Home," *TP*, August, 6, 1932; "Slaying Mystery Suspects Held Incommunicado While Fingerprints Are Studied," *TP*, August 7, 1932; "'Wildman' Dana, Guardian Charged with Murder," *TP*, August 9, 1932. See also H. Wells, "Crimson Crime at Glenburney Manor," June 1933. Several times, Sheriff Roberts repeated Dana's statement that he knew "nothing of the murder."

4. "Fingerprints May Be Dana's, States Bertillon Expert," *TP*, August 8, 1932.

5. "Investigation of Odell Ferguson Started Friday," *ND*, August 13, 1932; "Slaying Mystery Suspects Held Incommunicado While Fingerprints Are Studied," *TP*, August 7, 1932; "Bullet Riddled Body of Woman Found in Thicket," *ND*, August 6, 1932.

6. Zaida Wells attributes Alonzo Floyd's words to this moment. Z. Wells, *Merrill Murder Mystery*, 10. Merrill was found lying face upward in "Bullet Ridden Body of Woman Found in Thicket," *ND*, August 6, 1932; and "Merrill Murder Suspect, Killed Resisting Arrest in Pine Bluff, Identified," *TP*, August 15, 1932.

7. "Slaying Mystery Suspects Held Incommunicado While Fingerprints Are Studied," *TP*, August 7, 1932.

8. Ibid.

9. "Geiger, Overcoat Owner, Tries to Unravel Murder," *TP*, August 14, 1932.

10. Ibid.

11. "Slain at Home about Seven Thirty O'Clock in Evening," *ND*, August 9, 1932; "Fingerprints May Be Dana's, States Bertillon Expert," *TP*, August 8, 1932; "Bullet Riddled Body of Woman Found in Thicket," *ND*, August 6, 1932; "'Wildman' Dana, Guardian Charged in Merrill Murder," *TP*, August 9, 1932.

12. Information on James Chancellor from Jackson, Mississippi, City Directory, 1932. He also belonged to the International Association for Criminal Identification and was vice president of the state association.

13. "Bullet Riddled Body of Woman Found in Thicket," *ND*, August 6, 1932; "Slaying Mystery Suspects Held Incommunicado While Fingerprints Are Studied," *TP*, August 7, 1932. Dana told reporters about his hand during a jailhouse interview. "Dana's Life Filled with Tragedy and Futility," *TP*, August 9, 1932.

14. "Justice Must Be Meted Out for This Atrocious Crime," editorial, *ND*, August 5, 1932.

15. Z. Wells, *Merrill Murder Mystery*, 12.

16. "'Wildman' Dana, Guardian Charged in Merrill Murder," *TP*, August 9, 1932; "Fingerprints May Be Dana's, States Bertillon Expert," *TP*, August 8, 1932; "Fingerprints of Two Found Cause for the Charges," *ND*, August 9, 1932; "New Fingerprints of Dick Dana Are Being Compared," *ND*, August 9, 1932.

17. "Fingerprints of Two Found Cause for the Charges," *ND*, August 9, 1932; "New Fingerprints of Dick Dana Are Being Compared," *ND*, August 9, 1932.

18. "Slaying Mystery Suspects Held Incommunicado While Fingerprints Are Studied," *TP*, August 7, 1932.

19. "Coroner Abandons Attempt to Reopen Inquest in Murder," *TP*, August 11, 1932; "Merrill Murder Suspect, Killed Resisting Arrest in Pinc Bluff, Identified," *TP*, August 15, 1932.

20. "Coroner Abandons Attempt to Reopen Inquest in Murder," *TP*, August 11, 1932.

21. "Dick Dana and Miss Octavia Dockery Questioned by Officers Yesterday, Both Maintain That They Are Not Guilty," *ND*, August 11, 1932. On the Bertillon system, see "Bertillon System." Details of O'Neill's service in the New Orleans Police Department is confirmed through the 1920 and 1930 U.S. Federal Censuses and New Orleans City Directories.

22. "Investigation of Odell Ferguson Started Friday," *ND*, August 13, 1932.

23. Suggestion that Chancellor "broke under the strain" appears in "Geiger, Overcoat Owner, Tries to Unravel Murder," *TP*, August 14, 1932.

24. "May Call Darrow to Defense of Central Figures in Natchez Tragedy," *ND*, August 12, 1932.

25. "Dana Fingerprints Fully Identified, Authorities State," *TP*, August 10, 1932.

26. "Swelling Wave of Sympathy for Dick Dana and Miss Dockery Continues to Steadily Mount in This Community," *ND*, August 14, 1932; "Tide of Sympathy toward Dana and Octavia Dockery Evinced by Natchez Girls," *TP*, August 12, 1932.

27. "Swelling Wave of Sympathy for Dick Dana and Miss Dockery Continues to Steadily Mount in This Community," *ND*, August 14, 1932.

28. Ibid.

29. U.S. Federal Censuses for 1910, 1920, and 1930 document Sophie Friedman's whereabouts, dates of immigration, and parents' location. See also "Inquiry in Natchez Shifted to Skunk's Nest Area," *TP*, August 14, 1932.

30. "Chancellor Orders Release of Two on Own Recognizance," *ND*, August 16, 1932.

31. "Officers Placed," *ND*, August 16, 1932.

32. "Fingerprint Sets May Hold Key to Merrill Murder," *TP*, August 17, 1932.

33. "Chancellor Orders Release of Two on Own Recognizance," *ND*, August 16, 1932; "Octavia Dockery and Richard Dana Freed," *ND*, August 16, 1932.

CHAPTER SIX

1. "Slain Spinster's Own Gun Sought as Death Weapon," *TP*, August 11, 1932.

2. "Officers Placed on the Trail by Tip of Old Negro," *ND*, August 14, 1932.

3. Ibid.

4. Ibid.

5. Ibid.

6. "Deformed Hand Again to Fore in Murder Case," *ND*, August 16, 1932.

7. Ibid.; "Negro Definitely Linked," *TP*, August 15, 1932.

8. "Deformed Hand Again to Fore in Murder Case," *ND*, August 16, 1932; "Third Deformed Hand Figures in Merrill Enigma," *TP*, August 16, 1932.

9. "Third Deformed Hand Figures in Merrill Enigma," *TP*, August 16, 1932.

10. "Merrill Murder Suspect, Killed Resisting Arrest in Pine Bluff, Identified," *TP*, August 15, 1932.

11. "Officers Placed on the Trail by Tip of Old Negro," *ND*, August 14, 1932.

12. "Negro Definitely Linked," *TP*, August 15, 1932; "Trunk of GP Alias Lawrence Williams Reveals Several New Clues," *ND*, August 16, 1932.

13. Details of Meadie Pearls come from 1930 U.S. Federal Census. Pearls's daughter, Amelia, was identified later, but Charles East transcribed her letter addressed to local officials in Natchez in which she said George Pearls and Lawrence Williams were one and the same. "Amelia Garner to To Whom It May Concern," August 16, 1932, East Papers, LLMVC.

14. Coverage of sheriff's trip to Chicago, Williams's whereabouts, and the wire sent to detectives in Chicago are discussed in "Deformed Hand Again to Fore in Murder Case," *ND*, August 16, 1932.

15. "Abbot Says Evidence More Than Sufficant [*sic*]," *ND*, August 16, 1932; "Officers Believe Merrill Murder Mystery Is Solved," *ND*, August 17, 1932.

16. "Sheriff Roberts, Maurice O'Neill Arrive Today," *ND*, August 18, 1932.

17. "Fingerprints of Seven Were Taken Here Yesterday," *ND*, August 19, 1932. The paper reported that Pearls was allegedly a gang member.

18. Transcription of this letter comes from Charles East's notes during his meeting with O'Neill's daughter Marion Prevost. East Papers, LLMVC. These details were confirmed in Roberts's reports to the press. "Officers Believe Merrill Murder Mystery Is Solved," *ND*, August 17, 1932; "Fingerprints of Seven Were Taken Here Yesterday," *ND*, August 19, 1932.

19. U.S. Federal Census for 1930, Summit, Illinois, lists the address of George and Meadie Pearls as 7727 W. 62nd Street.

20. "Fingerprints of Seven Were Taken Here Yesterday," *ND*, August 19, 1932; "Prints of Minor, Six Others Taken as Police Renew Inquiry," *TP*, August 19, 1932.

21. "Prints of Minor, Six Others Taken as Police Renew Inquiry," *TP*, August 19, 1932; U.S. Federal Census—Slave Schedules, 1860, Concordia Parish, showed 111 slaves on Scotland plantation and 91 on St. Genevieve plantation.

22. "Latest Suspect in Merrill Case Spirited to Jail outside Natchez," *TP*, August 22, 1932; "Merrill Murder Suspects Held in Jail at Jackson," *TP*, August 24, 1932; "Officers Making Careful Check on Both Confessions," *ND*, August 25, 1932.

23. Emily Burns testified to this during her trial. "Jury Is Unable to Agree upon the Punishment," *ND*, November 27, 1932.

24. Ibid.

25. "Negro Woman Gives Details of Slaying Miss Merrill," *ND*, August 23, 1932; "Woman Confesses Presence at Scene of Merrill Murder," *TP*, August 23, 1932.

26. "Negress Says That Both at Merrill Home during Murder," *ND*, August 24, 1932. On the lynching, see "Negro Hanged by Citizens in Wisner Section," *ND*, November 20, 1932.

27. Burns confession, East Papers, LLMVC.

28. Emily Burns's second confession was edited and printed in the *Natchez Democrat.* "Negress Says That Both at Merrill Home during Murder," *ND*, August 24, 1932.

29. Ibid.

30. Ibid. The confession is located in Charles East's papers. On the back is written "Exhibit A," meaning it was used at her trial. Burns confession, East Papers, LLMVC.

31. "Negress Says That Both at Merrill Home during Murder," *ND*, August 24, 1932.

32. The double standard of southern womanhood stretches back to the period of antebellum slavery and continued well into the twentieth century. See White, *Ar'n't I a Woman?* The same double standards were applied to black women convicts. See LeFlouria, *Chained in Silence.*

33. "Officers Making Careful Check on Both Confessions," *ND*, August 25, 1932. The arrest of George "Doc" Smith took place while Dick Dana was being considered for a radio show. "Broadcast Plans for Dick Dana Show Progress," *ND*, August 29, 1932.

34. "Sheriff to Save Fingerprints for Merrill Jurors," *TP*, August 25, 1932; "Officers Making Careful Check on Both Confessions," *ND*, August 25, 1932.

35. "Action Checked with Confession at Crime Scene," *ND*, August 26, 1932.

36. "Merrill Murder Suspect, Killed Resisting Arrest in Pine Bluff, Identified," *TP*, August 15, 1932.

37. Ibid.

38. "Action Checked with Confession at Crime Scene," *ND*, August 26, 1932; "Sheriff Expects Development in Merrill Slaying," *TP*, August 26, 1932.

39. "Action Checked with Confession at Crime Scene," *ND*, August 26, 1932.

40. "Sheriff Expects to Close Inquiry during the Week," *ND*, August 30, 1932.

CHAPTER SEVEN

1. Advertisement for Pacific Whaling Company, *ND*, November 3, 1932. On Lew Nichols, see Vinnedge, *California's Whaling Coast*, 58.

2. "Old South's Society Is in Murder Drama," *Fitchburg (Mass.) Sentinel*, August 30, 1932; "Stranger Than Fiction," *Lima (Ohio) News*, August 15, 1932.

3. "Rich Woman Recluse Slain in Mississippi," *NYT*, August 6, 1932; "Elderly Recluse Is Slain in South," *Joplin (Mo.) Globe*, August 6, 1932; "Army Coat Is Clue to Recluse's Murder," *Atlanta Journal Constitution*, August 8, 1932; "Aged Recluse Slain; 4 Held," *Titusville (Ga.) Herald*, August 6, 1932.

4. "Fingerprints and Goats in Murder Case," *Star-Journal*, August 6, 1932; "Bloody Fingerprints and Goat Herd Link Eccentric Woman's Death, *Charleston Daily Mail*, August 8, 1932; "Hermit Named as Murderer," *Salt Lake City Tribune*, August 22, 1932

5. Bruce Catton, "A Story Stranger Than Fiction," *Freeport (Ill.) Journal Standard*, August 15, 1932.

6. See, for example, "Probe Death of Southern Belle," *Chronicle-Telegram* (Ohio), August 8, 1932.

7. "Natchez Recluse Shot to Death in Natchez Home," *TP*, August 6, 1932; "Rich Woman Recluse Slain in Mississippi," *NYT*, August 6, 1932.

8. Bruce Catton, "A Story Stranger Than Fiction," *Freeport (Ill.) Journal Standard*, August 15, 1932.

9. Zaida Wells, "Miss Jane Surget Merrill Was Lady of Education, Culture and Highly Refined," *ND*, August 12, 1932.

10. "Report on Slain Suspect's Prints May Solve Case," *TP*, August 15, 1932.

11. "Slaying Mystery Suspects Held Incommunicado While Fingerprints Are Studied," *TP*, August 7, 1932; "Coroner Abandons Attempt to Reopen Inquest in Murder," *TP*, August 11, 1932; "Probe Death of Southern Belle," *Chronicle-Telegram* (Ohio), August 8, 1932.

12. McKittrick's comments appear in "Report on Slain Suspect's Prints May Solve Case," *TP*, August 15, 1932.

13. "Stranger Spreads News of Murder," *TP*, August 10, 1932; "Hints of Contest on Merrill Will Heard in Natchez," *TP*, August 29, 1932; "Indiana Woman May Seek Share," *TP*, August 23, 1932; "Six Held in Jail Pending Merrill Murder Solution," *TP*, August 31, 1932; "Greenfield Woman Gets Word from Stranger of Recluse's Passing," *Kokomo (Ind.) Tribune*, August 19, 1932.

14. "Indiana Woman May Seek Share," *TP*, August 23, 1932.

15. On black male incarceration during this era, see Oshinsky, *"Worse Than Slavery"*; and Blackmon, *Slavery by Another Name*.

16. Calling it a "gun duel" was simply ratcheting up the language. "Natchez Sheriff Predicts 'Startling Development' in Merrill Murder Case," *TP*, August 21, 1932.

17. "Mississippi Woman Is Given Life, Accessory to Murder Plot," *Kansas City Plaindealer*, December 9, 1932. See also "Natchez Woman Gets Murder Investigation Spotlight," *Chicago Defender*, August 27, 1932; "Grand Jury of Dixie State to Probe Deaths," *Chicago Defender*, November 12, 1932; and "2 White, 2 Colored Arrested in Murder," *New York Amsterdam News*, August 24, 1932. The latter incorrectly referred to her as "Mrs. Emily Jones."

18. Unknown to Emily Scott, August 13, 1932, Emily T. Scott Papers, LLMVC.

19. "New Fingerprints of Dick Dana Are Being Compared," *ND*, August 9, 1932.

20. Ibid.; "Rich Woman Recluse Slain in Mississippi," *New York Times*, August 6, 1932; "Natchez Recluse Shot to Death in Natchez Home," *TP*, August 6, 1932; "Hermit Charged in Murder," *Jackson Daily News*, August 8, 1932.

21. "Finger Prints Made Basis of Murder Charge," *Jefferson City (Mo.) Post-Tribune*, August 10, 1932. For example, the photo caption for Dana and Dockery reads "Eccentric Recluse, Aged Sweetheart Held in 'Goat Feud' Murder," *Coshocton (Ohio) Tribune*, August 14, 1932.

22. "Pictures Taken of Dana and Miss Dockery," *ND*, August 9, 1932.

23. "Fingerprints Point Way to Two Slayers," *The Hutchinson News* (Kans.), August 10, 1932; "Pair Charged as Merrill Slayers," *The Kingsport Times* (Tenn.), August 9,

1932; "Southern Goat Castle Scene of a Tragedy," *Lebanon Semi-Weekly News* (Pa.), August 15, 1932.

24. "Dick Dana and Miss Octavia Dockery Who Are Being Held on Murder Charges and Whose Life Stories Are Both Fantastic and Weird," *ND*, August 11, 1932.

25. "Dana's Life Filled with Tragedy and Futility," *TP*, August 9, 1932; "Fallen Grandeur Bared by Murder," *Kingsport (Tenn.) Times*, August 17, 1932.

26. "Dick Dana and Miss Octavia Dockery Who Are Being Held on Murder Charges and Whose Life Stories Are Both Fantastic and Weird," *ND*, August 11, 1932.

27. Ibid.

28. Ibid.

29. Dockery was allowed this one interview, and it was first documented in the *Times-Picayune* and the *Natchez Democrat*. The story then appeared in the AP news-wire and was picked up by newspapers around the country. See "Life Story of Miss Dockery Reveals Struggle against Whim of Ironic Fate," *ND*, August 10, 1932; "Dick Dana and Miss Octavia Dockery Who Are Being Held on Murder Charges and Whose Life Stories Are Both Fantastic and Weird," *ND*, August 11, 1932; and "Death of Sister, Poverty, Drove Natchez Butterfly from Poetry to Pigsty," *TP*, August 10, 1932.

30. "Death of Sister, Poverty, Drove Natchez Butterfly from Poetry to Pigsty," *TP*, August 10, 1932.

31. "Dick Dana and Miss Octavia Dockery Who Are Being Held on Murder Charges and Whose Life Stories Are Both Fantastic and Weird," *ND*, August 11, 1932.

32. Ibid.

33. Ibid. Records show that Richard and Nydia Forman, along with Dick Dana and Octavia Dockery, became residents of Glenwood at the same time. See chapter 2.

34. Ibid.

35. Ibid.

CHAPTER EIGHT

1. Cox, "Revisiting the Natchez Pilgrimage," 349–55.

2. "Dick Dana and Miss Octavia Dockery Who Are Being Held on Murder Charges and Whose Life Stories Are Both Fantastic and Weird," *ND*, August 11, 1932.

3. "Natchez Sheriff Predicts 'Startling Development' in Merrill Murder Case," *TP*, August 21, 1932.

4. "Booster Displays Dana Souvenirs," *ND*, August 8, 1932.

5. Ibid.; "Swelling Wave of Sympathy for Dick Dana and Miss Dockery Continues to Steadily Mount in This Community," *ND*, August 14, 1932.

6. "Natchez Sheriff Predicts 'Startling Development' in Merrill Murder Case," *TP*, August 21, 1932.

7. Ibid.

8. "Merrill Murder Remains Puzzle to Authorities," *TP*, August 27, 1932.

9. "Gwen Bristow (1903–1980)." While one can compare Goat Castle with the house described in Faulkner's short story "A Rose for Emily," published in 1930, the most

common comparisons made at the time were with Edgar Allan Poe, especially his short story "The Fall of the House of Usher."

10. "Damask and Dirt Mingle in Dick Dana's 'Goat Castle,'" *TP*, August 14, 1932; "Debris Ankle Deep Fills Once Lovely Mansion," *TP*, August 14, 1932.

11. Ibid.

12. Ibid.

13. Ibid.

14. Ibid.

15. "Life Story of Miss Dockery Reveals Struggle against Whim of Ironic Fate," *ND*, August 10, 1932.

16. "Dana's Life Filled with Tragedy and Futility," *TP*, August 9, 1932"; "Investigation of Odell Ferguson Started Friday," *ND*, August 13, 1932; "Many Visitors View Glenwood during Weekend," *ND*, August 16, 1932. Trespassing at Elms Court described in "Crowd Applauds as Court Orders Release of Dana and Housekeeper," *TP*, August 16, 1932.

17. Discussion of visitors in "Sheriff to Save Fingerprints for Merrill Jurors," *TP*, August 25, 1932; "Admission to be Charged to Dana Property," *ND*, August 24, 1932.

18. "Admission to be Charged to Dana Property," *ND*, August 24, 1932.

19. Quote comes from "Swelling Wave of Sympathy for Dick Dana and Miss Dockery Continues to Steadily Mount in This Community," *ND*, August 14, 1932. Even as the investigation continued, visitors were turning out in droves to see Goat Castle. See "No Excitement Is Created Here by Confessions," *ND*, August 27, 1932; and "Sheriff to Save Fingerprints for Merrill Jurors," *TP*, August 25, 1932.

20. "No Excitement Is Created Here by Confessions," *ND*, August 27, 1932; "Merrill Murder Suspects Held in Jail at Jackson," *TP*, August 24, 1932.

21. "No Excitement Is Created Here by Confessions," *ND*, August 27, 1932; "Merrill Murder Suspects Held in Jail at Jackson," *TP*, August 24, 1932. On cleaning Glenwood, see "Sheriff to Save Fingerprints for Merrill Jurors," *TP*, August 25, 1932.

22. Notes on the goat flock appear in "Hints of Contest on Merrill Will Heard in Natchez," *TP*, August 29, 1932.

23. News of the piano donation appeared in "Six Held in Jail Pending Merrill Murder Solution," *TP*, August 31, 1932.

24. "Hundreds Hear Dana Concerts during Sunday," *ND*, September 6, 1932.

25. "Excursion Will Bring Many to Natchez Sunday," *ND*, September 10, 1932; "Excursion Here Brought Large Numbers," *ND*, September 13, 1932; "Three Excursions to Visit Here Next Sunday," *ND*, September 18, 1932.

26. "Abbott Announces W.S.M.B. Ready for Broadcast," *ND*, August 28, 1932; "Broadcast Plans for Dick Dana Show Progress," *ND*, August 29, 1932.

27. "Dana Will Not Broadcast Says E. H. Ratcliff," *ND*, August 30, 1932.

28. "Concert Given by Dick Dana in Woodville," *ND*, September 18, 1932; "Vicksburg Wants Dana to Appear There in Concert," *ND*, September 20, 1932.

29. "Dana-Dockery Entertainment Makes Big Hit," *ND*, October 13, 1932.

30. "Concert Given by Dick Dana in Woodville," *ND*, September 18, 1932; "Vicksburg Wants Dana to Appear There in Concert," *ND*, September 20, 1932; "Dana-

Dockery Concert Given at Sicily Island," *ND*, October 18, 1932; "Dana-Dockery Program Given at Jonesville," *ND*, October 19, 1932.

31. "Dana-Dockery Recital Makes Hit in Jackson," *ND*, October 26, 1932; Sansing, "Earl Leroy Brewer," accessed March 22, 2016.

32. "Dana Drops 'Wild Man' Role, Plans to Tour South," *TP*, September 18, 1932.

33. Ibid.

CHAPTER NINE

1. Weather reported in the *Natchez Democrat*, November 15, 1932.

2. Maurice O'Neill kept a number of items from the investigation following the trial. His daughter Marion Prevost inherited them, and in 1977 Charles East met with her and transcribed O'Neill's notes and the letters Roberts received. See East Papers, LLMVC.

3. "New Inquiry into Merrill Slaying Asked by Court," *TP*, November 15, 1932. Because no trial transcript exists, testimony is drawn from coverage by the *Natchez Democrat* and the *Times-Picayune*. However, subpoenas, affidavits, and jury instructions are all located in the records of the Adams County Circuit Court, Case File 4708, HNF.

4. "Merrill Murder Case Being Investigated by Grand Jury, Many Witnesses Called," *ND*, November 16, 1932; "Secrecy Shrouds Merrill Slaying Study by Jurors," *TP*, November 16, 1932.

5. "Merrill Murder Case Being Investigated by Grand Jury, Many Witnesses Called," *ND*, November 16, 1932. In a 1976 interview with Charles East, Tucker remained convinced that there was insufficient evidence to indict Dana and Dockery, stating that Joe Brown and Book Roberts were the ones who wanted to indict, not Tucker. But Brown and Roberts had investigated the case and Tucker had not. Clay Tucker to Charles East, Woodville, Mississippi, 1976, East Papers, LLMVC.

6. Details of McKittrick's interview appear in "Report on Slain Suspect's Prints May Solve Case," *TP*, August 15, 1932.

7. Grand Jury indictment, November 14, 1932, Adams County Circuit Court Records, Case File 4708, HNF.

8. "Slain Suspect, Woman Indicted in Merrill Case," *TP*, November 17, 1932; "Emily Burns Indicted for Murder of Miss Jane Merrill by County Grand Jury," *ND*, November 17, 1932.

9. "Trial of Emily Burns for Murder of Miss Jane Merrill Set for the Twenty-Fifth," *ND*, November 18, 1932. According to Charles East's transcriptions of Maurice O'Neill's notes, Emily Burns weighed 125 pounds in August. When she entered prison, the registrar listed her weight at 105 pounds.

10. Before 1940, capital punishment in Mississippi occurred by hanging. Cabana, "History of Capital Punishment," accessed March 31, 2016.

11. Wilfred A. Geisenberger, Subject File, MDAH. Details of the ages of the three attorneys are drawn from the 1930 U.S. Federal Census for Adams County.

12. "Emily Burns to be Placed on Trial Friday," *ND*, November 25, 1932; "State

Attempts to Picture Death of Miss Merrill," *TP*, November 26, 1932; "Confessions of Emily Burns to Officers Related," *ND*, November 26, 1932.

13. "State Attempts to Picture Death of Miss Merrill," *TP*, November 26, 1932.

14. "Confessions of Emily Burns to Officers Related," *ND*, November 26, 1932.

15. Ibid.

16. Ibid.; Burns confession, East Papers, LLMVC.

17. "Confessions of Emily Burns to Officers Related," *ND*, November 26, 1932; "State Attempts to Picture Death of Miss Merrill," *TP*, November 26, 1932.

18. "Confessions of Emily Burns to Officers Related," *ND*, November 26, 1932.

19. "State Attempts to Picture Death of Miss Merrill," *TP*, November 26, 1932.

20. "Jury Is Unable to Agree upon the Punishment," *ND*, November 27, 1932.

21. Ibid.

22. Ibid.

23. Ibid. Natchez City Directory for 1928 lists Annie Reed as living at 232 St. Catherine Street. Emily Burns lived with her mother at a duplex that contained a joint address of 228–230 St. Catherine Street, likely because they rented rooms in one.

24. "Jury Is Unable to Agree upon the Punishment," *ND*, November 27, 1932.

25. Ibid.

26. Ibid.

27. Ibid. All original witness subpoenas in the case are located in Adams County Circuit Court Records, Case File 4708, HNF. Natchez City Directory for 1929 showed Elmore as owner of East End Beer Parlor, although the paper called it a "store."

28. Stone's quotes appear in "Sheriff to Save Fingerprints for Merrill Jurors," *TP*, August 25, 1932.

29. Clifford Fields to Sheriff of Hinds County, November 22, 1932, Adams County Circuit Court Records, Case File 4708, HNF.

30. Affidavit in Support of Motion to Continue, November 25, 1932, ibid.

31. Ibid.

32. Ibid.

33. Ibid.

34. Ibid.

35. Ibid.

36. Z. Wells, *Merrill Murder Mystery*, 17.

37. Jury instructions by the state, *The State v. Emily Burns*, Adams County Circuit Court Records, Case 4708, HNF.

38. Ibid.

39. Ibid.

40. Jury instructions for the defendant, ibid.

41. Ibid.

42. Jury instructions by the state, ibid.

43. Ibid. Zaida Wells believed the reason Emily Burns did not receive the death penalty was due to Geisenberger's impassioned pleas for mercy during his closing arguments. Z. Wells, *Merrill Murder Mystery*, 17.

44. "Woman Convicted in Merrill Case; Faces Life Term," *TP*, November 27, 1932.

45. "Woman Involved in Merrill Death to Get Life," *TP*, November 28, 1932.

46. "Merrill Murder Accessory Given Life Term," *TP*, December 1, 1932.

47. "Prisoners Taken to Penitentiary," *ND*, December 6, 1932. Sergeant Tullos was killed five months later while taking convicts to the penitentiary from Hattiesburg. See "Chester J. Tullos," accessed April 4, 2016.

CHAPTER TEN

1. Cox, "Revisiting the Natchez Pilgrimage," 353–67; "Pilgrimage Week Begins Tomorrow, When Ante-bellum Days Will Be Re-Lived," *NYT*, April 2, 1933; Alfred C. Hottes to Mrs. Balfour (Katherine) Miller, February 3, 1933, Katherine Miller Scrapbook, HNF. Hottes was the editor of *Better Homes and Gardens*.

2. Goat Castle flyer, East Papers, LLMVC.

3. Dmitri, "So Red the Rose." Journalists in 1932 compared Goat Castle to something from an Edgar Allan Poe story, but as Faulkner became increasingly known throughout the decade, more journalists compared the case with his fiction.

4. H. Wells, "Crimson Crime at Glenburney Manor," May–September 1933. On Homer G. Wells see Przybyszewski, "Bloodhound Man," accessed May 18, 2016.

5. H. Wells, "Crimson Crime at Glenburney Manor," September 1933.

6. Ibid.

7. Ibid. African American newspapers also covered this story. See "Merrill Murder Suspects Sue Sheriff for $32,000," *Philadelphia Tribune*, August 17, 1933.

8. *Miss Octavia Dockery v. C. P. Roberts and National Surety Company of New York, New York*, Adams County Circuit Court Records, Case File 1822, HNF.

9. Ibid.

10. Ibid.

11. Ibid.

12. "Natchez Sheriff Predicts 'Startling Development' in Merrill Murder Case," *TP*, August 21, 1932.

13. *Miss Octavia Dockery v. C. P. Roberts and the National Surety Company of New York, New York*, Notice Under the General Issue, Adams County Circuit Court Records, Case File 1822, HNF.

14. Ibid.

15. Ibid.

16. Ibid.

17. Ibid.

18. "Dana and Dockery Indicted for Murder," *ND*, August 16, 1933; "Trial of Pair Set by Court for Wednesday," *ND*, November 16, 1933.

19. "Attorneys for Dana and Miss Dockery Want Suit Tried after Murder Hearing," *ND*, November 17, 1933.

20. Ibid.; "Trial of Pair Set by Court for Wednesday," *ND*, November 16, 1933; "Dana, Guardian Face Charges in Merrill Slaying," *TP*, November 16, 1933.

21. "Court Dismisses $32,000 Dana Suit against Sheriff," *TP*, November 18, 1933.

22. Ibid.; "Court Replaces Sheriff for Dana-Dockery Trial as Defense Charges Bias," *TP*, November 23, 1933.

23. "Attorneys for Dana and Miss Dockery Want Suit Tried after Murder Hearing," *TP*, November 17, 1933.

24. "Criminal Cases to Occupy Court during This Week," *ND*, November 19, 1933.

25. "Dana-Dockery Case Expected to Go to Trial," *ND*, November 21, 1933.

26. *The State v. Octavia Dockery*, Adams County Circuit Court Records, Case File 4746, HNF. See also "Court Grants Defense Motion for Severance," *ND*, November 23, 1933; and "Court Replaces Sheriff for Dana-Dockery Trial as Defense Charges Bias," *TP*, November 23, 1933.

27. *The State v. Octavia Dockery*, Adams County Circuit Court Records, Case File 4746, HNF.

28. "Mystery Woman of 'Goat Castle' Faces Trial Today in Merrill Murder Case," *TP*, November 27, 1933.

29. "Court Grants Defense Motion for Severance," *ND*, November 23, 1933. On the trial-weary public, see "Mystery Woman of 'Goat Castle' Faces Trial Today in Merrill Murder Case," *TP*, November 27, 1933.

30. "Dockery Defense May Base Case on Two Witnesses," *TP*, November 28, 1933.

31. Ibid.

32. "Mystery Woman of 'Goat Castle' Faces Trial Today in Merrill Murder Case," *TP*, November 27, 1933.

33. Ibid.

34. "Regular Panel, Special Venire Exhausted Monday," *ND*, November 28, 1933.

35. "Further Action Not to be Taken at Present Term," *ND*, November 29, 1933.

36. Ibid.

37. Bristow's account appeared in "Dana, Guardian Sent Home Free after Mistrial," *TP*, November 29, 1933.

38. Ibid.

CHAPTER ELEVEN

1. Details on Ola Mae Spickard, Jackson, Mississippi, City Directories, 1920, 1930; Series 1567: Convict Registers, 69, Department of Corrections, Mississippi State Penitentiary, MDAH.

2. Series 1567: Convict Registers, 69, Department of Corrections, Mississippi State Penitentiary, MDAH.

3. Ibid.

4. Foreman and Tatum, "Short History of Mississippi's State Penal Systems," 255. On the broader history of Parchman, see Oshinsky, *"Worse Than Slavery"*; and Taylor, *Down on Parchman Farm*. On the treatment of women in Jim Crow–era prisons, especially the case of Georgia, see LeFlouria, *Chained in Silence*.

5. *Biennial Reports of the Board of Trustees of the Mississippi State Penitentiary*, 1933–1939; Board Files, 1907–1976, Mississippi State Penitentiary, MDAH; Oshinsky, *"Worse Than Slavery,"* 172.

6. *Biennial Report of the Board of Trustees of the Mississippi State Penitentiary*, 1933, 9–10.

7. "My Prison Life," by Fanny Walden, February 28, 1935, David Cohn Papers, Archives and Special Collections, J. D. Williams Library, University of Mississippi.

8. On mercy courts, see Taylor, *Down on Parchman Farm*, 54–55.

9. Sansing, "Paul B. Johnson," accessed April 20, 2016.

10. "Governor Opens Mercy Court," *ND*, December 18, 1940.

11. Pardons, Series 926, Records of the Office of the Governor, MDAH; "Emily Burns Is Given Freedom by Gov. Johnson," *ND*, December 19, 1940; "Governor Frees Natchez Suspect in Castle Killing," *TP*, December 19, 1940.

12. Alfred Smith's daughters Linda Griffin and Phyliss Morris described his heroic effort to the author, May 17, 2016, Natchez, MS.

EPILOGUE

1. "Denies Intention to Evict Couple from 'Goat Castle' at Natchez," *TP*, June 26, 1937.

2. "Dana, Guardian Lose Ruling for 45-Acre Estate," *TP*, June 6, 1939.

3. "Hoosier Woman Claims Estate in Southland," *Kokomo (Ind.) Tribune*, August 18, 1933; "Withdraws Claim to Estate," ibid., August 19, 1935.

4. "R. C. Dana, Master of 'Goat Castle,' Freed with Guardian in Strange Natchez, Miss., Murder Case of 1932 — Stricken at 77," *NYT*, December 12, 1948.

5. *Miss Octavia Dockery v. Seaman Zerkowsky, Isaac Zerkowsky, Sam Zerkowsky and Mrs. Jeanette Habas*, Adams County Chancery Court Records, Case File 11,795, HNF. See also "Marriage of Pair at 'Castle' Denied," *TP*, February 27, 1949; "She's Not His Wife, Defense Says of Suit," *Delta Times-Democrat* (Greenville, Miss.), February 27, 1949. Details of Dockery's health and stay at the charity hospital appear in "Octavia Dockery, 84, Lived in 'Goat Castle,'" *NYT*, April 23, 1949.

6. "Octavia Dockery, 84, Lived in 'Goat Castle,'" *NYT*, April 23, 1949; "Death Won Case for Miss Dockery, Principal in Goat Castle Suit," *Delta Times-Democrat* (Greenville, Miss.), April 25, 1949; "Death Removes 'Goat Castle's' Last Occupant," *Anniston (Ala.) Star*, April 24, 1949; "Miss Octavia Dockery," *Gaston (N.C.) Gazette*, May 14, 1949.

7. Duncan Morgan, discussion with author, Natchez, Mississippi, March 8, 2012.

8. Birdia Green, telephone discussion with author, May 3, 2016.

9. Natchez City Directory, 1950.

10. Ibid., 1950, 1955. Author's discussions with Doris Maynard and Birdia Green revealed Lee Randolph's role as deacon and descriptions of his size. Emily Burns's death was recorded in the family Bible as September 1969, Smith family Bible, Natchez, Mississippi.

11. Based on author's conversation with Birdia Green, Phyliss Morris, and Linda Griffin, October 9, 2015, Natchez, Mississippi.

BIBLIOGRAPHY

ARCHIVAL COLLECTIONS

Baton Rouge, La.
    Special Collections, Hill Memorial Library, Louisiana State University Libraries
        Louisiana and Lower Mississippi Valley Collections
            Charles B. Dana and Family Papers
            Charles East Papers
            Thomas H. and Joan W. Gandy Photograph Collection
            Emily T. Scott Papers
Jackson, Miss.
    Mississippi Division of Archives and History
        Adams County Certificates of Death
        Department of Corrections, Mississippi State Penitentiary
            Biennial Reports of the Board of Trustees, 1931–1939
            Board Files, 1907–1976
            Series 1556: Statistics Register
            Series 1557: Board Minutes
            Series 1567: Convict Registers
            Series 1571: Monthly Roll Call Ledger
        Octavia Dockery Papers, 1882–1889
        Mississippi State Penitentiary (Parchman) Photo Collections
        Mississippi Supreme Court
            Series 208: Case Files
        Records of the Office of the Governor
            Pardon and Suspension Files, Series 912
            Pardons, Series 926
        Subject Files
            Wilfred A. Geisenberger
            Goat Castle
            Duncan G. Minor
            Stephen Minor
Natchez, Miss.
    Adams County Courthouse
        Circuit Court Ledgers

Historic Natchez Foundation
    Adams County Chancery Court Records
    Adams County Circuit Court Records
    Adams County Historic Sites Subject Files
        Elms Court
        Glenburnie
        Oakland
    Adams County Probate Records
    Dicks Family Collection
    Dunbar Merrill Flinn Collection
    George Kelly Letters
    Katherine Miller Scrapbook
    Earl Norman Photograph Collection
Northampton, Mass.
    Sophia Smith Collection, Smith College
        Sophie Friedman Papers
University, Miss.
    J. D. Williams Library, University of Mississippi
        Archives and Special Collections
            Roane Fleming Byrnes Collection
            David Cohn Papers
Washington, D.C.
    National Archives and Records Administration
        Records of the Southern Claims Commission, Records of the General
            Accounting Office, Record Group 217

NEWSPAPERS

Anniston (Ala.) Star
Atlanta Journal Constitution
Charleston (W.Va.) Daily Mail
Chicago Defender
Chronicle-Telegram (Ohio)
Coshocton (Ohio) Tribune
Daily Arkansas Democrat
Delta Times-Democrat (Miss.)
Evening Star (Washington, D.C.)
Evening World (New York)
Fitchburg (Mass.) Sentinel
Freeport (Ill.) Journal Standard
Gaston (N.C.) Gazette
Hutchinson (Kansas) News
Jackson (Miss.) Daily-Times
Jefferson City (Mo.) Post-Tribune

Joplin (Mo.) Globe
Kansas City Plaindealer
Kingsport (Tenn.) Times
Kokomo (Ind.) Tribune
Memphis Commercial Appeal
Milwaukee Daily Sentinel
Natchez Democrat
New Orleans Times-Picayune
New York Amsterdam News
New York Sun
New York Times
Philadelphia Tribune
Pittsburgh Dispatch
Salt Lake City Tribune
Star-Journal (Ohio)
Titusville (Ga.) Herald

GOVERNMENT RECORDS
(SOURCES AVAILABLE AT ANCESTRY.COM)

Mississippi, Wills and Probate Records, 1877–1920
New England, United Methodist Church Records, 1787–1922
New Jersey, Death and Burials Index, 1798–1971
Pennsylvania, Passenger and Crew Lists, 1800–1952
Spanish-American War Military and Naval Service Records, 1898–1902
U.S. Federal Census, 1850–1940
U.S. Federal Census—Slave Schedules, 1860
U.S. World War I Draft Registration Cards, 1917–1918

CITY DIRECTORIES (AVAILABLE AT ANCESTRY.COM)

Jackson, Mississippi, City Directory, 1920, 1930–1932
Memphis, Tennessee, City Directories, 1880–1920
Natchez, Mississippi, City Directories, 1900–1970
New Orleans City Directories
Newport, Rhode Island, City Directory, 1867–1868
New York City Directories, 1880–1900

PUBLISHED PRIMARY SOURCES

Biographical and Historical Memoirs of Mississippi. Vol. 2. Chicago: Godspeed
    Publishing, 1891.
The Commercial and Financial Chronicle. Vol. 2. 1866.
General Catalogue of Dartmouth College. 1880.

Hearing before Senate Executive Committee on Freedmen and Abandoned Lands. 39th Cong., 1st sess., 1865.

Journal of the Thirty-Fifth Convention of the Protestant Episcopal Church for the Diocese of Mississippi. 1861.

Journal of the Proceedings of the Protestant Episcopal Church, Mississippi Diocese. 1867.

UNPUBLISHED PRIMARY SOURCES

Smith family Bible, Natchez, Mississippi

Smith family portrait, ca. 1913

DISCUSSIONS WITH AUTHOR, NATCHEZ, MISSISSIPPI

Ballard, Sallie

Blankenstein, Kathie

Davis, Felice

Green, Birdia

Green, Daisy

Griffin, Linda

Maynard, Doris

Morgan, Duncan

Morris, Phyliss

SECONDARY SOURCES

Anderson, Aaron. *Builders of the New South: Merchants, Capital, and the Remaking of Natchez, 1865–1914.* Jackson: University of Mississippi Press, 2013.

Anderson, William J. *Life and Narrative of William J. Anderson.* Chicago: Daily Tribune Book and Job Printing Office, 1857.

Arey, Frank. "Thomas Pleasant Dockery, 1833–1898." *Encyclopedia of Arkansas History and Culture.* http://www.encyclopediaofarkansas.net/encyclopedia/entry -detail.aspx?entryID=1191.

Baptist, Edward E. *The Half Has Never Been Told: Slavery and the Making of American Capitalism.* New York: Basic Books, 2014.

Barnett, Jim, and H. Clark Burkett. "The Forks of the Road Slave Market at Natchez." *Journal of Mississippi History* 63 (Fall 2001): 169–87.

"Battle of Port Gibson," *National Park Service.* http://www.nps.gov/vick/history culture/battleportgibson.htm.

Blackmon, Douglas J. *Slavery by Another Name: The Re-enslavement of Black Americans from the Civil War to World War II.* New York: Anchor, 2009.

Boltwood, Edward. *The History of Pittsfield, Massachusetts: From the Year 1876 to the Year 1916.* Pittsfield, Mass.: Eagle Printing and Binding Co., 1916.

Brooke, Steven. *The Majesty of Natchez*. Gretna, La.: Pelican, 2007.

Broussard, Joyce L. "Occupied Natchez, Elite Women, and the Feminization of the Civil War." *Journal of Mississippi History* 70 (2008): 179–207.

Cabana, Donald A. "The History of Capital Punishment in Mississippi: An Overview." *Mississippi History Now*. http://mshistorynow.mdah.state.ms.us/articles /84/history-of-capital-punishment-in-mississippi-an-overview.

Callon, Sim, and Carolyn Vance Smith. *The Goat Castle Murder: A True Natchez Story That Shocked the World*. Natchez, Miss.: Plantation, 1985.

Cashin, Joan. "The Structure of Antebellum Families: 'The Ties That Bound Us Was Strong.'" *Journal of Southern History* 56, no. 1 (February 1990): 55–70.

Collier, Louise Wilbourn. *Pilgrimage: A Tale of Old Natchez*. Gretna, La.: Pelican, 1994.

Cook, Florence Elliott. "Growing Up White, Genteel, and Female in a Changing South, 1865–1915." Ph.D. diss., University of California at Berkeley, 1992.

Cox, Karen L. *Dreaming of Dixie: How the South Was Created in American Popular Culture*. Chapel Hill: University of North Carolina Press, 2011.

———. "Revisiting the Natchez Pilgrimage: Women and the Creation of Mississippi's Heritage Tourism Industry." *Journal of Mississippi History* 74, no. 4 (Winter 2012): 349–71.

Davis, Jack E. *Race against Time: Culture and Separation in Natchez since 1930*. Baton Rouge: Louisiana State University Press, 2001.

Deyle, Steven. *Carry Me Back: The Domestic Slave Trade in American Life*. New York: Oxford University Press, 2005.

Dmitri, Ivan. "So Red the Rose." *Saturday Evening Post*, March 4, 1939, 18–23.

Dolkensky, Suzanne T. "Natchez in 1920: On the Threshold of Modernity." *Journal of Mississippi History* 73, no. 2 (Summer 2011): 1–35.

Dockery, Octavia. "Held by the Enemy." *The Blue and the Gray*, July 1893, 334–36.

Foreman, Paul B., and Julien R. Tatum. "The Short History of Mississippi's State Penal Systems." *Mississippi Law Journal*, April 1938, 255–78.

"Glenburnie." *National Register of Historic Places Inventory—Nomination*. National Park Service, 1976. http://npgallery.nps.gov/nrhp/AssetDetail?assetID =370a241d-b7b4-4d2b-bf94-574a4f71af91.

Gross, Kali Nicole. "African American Women, Mass Incarceration, and the Politics of Protection," *Journal of American History* 102, issue 1 (June 2015): 25–33.

Hoelscher, Steven. "The White-Pillared Past: Landscapes of Memory and Race in the American South." In *Landscape and Race in the United States*, edited by Richard H. Schein, 39–61. New York: Routledge Press, 2006.

Hunter, Tera W. *To 'Joy My Freedom: Southern Black Women's Lives and Labors after the Civil War*. Cambridge, Mass.: Harvard University Press, 1998.

Ingraham, Joseph Holt. *The South-West by a Yankee*. New York: Harper and Brothers, 1835.

Jenkins, Kathleen M. "Melrose, a Multifaceted Jewel in the NPS Crown: Interdisciplinary Contributions to Historic Preservation and Museum Collection

Management." In *Crossing Boundaries in Park Management: Proceedings of the
  11th Conference on Research and Resource Management in Parks and on Public
  Lands*, edited by David Harmon, 371–74. Hancock, Mich.: George Wright Society, 2001.

Johnson, Walter. *River of Dark Dreams: Slavery and Empire in the Cotton Kingdom.*
  Cambridge, Mass.: Belknap Press, 2013.

———. *Soul by Soul: Life inside the Antebellum Slave Market.* Cambridge, Mass.:
  Harvard University Press, 2000.

Kane, Harnett T. *Natchez on the Mississippi.* New York: William Morrow, 1947.

Lauderdale, Vance. "Meet Homer G. Wells—Famous Memphis Detective and
  'Bloodhound Man.'" *Memphis: The City Magazine*, November 2011, http://
  memphismagazine.com/ask-vance/meet-homer-g-wells-memphis-detective
  -and-bloodhound-man/.

Lebsock, Suzanne. *A Murder in Virginia: Southern Justice on Trial.* New York:
  W. W. Norton, 2004.

LeFlouria, Talitha L. *Chained in Silence: Black Women and Convict Labor in the
  New South.* Chapel Hill: University of North Carolina Press, 2015.

Lemann, Nicholas. *The Promised Land: The Great Black Migration and How It
  Changed America.* New York: Vintage Books, 1991.

Llewelyn, Michael. *The Goat Castle Murder: A Novel.* Seattle: Water Street Press,
  2016.

Lomax, Alan. *The Land Where the Blues Began.* New York: New Press, 1993.

Mansell, Jeffrey. Histories of "Elms Court" and "Oakland." Natchez, Miss.:
  Natchez National Historic Park, National Park Service, n.d.

Marszalek, John F., ed. *The Papers of Ulysses S. Grant.* Digital ed. Starkville:
  Mississippi State University, 2008.

Matrana, Marc R. *Lost Plantations of the South.* Jackson: University of Mississippi
  Press, 2009.

McCurry, Stephanie. *Masters of Small Worlds: Yeoman Households, Gender Relations, and the Political Culture of the Antebellum South Carolina Low Country.*
  New York: Oxford University Press, 1995.

McMillen Neil R. *Dark Journey: Black Mississippians in the Age of Jim Crow.*
  Urbana: University of Illinois Press, 1990.

Miller, Paul F. *Lost Newport: Vanished Cottage of the Resort Era.* Bedford, Mass.:
  Applewood Books, 2010.

Oliver, Nola Nance. *This Too Is Natchez.* New York: Hastings House, 1953.

Oshinsky, David M. *"Worse Than Slavery": Parchman and the Ordeal of Jim Crow
  Justice.* New York: Free Press, 1996.

Palmer, Louis. "Bourgeois Blues: Class, Whiteness, and Southern Gothic in Early
  Faulkner and Caldwell." *Faulkner Journal*, Fall/Spring 2007, 120–39.

Phillips, Jason. "Reconstruction in Mississippi, 1865–1876." *Mississippi History
  Now*, May 2006. http://mshistorynow.mdah.state.ms.us/index.php?id=204.

Przybyszewski, Chris. "The Bloodhound Man." *Memphis Flyer*, July 23, 2001.

http://www.memphisflyer.com/memphis/the-bloodhound-man/Content?oid
=1117349.

Rabinowitz, Howard N. *Race Relations in the Urban South, 1865–1890.* Athens: University of Georgia Press, 1996.

Reed, Christopher Robert. *The Depression Comes to the South Side: Protest and Politics in the Black Metropolis, 1930–1933.* Bloomington: Indiana University Press, 2011.

Riis, Jacob A. *How the Other Half Lives: Studies among the Tenements of New York.* New York: Charles Scribner's Sons, 1890.

Sansing, David G. "Earl Leroy Brewer: Thirty-Eighth Governor of Mississippi, 1912–1916." *Mississippi History Now,* http://mshistorynow.mdah.state.ms.us /index.php?s=extra&id=139.

———. "Paul B. Johnson: Forty-Sixth Governor of Mississippi, 1940–1943." *Mississippi History Now,* http://mshistorynow.mdah.state.ms.us/index.php?s=extra &id=146.

Sansing, David G., Sim C. Callon, and Carolyn Vance Smith. *Natchez: An Illustrated History.* Natchez, Miss.: Plantation.

Scarborough, William Kauffman. *Masters of the Big House: Elite Slaveholders of the Mid-Nineteenth-Century South.* Baton Rouge: Louisiana State University Press, 2003.

Schroeder, John D. "Summit, IL." *Encyclopedia of Chicago.* Chicago: Chicago Historical Society, 2005. http://www.encyclopedia.chicagohistory.org/pages /1220.html.

Sharpless, Rebecca. *Cooking in Other Women's Kitchens: Domestic Workers in the South, 1865–1960.* Chapel Hill: University of North Carolina Press, 2010.

Simon, John Y., ed. *The Personal Memoirs of Julia Dent Grant (Mrs. Ulysses S. Grant).* Carbondale: Southern Illinois University Press, 1988.

Smith, Erin A. *Hard-Boiled: Working-Class Readers and Pulp Magazines.* Philadelphia: Temple University Press, 2000.

Street, James. *Look Away! A Dixie Notebook.* 1936; reprint, Westport, Conn.: Greenwood Press, 1977.

Taylor, Williams Banks. *Down on Parchman Farm: The Great Prison in the Mississippi Delta.* Columbus: Ohio State University Press, 1999.

Tidwell, John Edgar, and Mark A. Sanders, eds. *Sterling A. Brown's "A Negro Looks at the South."* New York: Oxford University Press, 2007.

Trotti, Michael Ayers. *The Body in the Reservoir: Murder and Sensationalism in the South.* Chapel Hill: University of North Carolina Press, 2008.

Various Artists. *Jailhouse Blues.* Rosetta Records, RR 1316, vinyl LP. 1987.

Vinnedge, Dale. *California's Whaling Coast (Images of America).* Charleston, S.C.: Arcadia, 2014.

Wells, Homer G. "The Crimson Crime at Glenburney Manor." Five-part series in *Master Detective,* May–September 1933.

Wells, Zaida Marion. *The Merrill Murder Mystery.* Natchez, Miss., n.d.

White, Deborah Gray. *Ar'n't I a Woman? Female Slaves in the Plantation South.*
New York: W. W. Norton, 1999.

Wilkerson, Isabel. *The Warmth of Other Suns: The Epic Story of America's Great
Migration.* New York: Vintage Books, 2010.

Wilson, James Harrison. *The Life of Charles A. Dana.* New York: Harper and
Brothers, 1907.

Wilson, Mark R. "Food Processing: Regional and National Market." *Encyclopedia
of Chicago.* Chicago: Chicago Historical Society, 2005. http://www.encyclopedia
.chicagohistory.org/pages/1220.html.

Wright, Richard. *Black Boy (American Hunger): A Record of Childhood and Youth.*
New York: Perennial Classics, 1998.

WEBSITES

"The Bertillon System." National Library of Medicine. Online exhibit "Visible
Proofs." https://www.nlm.nih.gov/visibleproofs/galleries/technologies/bertillon
.html.

"Chester J. Tullos." Officer Down Memorial Page. https://www.odmp.org/officer
/13492-sergeant-chester-j-tullos.

"Doane Academy — Our History." https://www.doaneacademy.org/about/our
-history.

Find a Grave. http://www.findagrave.com.

"Gwen Bristow (1903–1980)." Alabama Women's Hall of Fame, 2005. http://www
.awhf.org/bristow.html.

"King's Daughters — History." https://www.kingsdaughters.org/who-we-are
/history/.

"The Spread of U.S. Slavery, 1790–1860." http://lincolnmullen.com/projects
/slavery/.

INDEX

Page numbers in *italics* refer to illustrations.

Abbott, Sam, 127, 128, 129

Abbott, Walter, 73, 92, 93, 135, 137, 142

Adams County: black population in, 58; slave population in, 12

Adams County Circuit Court, 132–33, 145, 155, 157, 160

Adams County jail: Black and Burns in, 90, 93; Dana and Dockery in, 5, 80–86, 93, 155

African Americans. *See* Blacks

Alexandria, Va., Christ Church of, 36–37, 112

Aliases: black use of, 58; of Williams, 58, 88, 93, 194n13

Allen, George, 74, 75–77, 87

American Civil Liberties Union, 84

American Civil War. *See* Civil War

American Heritage Publishing, 14

Anderson, Charles, 102, 139, 142

Anderson, William, 11

Antioch Baptist Church, 3, 56, 102, 161, 167, 174

Architecture: Greek Revival, 2, 17; of Natchez mansions, 6–7

Aristocracy, southern: Dana as descendant of, 2, 111–12; Dockery as descendant of, 2, 111, 115; estates of, 8–9; Merrill in, 1–2, 6, 17, 105; in press coverage of Merrill murder, 1–2, 105, 111–12

Arkansas. *See* Pine Bluff

Armfield, John, 10

Army. *See* Confederate army; Union army

Arrests: of Black, 5, 90; of Burns, 2–3, 5, 90, 97; of Dana, 2, 4–5, 75, 154, 155; of Dockery, 2, 4–5, 75, 154, 155; of Ferguson, 78; of Geiger, 78; of Newell, 97, 100; of Smith (George), 100, 195n33

Associated Press, 124

Atlanta Journal Constitution, 104

Atlantic Monthly, 7

Audubon, John James, 8

Austin, H. L., 107

Bahin, Charlie, 70, 71

Baker, Duncan, 39, 187n11

Baker, Mrs. H. L., 139

Baker-Grand Theatre, 71, 142, 187n11

Ballistics tests, 93, 95, 100, 137, 140

Barnum, P. T., 8

Belgium, Merrill (Ayres) as ambassador to, 21–22, 104–5, 184n10

Bell, Abigail, 54, 188n4

Bennett, Bob, 158

Benoist, E. E., 136

Bertillon, Alphonse, 82–83

Better Homes and Gardens, 148

Black, James, 53, 54, 56–57

Black, Nellie Smith: arrest of, 5, 90, 93; birth of, 54; boarders in home of, 57, 61, 89; after Burns's release from prison, 173; in Burns's trial, 140; family of, 54, *55*; interrogation of, 93; marriage of, 54; as material witness, 100; on night of murder, 64; photographs of, *55*, *91*; time spent in jail,

93, 100, 102, 131; in Wells's retelling
of murder, 150–51; work as laundress,
57
Black Codes, 58
Black newspapers, 108
Blacks: coded language used for, 81;
in criminal justice system of South,
2–3, 78, 81, 90, 100, 107; employment opportunities for, 56–57, 172;
Great Migration of, 12–13, 53, 60;
nicknames and aliases used by, 58,
65, 190n4; population in Mississippi,
58; in Reconstruction era, 58–60; in
Union army during Civil War, 11;
women (See Black women)
Blacks, in Natchez, 53–62; in Burns's
trial, 136; community of, 54–56; employment opportunities for, 56–57,
172; after end of slavery, 12–13, 55–56;
memory of Merrill murder among,
173; in middle class, 13; population
of, 55, 61; residential segregation of,
54–56; sharecropping by, 12, 13; as
suspects in Merrill murder, 78, 81,
88; in tourism industry, 7, 148; as
witnesses in Merrill murder, 95–96,
100, 136
Black women: citizenship rights of, 100;
double standard for, 99–100, 173,
195n32; employment options for, 57,
172; in Parchman prison, 161; stereotypes of, 151; vs. white women, as
ladies, 99–100
Blue and the Gray, The (magazine), 45
Blues, 164
Bluff City Undertaking Company, 57,
189n13
Bowers, Mary, 162
Boyd, Willie, 1, 69–71, 78, 191n14
Boyt, E. C., 87, 185n34
Brandon, Gerard, 133, 134, 152, 155–56
Brandon and Brandon (firm), 152
Brewer, Earl, 128

Bristow, Gwen, 106, 120–22, 160, 197n9
Brown, Joseph, 81, 82, 132–33, 199n5
Brown, Sterling, 14
Bruce, Blanche, 60
Bulger, Thomas, 45
Bullwhip, in Burns's interrogation, 96,
136, 138, 141
Burns, Edward, 57, 189n12
Burns, Emily ("Sister"), 90–91; birth
of, 53, 54; boarders in home of, 57,
61; church of, 3, 56, 102, 161, 167, 174;
death of, 4, 174, 203n10; in Dockery's
trial, as witness, 157, 158, 164; education of, 56, 57; family of, 53–54, 55,
56–57, 188n4; grave of, 3; home of,
166–67, 173–74, 200n23; life after
prison, 4, 166–67, 173–74; marriages
of, 57, 174, 189n12; at Parchman
prison, 3, 146, 161–66; photographs
of, 55, 91; physical appearance of,
57, 133, 161, 199n9; suspension of
sentence and release of, 4, 165–66,
173; Williams's introduction to, 58;
Williams's move into home of, 5, 58,
61–62; Williams's relationship with,
5, 62; Williams's threat against, 65,
90, 98, 190n5; work as laundress, 53,
57–58; work as seamstress, 167, 173
Burns, Emily, in Merrill murder: as
accessory to murder, 100, 132, 133,
143, 158; arraignment of, 133; arrest
of, 2–3, 5, 90, 93, 97; attorney for, lack
of, 93, 131; charges against, 97, 100,
131; confession of, 5, 96–102, 135, 144;
fingerprints of, 98, 102; grand jury indictment of, 132–33; innocence of, 5,
145–46, 165–66; interrogation of, 93,
95–98; in jail awaiting grand jury, 102,
131; press coverage of, 104, 107–8; in
reenactment of crime, 101–2, 137, 142;
role of, 64–68, 145–46; treatment in
jail, 96, 99–100, 136, 138, 141–42; as
victim, 173

Burns, Emily, trial of, 133–46; attorneys appointed for, 133, 157; ballistics in, 137, 140; Burns's confession in, 135, 144; Burns's testimony in, 141–42, 144; conviction in, 144–45; death penalty in, 134, 144–45; fingerprints in, 140–41; insanity defense in, 137, 138–40, 143; jury in, 5, 134, 142–45; as only trial for Merrill murder, 2–3, 133; planned robbery of Merrill in, 143; records of, 199n3; reenactment of crime in, 137, 142; sentencing in, 3–4, 144–45, 200n43; spectators at, 134, 137; speed of, 5, 133, 142, 144, 145; start of, 134; suspension of sentence after, 4, 165–66, 173; testimony of witnesses in, 134–41, 158
Burr, Aaron, 8

Callon, Sim, *The Goat Castle Murder*, 14–15
Capital punishment. *See* Death penalty
Car(s): of Merrill, 30, 87, 185n34; tourism by, 7
Catholic Church, 13
Catton, Bruce, 104, 105
Census, U.S., 12
Chamberlain-Hunt Academy, 39, 111, 186n8
Chancellor, James: breakdown of, 84; in Burns's trial, 140–41; career of, 80, 192n12; in murder investigation, 80, 81, 83–84, 94, 97, 100, 102
Charleston Daily Mail, 104
Chew, J. C., 41–42
Chicago: Merrill murder investigation in, 92–95, 137; Williams's life in, 5, 53, 60–61, 94, 194n19
Chickens, at Glenwood, 31, 48
Christ Church (Alexandria, Va.), 36–37, 112
Citizenship, black, 58, 60, 100
Civil rights, 100, 131, 174

Civil War: black soldiers in, 11; Dockery family affected by, 40–42; Merrill family affected by, 17–20; Natchez in, 11–12, 18–20, 25–26; Port Gibson in, 37–38, 40; Vicksburg in, 17–18, 37, 40, 42
Clark, W. E., 137
Clothes: of Dana, 75, 78, 109, 128, 129, 159; of Dockery, 158–59; of Merrill, 29, 105; of Williams, 68, 98, 135, 138, 139
Cohn, David, 7
Community memory, of Merrill murder, 3, 173
Comstock School for Girls, 41, 113
Concordia Parish, La.: Merrill family plantations in, 19, 22, 31, 66, 95; slave population in, 12
Confederate army: defeat of, 12; Dockery (Thomas) in, 40–43; at Port Gibson, 37; at Vicksburg, 17–18
Confederate guerrillas, 20, 25
Congress, U.S.: on African slave trade, 10; on Reconstruction, 60
Connor, Mike, 165
Contraband, slave, 20
Corban, Robert: arraignment of Burns by, 133; arraignment of Dana and Dockery by, 155; in Burns's sentencing, 145; in Burns's trial, 134, 137, 144; in civil lawsuit against Roberts, 156; in Dockery's trial, 157, 159–60; in Geiger's trial, 157; instructions to grand jury by, 132
Corn Products Refining Company, 61
Cotton industry: Merrill family in, 19–20; in Natchez economy, 8, 9, 12; slaves in, 9, 53–54; Surget family in, 17
Cotton Kingdom, 1, 12, 19
Cousins, marriage of, 24
Crime stories, popularity of, 4, 103–4
Criminal justice system, of Jim Crow

South, blacks in, 2–3, 78, 81, 90, 100, 107
"Crimson Crime at Glenburney Manor, The" (Wells), 14, 150–51
Curtis, Zula, 61, 89–90, 136, 158
Cutrer, Richard, 85–86, 95

Dana, Charles, Jr. (brother of Dick), 35, 37, 38–39
Dana, Charles Anderson, 35
Dana, Charles Backus (father of Dick), 35–38, *36*, 48, 112, 118, 122
Dana, Dick (Richard Henry Clay), 35–51; birth of, 38; black community's interactions with, 172; in boarding-houses, 39, 46, 112; childhood of, 5, 38–39; civil lawsuit against Roberts, 147, 151–56; clothes of, 75, 78, 109, 128, 129, 159; death of, 170; diary of, 47, 187n12; Dockery on marriage to, 171; Dockery's introduction to, 39; education of, 39, 111, 186n8; family of, 35–39, 112; feud with Merrill, 4, 30–34; grave of, 3, 170; guardianship of, 3, 31, 48, 112, 186n37; home of (*See* Glenwood); income of, lack of, 47; injury to fingers of, 39, 80, 112, 187n10; mental health problems of, 30–31, 47–51, 109, 186n37; music ca-reer of, 39, 112, 125–28, 187n11; nick-names for, 65, 154–55, 190n4; pho-tographs of, *110*, *126*, *148*; physical appearance of, 50, 109, 159, 190n10; public performances by, 125–29, 154–55; radio broadcast by (proposed), 127–28, 195n33; in tourism at Glen-wood, 124–29; after trial, life of, 169–71; Williams's introduction to, 62, 63, 89, 190n1
Dana, Dick, in Merrill murder, 75–86; as accessory to murder, 155–56; alibi of, 79–80; arraignment of, 155; arrest of, 2, 4–5, 75, 154, 155; attorneys of,

84, 85, 155–56; Burns's confession on, 97–98, 100–102, 135; charges against, 4, 81, 97, 101; claims of innocence by, 81–82; clothes of, 75, 78; as early sus-pect, 4–5, 75, 78–80; fingerprints of, 4, 81–82, 84, 90, 100, 102, 141; grand jury on, 132–33, 156; indictment of, 132–33, 147, 155–56, 199n5; jailhouse photos of, 6, 109–10, *110*; local sym-pathy for, 84–86, 115; press coverage of, 2, 5–6, 81–82, 104, 108–12, 159; questioning of, 69, 75, 79–80, 82, 84, 191n13; release from jail, 86, 93, 97, 99, 115, 132, 156–57; Roberts on guilt of, 82, 97, 129, 147, 154; role of, 63–69, 146; trial of, 156–57, 160; in Wells's retelling of murder, 151
Dana, Elvira Close, 37–39, 186n8
Dana, Richard Henry, 35
Darrow, Clarence, 84
Death penalty: in Burns's trial, 134, 144–45; in Dockery's trial, 159–60; by hanging, in Mississippi, 134, 199n10
Delta Times-Democrat, 171
Dickson, Archibald: as custodian of Glenwood, 118–19; and Dana and Dockery's release from jail, 86; at Forman's boardinghouse, 39, 46; and reenactment of crime, 101; on visitors to Glenwood, 118–20, 124
Doane, George, 21
Doane Academy, 184n9
Dockery, Ann, 40
Dockery, Frederika Toelle, 41–42
Dockery, John, 39–40
Dockery, Laura West (mother of Octa-via), 40–41, 42, 45–46, 113
Dockery, Nydia (sister of Octavia). *See* Forman, Nydia Dockery
Dockery, Octavia, 39–51; birth of, 39, 41, 43; black community's interac-tions with, 172–73; as boarder on Pine Street, 47, 188n38; on Burns's

conviction, 147; childhood of, 41–43, 113; civil lawsuit against Roberts, 147, 151 56, 160; clothes of, 158–59; Dana's introduction to, 39; death of, 171; after death of sister, 47–48, 114; education of, 41, 113; family of, 39–43, 113; feud with Merrill, 4, 30–34, 51; Geiger's lawsuit against, 102; grave of, 3, 173; as guardian of Dana, 3, 48, 112; home of (*See* Glenwood); income earned by, 47, 50–51; living with Formans, 39, 43, 46–47; on marriage to Dana, 171; Merrill's lawsuits against, 32–34, 51; as "Mistress of Goat Castle," 3, 109, 173; nicknames for, 65, 154–55, 190n4; photographs of, *44, 110, 148, 152*; physical appearance of, 43; public performances by, 128–29, 154–55; Reed's courtship of, 44–45, 187n29; on theft at Glenwood, 119; in tourism at Glenwood, 119, 124–29; after trial, life of, 169–71, 173–74; wealth of family of, 40; Williams's introduction to, 62, 63, 89, 172, 190n1; writing career of, 44–46, 114

Dockery, Octavia, in Merrill murder, 75–86; as accessory to murder, 155–56; alibi of, 158; arraignment of, 155; arrest of, 2, 4–5, 75, 154, 155; attorneys of, 84, 85, 155–56; Burns's confession on, 97–98, 100–102, 135; charges against, 4, 81, 97, 101; claims of innocence by, 81, 153; as early suspect, 4–5, 75, 78–80; fingerprints of, 4, 81–82, 84, 100; grand jury on, 132–33, 156; indictment of, 132–33, 147, 155–56, 158, 199n5; jailhouse photos of, 6, 109–10, *110*; local sympathy for, 84–86, 115; press coverage of, 2, 5–6, 85, 104, 108–15, 159, 197n29; questioning of, 82; on reenactment of crime, 101; release from jail, 86, 93,

97, 99, 115, 132, 156–57; Roberts on guilt of, 82, 97, 129, 147, 154; role of, 63–69, 146; trial of, 156–60, 164; in Wells's retelling of murder, 151; on Williams's role in murder, 101

Dockery, Thomas Pleasant (father of Octavia), 39–43, 113, 187n24

Dogs: owned by Merrill, 65, 66, 69; in search for gun, 87; in search for Merrill's body, 74, 75–77, 136

Domestic work, by black women, 57, 172

Dumas, A. W., 139–40

East, Charles, 14, 194n13, 199nn2, 5

Elmore, Sarah, 140, 200n27

Elms Court: architectural style of, 17; changes in ownership of, 29; McKittrick family at, 106, 120, 124; as Merrill's home, 11, 13, 28; spelling of name, 183n10; tourists at, 124; as wedding gift to Merrill's parents, 17

Engle, C. F., 156

Europe: Merrill family in, 21–22; tourists from Natchez in, 9

"Fall of the House of Usher" (Poe), 118, 198n9

Farris, Laurin, 138, 191n16

Faulkner, William, 4, 150, 169, 197n9, 201n3

Ferguson, Odell: arrest of, 78; as early suspect in murder, 77, 78; on first encounter with Dana, 35; interrogation of, 78, 82, 102; on night of murder, 77, 99

Ferries, across Mississippi River, 7

Fields, Clifford, 140–41

Fingerprints, 80–84; of Burns, 98, 102; in Burns's trial, 140–41; of Dana, 4, 81–82, 84, 90, 100, 102, 141; of Dockery, 4, 81–82, 84, 100; and grand jury,

100; of Minor, 95; O'Neill on, 83–84, 95, 97; third set of, 82, 87, 92, 94; of Williams, 92, 94
Fire, at Rhythm Club, 166
Fiveash, W. D., 88, 91
Floyd, Alonzo, 77, 78, 95
Ford, Henry, 7
Forks of the Road (slave market), 10, 11, 13, 54, 56
Forman, Nydia Dockery: childhood of, 41–42, 113; Dana in boardinghouse of, 39, 46, 114; death of, 47–48; Dockery living with, 39, 43, 46–47, 113; at Glenwood, 46–47, 114, 197n33; marriage of, 42–43
Forman, Richard: Dana in boardinghouse of, 39, 46, 112; death of, 47–48, 114; Dockery living with, 39, 43, 46–47, 113; at Glenwood, 46–47, 114, 197n33; marriage of, 42–43
Forman, Sadie, 39, 47, 188n36
Fort Rosalie, 8
Foster, Stephen, 128
France, Merrill family in, 22
Franklin, Isaac, 10
Franklin and Armfield, 10
Freedmen's Bureau, 60
Friedman, Sophie, 85, 129

Garner, Amelia, 61, 91, 94, 194n13
Gayoso de Lemos, Manuel, 8
Geiger, John: arrest of, 78; on black suspects, 78, 81; departure from Skunk's Nest, 50–51, 65, 75, 78, 102; injury to hand of, 90; interrogation of, 78, 82; lawsuit against Dockery, 102; overcoat of, 50–51, 65–66, 75, 78, 79; on trial for desertion of children, 157
Geisenberger, Abraham, 32, 34, 134
Geisenberger, Wilfred A., 133–45; appointment as Burns's attorney, 133; career of, 134; cross-examination of Stone by, 135–36; defense presented by, 137, 138–42, 143, 145; instructions to jury by, 143–44; pleas for mercy by, 145, 200n43
Gibbons, James, 24
Gibson, Charles Dana, 35
Glenburnie (Merrill's home): cash kept at, 63, 66; Dana and Dockery's fingerprints in, 4, 81–82; Dockery's hogs at, 31–34; location of, 29; Merrill's purchase of, 29; Minor's inheritance of, 95; Minor's move into, 106; Minor's nightly visits to, 1, 29, 34, 63; photograph of, 64; size of, 31, 66
Glenwood ("Goat Castle"), 118–29; admission charged for, 124–27, 148, 150; blood found inside, 79; changes in ownership of, 50; Dana and Dockery as squatters in, 5–6, 48, 50, 157; Dana and Dockery's move into, 30–31, 47–51, 114, 197n33; Dana family's purchase of, 38; Dana's childhood in, 5, 38–39; Dickson as custodian of, 118–20; dilapidated condition of, 6, 48, 84, 118, 120; Dockery as mistress of, 3, 109, 173; Dockery's five-year lease on, 49–51; Formans living in, 46–47, 114, 197n33; goats at (See Goats, at Glenwood); hogs at, 31–34, 51, 63, 67, 73; location of, 30; Minor's purchase of, 30–31, 47, 49; nicknames for, 2, 6, 65, 154–55, 190n4; photographs of, 49, 121, 123; press coverage of, 104, 120–22; property tax payments on, 5, 30–31, 47, 49, 170; razing of, 171; residents of (See Dana, Dick; Dockery, Octavia); size of, 38; theft at, 118–19, 153; tourists at, 84–85, 118–20, 124–29, 148–50, 149; after trials, life at, 169–71; Zerkowsky mortgage on, 157, 169–71
Gloucester, 29
Goat Castle. See Glenwood
"Goat Castle murder," 2, 6

Goat Castle Murder, The (Callon and Smith), 14–15
Goat Castle Murder, The (Llewelyn), 15
Goats, at Glenwood: Dockery's acquisition of, 31; on Glenburnie property, 31, 51, 63, 67, 69, 75, 79, 82; inside house, 6, 48, 114, 120, 125, *148*; after murder trials, 169, 170; photographs of, *148*; press coverage of, 6, 104, 120–22, 125, *148*; tourists and, 125
Goldberger, Louis, 85
Goldberger, Mollie, 85
Gone with the Wind (Mitchell), 13
Goodman, Walter, III, 25
Goodman, Walter, Jr., 20, 24–25, 184n7
Goodman, Walter, Sr., 184n7
Goodman and Merrill (firm), 20, 184n7
Grand jury: Burns and Black in jail awaiting, 102, 131; evidence presented to, 100, 132; first meeting of, 132–33; indictments by, 132–33, 156; judge's instructions to, 132; preparation for meeting of, 102
Grant, Julia, 21–22
Grant, Ulysses S.: in Civil War, 17–18, 19–20, 37–38, 42; death of, 42, 187n24; European tour by, 21–22
Great Depression: Burns in, 58; Parchman prison in, 162–63; popularity of true crime stories in, 4, 103–4; tourism during, 7; unemployment in, 61, 62; Williams in, 5, 61
Great Migration, 12–13, 53, 60
Greek Revival architecture, 2, 17
Green, Birdia, 173
Grist, Nellie, 107, 170
Guns, in Merrill murder: ballistics tests on, 93, 95, 137, 140; in Burns's trial, 137, 140; number of shots fired, 190n9; owned by Merrill, 67, 68, 87; owned by Williams, 66–67, 68, 88, 93, 100, 137

Habas, Jeanette, 171
Habeas corpus, 85–86, 93, 97, 100, 132
Hacher, M. C., 1, 69–70, 191n14
Hanging, capital punishment by, 134, 199n10
Harbor View (Newport), 20
"Held by the Enemy" (Dockery), 45
Henry Street settlement, 23–24
Henslee, Robert, 87–88, 108, 138
Hinds County jail: Burns in, 97, 100; Newell in, 97, 100
Hogs, at Glenwood, 31–34, 51, 63, 67, 73
Holy Family Catholic Church, 13, 56, 173
Hoover, Herbert, 104
House, William, 97
Housing, segregation in, 54–56
How the Other Half Lives (Riis), 23

Illinois Central Railroad, 61, 85, 94
Ingraham, Joseph, *The South-West by a Yankee*, 10
Insanity defense, in Burns's trial, 137, 138–40, 143
Investigation. *See* Merrill murder investigation
Italian immigrants, 13

Jackson, Ed, 170
Jail. *See* Adams County jail; Hinds County jail; Parchman
Jefferson Academy, 8
Jefferson County, slave population in, 12
Jenkins, Hyde, 96, 132, 135, 138
Jernigan, Mary, 161–62
Jewish community, in Natchez, 12, 85
Jim Crow South: blacks in criminal justice system of, 2–3, 78, 81, 90, 100, 107; civil rights in, 131; coded language in, 81; mob violence in, 97
Jobs: for black men and women, 56–57; during Great Depression, 61, 62

Johnson, Barney, 136
Johnson, Ben, 138
Johnson, Paul B., Sr., 4, 165–66, 173
Joplin Globe, 104
Jubilee Trail (Bristow), 120
Junkin, John R.: in Burns's trial, 138, 140, 141–42; at grand jury, 132; in murder investigation, 92, 93, 96, 102, 135
Jury, in Burns's trial, 142–45; as all white men, 5, 134, 142; deliberation by, 142, 144; instructions given to, 143–44; selection of, 134; verdict of, 144–45. *See also* Grand jury
Jury, in Dockery's trial, 159–60
Justice system, of Jim Crow South: blacks in, 2–3, 78, 81, 90, 100, 107

Kane, Harnett, *Natchez on the Mississippi*, 14
Kansas City Plaindealer, 108
Kelly, George, 64
Kennedy, Laurens, 30, 32–33, 85, 156
Kingsberry, Herbert, 138
King's Daughters, 23–24
Kingsley, Charles, *Twenty-Five Village Sermons*, 48
Kuehnle, Joseph, 80, 86, 125
Ku Klux Klan, 60

Lamp, used during Merrill murder, 67–68; Burns's confession regarding, 97–98, 102, 135, 190n11; at Burns's trial, 135, 141; discovery of, in search for body, 75–77, 190n11
Laub, Saul, 12, 107
Laundry work, 53, 57–58
Lawsuits: against Dockery, by Geiger, 102; against Dockery, by Merrill, 32–34, 51; against Minor, by Grist, 170; against Roberts, by Dana and Dockery, 147, 151–56, 160
Lee, Robert E., 36, 48, 112
Lespedeza, 31–32

Lincoln, Abraham, 35, 74
Lind, Jenny, 8
Lindbergh, Charles, 103
Llewelyn, Michael, *The Goat Castle Murder*, 15
Logan, William E., 133, 134, 156–57
Louisiana: lynchings in, 97; Merrill family plantations in, 19, 22, 31, 66, 95; slave population in, 12; slave trade in, 9–10, 54
Love, Pearly, 161
Lynchings, 81, 97

MacRae, Catharine, 106
Maine, USS, 38
Marriage: among aristocracy, 17, 21; of cousins, 24
Mask, Pleasant Thomas, 41
Master Detective, 150–51, 189n16, 191n11
McKittrick, Charlotte Surget, 106, 120, 124
McKittrick, David, 106, 120, 124, 133
McMurran family, 8–9
Media coverage. *See* Press coverage
Melrose (estate), 8–9
Memory, community, of Merrill murder, 3, 173
Merrill, Anna (great-aunt of Jennie), 184n7
Merrill, Ayres P., III (brother of Jennie), 22
Merrill, Ayres P., Jr. (father of Jennie), 17–22; as ambassador to Belgium, 21–22, 104–5, 184n10; death of, 20, 22; in firm of Goodman and Merrill, 20, 184n7; marriage of, 17; photograph of, *19*; in press coverage of murder, 104–5; slaves owned by, 11, 19; Union sympathies of, 18–21; wealth of, 11, 20
Merrill, Catherine (sister of Jennie), 21–22

Merrill, Dunbar (brother of Jennie), 22, 24

Merrill, Frank (brother of Jennie), 22

Merrill, Jane Surget (mother of Jennie), 17, 20

Merrill, Jennie (Jane Surget): birth of, 17–18, 25, 184n3, 185n24; childhood of, 21–22; clothes of, 29, 105; after death of father, 22–23; education of, 21; family of, 11, 17–22; full name of, 17; funeral of, 80; Goodman's courtship of, 24–25; grave of, 3; guns of, 67, 68, 87; home of (*See* Elms Court; Glenburnie); in King's Daughters, 23–24; lawsuits against Dockery, 32–34, 51; Minor's courtship of, 25, 27–29, 106; Minor's nightly visits to, 1, 29, 34, 63; murder of (*See* Merrill murder); in New York, 20, 23–24, 29, 184n7; photograph of, *18*; physical appearance of, 67, 106; in planter aristocracy, 1–2, 6, 17, 105; as recluse, 1, 2, 29–30, 34, 105; return to Natchez in 1890s, 24, 29; rumored marriage to Minor, 106–7; wealth of, 11, 17, 20, 66, 95, 171–72; Williams's search for work with, 62, 63, 82, 88, 89; will of, 95, 103, 107, 170

Merrill, Minnie (sister of Jennie), 21–22

Merrill murder, 63–71; books about, 14–15; community memory of, 3, 173; date of, 3, 4; discovery of body after, 77; disposal of body in, 4, 67–68, 102; dog owned by Merrill in, 65, 66, 69; facts of crime, 4–5, 63–71; as "Goat Castle murder," 2, 6; guns in (*See* Guns); investigation of (*See* Merrill murder investigation); lamp in (*See* Lamp); map of vicinity of, *76*; Minor on night of, 1, 69–71, 73; overcoat in (*See* Overcoat); phone call reporting, 70–71, 191n16; planned robbery in, 63–69, 97, 98, 135, 143, 172; press cov-

erage of (*See* Press coverage); search for body after, 73–77, 95, 136; wounds to Merrill in, 67, 77, 136, 190n9

Merrill murder investigation, 73–102; arrests in (*See* Arrests); ballistics tests in, 93, 95, 100; black suspects in, 78, 81, 88; black witnesses questioned in, 95–96, 100; charges against Burns in, 97, 100, 131; charges against Dana and Dockery in, 4, 81, 97, 101, 155–56; in Chicago, 92–95, 137; confession by Burns in, 5, 96–102, 135, 144; early suspects in, 4–5, 75, 78–80; fingerprints in (*See* Fingerprints); in Pine Bluff, 92–95; questioning of Dana in, 69, 75, 79–80, 82, 84, 191n13; reasons for reopening of, 158; reenactment of crime in, 101–2, 137, 142; search for body in, 73–77, 95, 136; search for gun in, 87; search for Williams in, 82, 86, 87–92. *See also specific suspects*

Merrill Murder Mystery, The (Wells), 14, 191n16

Merrill murder trial. *See* Burns, Emily, trial of

Middle class, black, 13

Miller, Katherine, 148

Minor, Duncan, 25–30; birth of, 25, 185n24; courtship of Merrill, 25, 27–29, 106; as cousin of Merrill, 1, 25; death of, 170; in Dockery's trial, 158; education of, 27; family of, 25–27; fingerprints of, 95; Glenwood bought by, 30–31, 47, 49; home of, 1, 25, 27; in Merrill's will, 95, 107, 170; as murder suspect, 95, 131–32; nightly visits to Glenburnie, 1, 29, 34, 63; on night of murder, 1, 69–71, 73; photographs of, *26*, *74*; press coverage of, 104, 106, 111; at reenactment of crime, 142; rumored marriage to Merrill, 106–7; in search for body, 77, 95; Williams's

search for work with, 61, 62, 63, 82, 88, 89, 108
Minor, James, 27
Minor, John, 25–26
Minor, Kate, 25–27, 29
Minor, Stephen, 25
Mississippi: black population of, 58; capital punishment by hanging in, 134, 199n10; Reconstruction in, 58–60. *See also specific cities*
Mississippi Central Railroad, 127
Mississippi River: bridge across, 7, 12; in Civil War, 18, 37; ferries across, 7
Mississippi State Penitentiary. *See* Parchman
Mississippi Supreme Court, 160, 170
Mississippi Territory, Natchez as capital of, 8
Mistrial, in Dana and Dockery's cases, 160
Mitchell, Margaret, *Gone with the Wind*, 13
Mob violence, 97
Model T cars, 7, 30
Morgan, Duncan, 173
Movies, set in Old South, 13, 117
Mulvihill, Pat, Jr., 31, 48–49, 155
Murder. *See* Merrill murder
"My Prison Life" (Walden), 164

Natchez, Miss., 6–14; blacks in (*See* Blacks, in Natchez); in Civil War, 11–12, 18–20, 25–26; cotton in economy of, 8, 9, 12; decline of, 12; as epicenter of Old South, 1, 2, 14; establishment of, 7–8; Jewish community in, 12, 85; location of, 2; mansions and estates of, 6–7, 8–9, 12–13; origins of name, 7; planter aristocracy of, 1–2, 6; race relations in, 14, 171–73; slave population in, 12; slave trade in, 10–11; tourism in, 6–7, 117, 147–49, 169. *See also specific residents and sites*

Natchez City Cemetery, 3, 43
Natchez Democrat: on Burns's confession, 97, 99, 140; on Dana and Dockery's trials, 160; on Dana's aristocratic heritage, 112; on Dana's clothes, 78; on Dockery's aristocratic heritage, 115; Farris's 1979 interview with, 191n16; on Merrill as recluse, 105; on photos of Dana and Dockery, 110; plea for justice in, 81; vs. *Times-Picayune*, coverage in, 190n3, 191n14; on tourism at Glenwood, 124; on Williams, 108
Natchez Garden Club: Jewish members of, 12; pilgrimages of, 7, 117, 147–48, 150, 169
"Natchez Gothic" (East), 14
Natchez Indians, 7
Natchez on the Mississippi (Kane), 14
Natchez Trace, 10
"Natchez Under-the-Hill," 9
National Box Factory, 56–57
National Surety Company of New York, 152
Native Americans, 7
Newell, Edgar Allen Poe: as accessory to murder, 132; alibi of, 151; arrest of, 97, 100; as boarder in Burns's house, 57, 61; Burns's confession on, 97–102, 135; in Burns's trial, 135, 139; in Dockery's trial, 158; embalming work by, 57, 172, 189n13; grand jury on, 132–33; release from jail, 102, 132; role in Merrill murder, 64, 66–68, 190n3; in Wells's retelling of murder, 151
New Orleans, La.: Merrill in, 27, 28; slave trade in, 9–10, 54
New Orleans Times-Picayune: on Burns's conviction, 145; on Dana, 109; on Dana and Dockery's trials, 158, 160; on Glenwood, 120–21, 125; on Merrill's life, 106; vs. *Natchez*

Democrat, coverage in, 190n3, 191n14; on Williams's death, 108

Newport, R.I., Merrill family home in, 20

Newspapers, black, 108. *See also* Press coverage; *specific publications*

"New Woman," 43–44

New York Amsterdam News, 108

New York City: Dockery family in, 41–43, 113; King's Daughters in, 23–24; Merrill in, 20, 23–24, 29, 184n7; Minor family in, 26

New York Sun, 35, 38, 111

New York Times: on Dana's death, 170; on Dana's life, 109; on Dockery (Thomas), 41–42; on Dockery's (Octavia) death, 171; on Merrill murder, 4, 104, 105; on Merrill's life, 105; on Natchez during Civil War, 11; on tourism in Natchez, 148

New York World, 42

Nichols, "Whalebone Lew," 103

Nicknames: black use of, 58, 65, 190n4; of Dana, 65, 154–55, 190n4; of Dockery, 65, 154–55, 190n4; of Glenwood, 2, 6, 65, 154–55, 190n4; of Roberts, 73–74; of Williams, 58, 189n14

Norman, Earl, 110

Nostalgia, 13, 14, 42

Nutt, Julia, 25–26

Oakland (Minor family home), 1, 25, 27

"Old Black Joe" (Foster), 128

Old South: movies set in, 13, 117; Natchez as epicenter of, 1, 2, 14; planter class in (*See* Aristocracy); press coverage of decline of, 105; tourism in, 6–7

O'Neill, Maurice: ballistics test by, 93, 95, 100; in Burns's trial, 136–37, 140; career of, 82–83; case notes kept by, 199n2; in Chicago, 92, 94–95, 137; in Dockery's trial, 158; on fingerprint

evidence, 83–84, 95, 97; murder investigation joined by, 82–83, 88, 92; photograph of, *83*; in search for Williams, 86

Overcoat, in Merrill murder, 65–66, *79*; Burns's confession on, 97, 98, 101, 135; at Burns's trial, 135; Geiger questioned about, 78; Geiger's lawsuit for return of, 102; in search for body, 75

Pacific Whaling Company, 103

Pantoliano, Thomas, 128

Parchman (Mississippi State Penitentiary), 161–66; Burns at, 3, 146, 161–66; conditions at, 162–63; establishment of, 162; labor by inmates at, 162–64; mercy courts at, 165–66; population of, 162, 163; sewing room at, 162, *163*, 166, 167; women in, 161–62, 164

Pearls, George. *See* Williams, Lawrence

Pearls, Meadie, 61, 62, 91–92

Pemberton, John C., 18

Peoples' Undertaking Establishment, 92, 94

Perry, Percy, 96, 100

Pine Bluff (Arkansas): murder investigation in, 92–95; Williams's death in, 5, 87–88, 91, 93

"Pink." *See* Williams, Lawrence

Pinkney Williams. *See* Williams, Lawrence

Plantations: former slaves on, 59; of Merrill family, 11, 19, 22, 31, 66, 95; nostalgia for, 13; slaves on, 10, 12; of Surget family, 17. *See also* Cotton

Planter aristocracy. *See* Aristocracy

Poe, Edgar Allen, 4, 111, 118, 120, 198n9, 201n3

"Poe." *See* Newell, Edgar Allen Poe

Poll taxes, 160

Port Gibson, Miss., Civil War in, 37–38, 40

Press coverage: of Merrill (Ayres) as ambassador to Belgium, 22, 184n10; of tourism in Natchez, 7

Press coverage, of Merrill murder, 103–15; aristocracy in, 1–2, 105, 111–12; in black newspapers, 108; Burns in, 104, 107–8, 145; Dana in, 2, 5–6, 81–82, 104, 108–12, 159; Dockery in, 2, 5–6, 85, 104, 108–15, 159, 197n29; Glenwood in, 104, 120–22; goats in, 6, *48*, 104, 120–22, 125; Merrill's life in, 1–2, 104–6, 111; Minor in, 104, 106, 111; reasons for intensity of, 4; sample headlines from, 4, 6, 104; Williams in, 104, 107–8. *See also specific publications*

Prevost, Marion, 199n2

Princeton University, 27

Property taxes, on Glenwood, 5, 30–31, 47, 49, 170

Quitman, Frederick, 9

Race relations, in Natchez, 14, 171–73

Racial segregation, residential, 54–56. *See also* Jim Crow South

Randolph, Lee, 174

Ransom, Thomas, 20

Ratcliff, Ed: in civil lawsuit against Roberts, 155–56; on radio broadcast by Dana, 127–28; son of, 84; on theft at Glenwood, 119; writ of habeas corpus by, 85

Ratcliff, Lee, 84

Reconstruction, 58–60

Red Star Line, 22

Reed, Annie, 138, 200n23

Reed, Ethel, 161

Reed, Richard, 44–45, 187n29

Revels, Hiram, 56, 60

Rhode Island, Merrill family home in, 20

Rhythm Club fire, 166

Riis, Jacob, 23, 29

Roads, to Natchez, 7, 12

Roberts, Calpernia, 73

Roberts, Clarence Powell ("Book"), 80–102; black community's interactions with, 172; on Burns's confession, 97; on Burns's conviction, 147; on Burns's role in murder, 100, 102; in Burns's trial, 137, 138–39, 140; career of, 73; Dana and Dockery questioned by, 75, 80, 82, 84; Dana and Dockery's civil lawsuit against, 147, 151–56, 160; in Dana and Dockery's trials, 157, 160; family of, 73; on fingerprint evidence, 80, 81, 82, 97, 100, 102; at grand jury, 132; on guilt of Dana and Dockery, 82, 97, 129, 147, 154; on indictment of Dana and Dockery, 132, 147, 155–56, 199n5; and jailhouse photos of Dana and Dockery, 110; origins of nickname, 73–74; phone call on night of murder to, 70–71; photograph of, *74*; in reenactment of crime, 101–2, 142; in search for Merrill's body, 73–77; in search for murder weapon, 87; in search for Williams, 82, 86, 87–92; Skunk's Nest shut down by, 50; on tall man involved in murder, 190n10; temporarily relieved of sheriff duties, 157, 159; and theft at Glenwood, 119–20; unsolicited advice in letters to, 131–32; in Wells's retelling of murder, 150–51; on Williams's role in murder, 100

Roberts, Quitman, 73

Rollins, Henry, 32, 34

Roosevelt, Franklin Delano, 103, 165

"Rose for Emily, A" (Faulkner), 197n9

Ryan, Mike: in feud between Merrill and Dockery, 32, 33–34, 186n39; in murder investigation, 79, 80, 82, 186n39; in search for Merrill's body, 73

Salt Lake City Tribune, 104

Saturday Evening Post, 46, 150

Schizophrenia, 140
Schumaker, William, 92
Scopes Monkey Trial, 84
Segregation, residential, 54–56
Serio, Barnett, 70
Serio, Joe, 70, 73, 75, 87
Sharecropping, 12, 13
Sims, A. E., 138
Sims, Edward, 140
"Sister." *See* Burns, Emily
Skinner's Cemetery, 3
Skunk's Nest: Geiger's departure from,
  50–51, 65, 75, 78, 102; shut down by
  sheriff, 50
Slaves: in cotton industry, 9, 53–54; de-
  scendants of, 12–13, 53; emancipation
  of, 12–13; former, hiring of, 19–20,
  59; on Natchez estates, 8–9; number
  of, in South, 9; owned by Dockery
  family, 40; owned by Merrill family,
  11, 19; owned by Surget family, 17;
  population of, 12
Slave trade: African vs. domestic, 10;
  in Natchez, 10–11; in New Orleans,
  9 10, 54
Sledge, Rubin, 162
Smith, Agnes, 54, *55*, 188n4
Smith, Alfred, 166, 203n12
Smith, Carolyn Vance, *The Goat Castle
  Murder*, 14–15
Smith, George "Doc," *55*, 100, 195n33
Smith, Ned, 157, 159
Smith, Nellie. *See* Black, Nellie Smith
Smith, Nettie, 71
So Red the Rose (Young), 13
South. *See* Jim Crow South; Old South
Southern aristocracy. *See* Aristocracy
Southern Claims Commission, 26–27
South-West by a Yankee, The (Ingra-
  ham), 10
Spain, Thomas H., 25
Spanish-American War, 38–39
Spickard, Ola Mae, 161

Stallone, Eduardo, 13
Stallone, Maria, 13
Stanton, Effie, 34, 66, 95
Star-Journal, 104
State v. Emily Burns. See Burns, Emily,
  trial of
State v. Octavia Dockery, 156–60
State v. Richard Dana, 156–57, 160
Stereotypes, of black women, 151
St. Mary's Hall, 21, 184n9
Stone, Joseph: in Burns's trial, 134–36,
  140; Dana and Dockery arrested
  by, 155; in murder investigation, 93,
  96–97, 99, 100; photograph of, *79*
St. Paul's School, 27
Sturdivant, S. J., 77
Summit, Ill., 61
Sunny South (magazine), 45
Surget, Francis, 17
Surget, Jacob, 26, 27
Surget, Jane. *See* Merrill, Jane Surget
  (mother of Jennie)
Surget family, 17, 25

Tann, O. G., 163
Taxes: poll, 160; property, on Glen-
  wood, 5, 30–31, 47, 49, 170
Tenements, in New York, 23–24
Terrell, Louis, 66, 92, 94, 137
Textile industry, 9
Thomas, Samuel, 60
Titusville Herald, 104
Tobacco farming, 9
Toelle, Frederika. *See* Dockery, Freder-
  ika Toelle
Tourism: in Europe, 9; at Glenwood,
  84–85, 118–20, 124–29, 148–50,
  149; in Natchez, 6–7, 117, 147–49,
  169
Trains, to Natchez, 7, 12
Trial: of Burns (*See* Burns, Emily, trial
  of); of Dana, 156–57, 160; of Dockery,
  156–60, 164; of Geiger, 157

Trinity Episcopal Church (Natchez), 38, 80, 170
True crime stories, popularity in Great Depression of, 4, 103–4
Truly, Everett, 155
Tucker, Clay: in Burns's trial, 134–35, 137, 138; in Dana and Dockery's trial, 157; on indictment of Dana and Dockery, 132, 147, 155, 156, 199n5; in murder investigation, 92, 101; in release of Dana and Dockery from jail, 86, 132
Tullos, Chester, 146, 201n47
Twenty-Five Village Sermons (Kingsley), 48
Two Years before the Mast (Dana), 35

Union army: black soldiers in, 11; in Natchez, 11, 18–20, 25; in Port Gibson, 37–38; in Vicksburg, 17–18
United Press International, 124

Vagrancy laws, 58–59
Vanderbilt University, 39, 111
Vardaman, James K., 162
Vicksburg, Miss.: in Civil War, 17–18, 37, 40, 42; Freedmen's Bureau in, 60
Violence, mob, 97
Virginia, slave trade in, 10

Walden, Fanny, "My Prison Life," 164
Washington, Booker T., 74
Washington, George, 36
Wealth: of Dockery family, 40; of Merrill family, 11, 17, 20, 66, 95, 171–72; in Natchez, during Civil War, 11; of Surget family, 17, 25
Wells, Homer G.: "The Crimson Crime at Glenburney Manor," 14, 150–51; *Master Detective*, 150–51, 189n16
Wells, Zaida Marion: on black vs. white suspects, 81; on Burns's sentence, 200n43; on Burns's trial, 140, 142–43; on fingerprint evidence, 140; *The*

Merrill Murder Mystery, 14, 191n16; on Merrill's life, 105–6; on night of murder, 71, 105, 142–43
Whale display, 103
White, Hugh, 165, 166
White women: in aristocracy, expectations for, 17; vs. black women, as ladies, 99–100; at Parchman prison, 161–62; service clubs of, 23
Wilds Pond, 77, 87
Will, of Merrill, 95, 103, 107, 170
Williams, Lawrence (alias George Pearls and Pinkney Williams): aliases of, 58, 88, 93, 194n13; birth of, 53, 58, 188n1; Burns's introduction to, 58; Burns's relationship with, 5, 62; in Chicago, 5, 53, 60–61, 94, 194n19; childhood of, 58; clothes of, 68, 98, 135, 138, 139; criminal record of, 94; Dana and Dockery's introduction to, 62, 63, 89, 172, 190n1; daughter of (Amelia), 61, 91, 94, 194n13; death of, 5, 87–88, 91, 93, 108; family of, 58, 61, 188n1; funeral for, 92; injury to hand of, 89–90; jobs held by, 61, 62, 172; move into Burns's home, 5, 58, 61–62; photograph of, 59; physical appearance of, 58, 189n15; search for work with Minor and Merrill, 61, 62, 63, 82, 88, 89, 108; second wife of (Meadie), 61, 62, 91–92; trunk of, 59, 68, 89, 90–91, 189n16; use of nickname "Pink" for, 58, 189n14
Williams, Lawrence, in Merrill murder, 87–94; Burns's confession on, 97–102, 135; at Burns's trial, 135–39; Burns threatened by, 65, 90, 98, 190n5; at Dockery's trial, 158; fingerprints of, 92, 94; flight after, 5, 68, 87–88, 98; grand jury on, 132–33; gun of, 66–67, 68, 88, 93, 100, 137; identification of, 92–94, 137; as murder suspect, 5; postmortem convic-

tion of, 5, 133, 134; press coverage of, 104, 107–8; role of, 63–68; search for, 82, 86, 87–92; true bill against, 133

Williams, Meadie. *See* Pearls, Meadie

Winston, Louis, 89, 90, 136

Wisner, La., lynching in, 97

Women: double standard for, 99–100, 173, 195n32; at Parchman prison, 161–62, *163*, 164. *See also* Black women; White women

Wright, Richard, 12–13

Yazoo and Mississippi Valley Railroad, 127

Young, Stark, *So Red the Rose*, 13

Zeeland, SS, 22

Zerkowsky, Charles, 56, 150, 169

Zerkowsky, Isaac, 156–57, 170, 171

Zerkowsky, Sam, 171

Zerkowsky, Seaman, 170, 171

Zerkowsky family, 169–71